**MOVIES OF THE 90**

JÜRGEN MÜLLER (ED.)

# MOVIES OF THE 90s

**IN COLLABORATION WITH
HERBERT KLEMENS FILMBILD FUNDUS ROBERT FISCHER**

**TASCHEN**

KÖLN LONDON LOS ANGELES MADRID PARIS TOKYO

# 20 CAMERA SHOTS
# FOR 6 SECONDS OF FILM
## Remarks on cinema of the 90s

Movies of the 90s contain imperceptible images. Shots can be accelerated so that they lie below the perception threshold. An example of such acceleration occurs at the end of Jonathan Demme's *The Silence of the Lambs* (1991, p. 48), in what is perhaps the shortest showdown in cinematic history. The exchange of fire between the FBI agent Clarice Starling and the mass-murderer Buffalo Bill takes no more than six seconds, even though it comprises twenty camera shots. It seems odd to devote only six seconds to the most exciting part of a two-hour film, but Demme allows the climax to implode in the true sense of the word and uses extremely powerful visual images.

The director skilfully and expertly creates the build-up to the showdown: after a tense parallel montage, at the end of which we expect the mur-

derer to be caught, it is not the FBI task force that is standing at his door but Clarice on her own. She doesn't know it, but she has found Buffalo Bill. Before she realises who it is standing in front of her, he is able to take refuge in his cellar, where he is holding his latest victim captive. The murderer switches off the light when the FBI agent follows him into the cellar. While her adversary watches, Clarice gropes uncertainly in the dark. Throughout this scene, the audience sees through Buffalo Bill's eyes, his night-vision device turning everything a ghostly green. During the chase, Clarice's irregular, panic-stricken breathing is all that can be heard. Only when the young agent hears the pistol being cocked behind her is she able to guess the murderer's position. At the speed of light, she spins round and the gunfight begins. In the silence, the cocking of the gun sounds like a thunderclap, as

though we are hearing it through Clarice's ears, for in the darkness she has become acutely sensitive to even the tiniest of sounds. When we in turn find ourselves in absolute darkness, we not only hear through the ears of the FBI agent, but also see through her eyes.

The next shot shows the flash from Bill's revolver, which is reflected in the lenses of his night-vision device. The explosion from the gun looks like an abstract painting, and the fight does in fact develop into a symbolic duel. Whereas at first the murderer had the advantage in the darkness, the situation changes when the shooting match begins, as the adversaries dazzle each other when shots are exchanged. The flash from the gunshot allows the camera to show the murderer, who has been hit. This is then followed by a black screen, which lasts longer than the view of the people. Again we see a shot being fired, then another black screen. Now the audience can make out Clarice taking aim, but she is blinded by the shot fired from Bill's pistol. A black screen and renewed gunfire. The FBI agent shoots with her eyes shut. Another gunshot. Again the audience sees Clarice shooting. A black screen. Bill has been hit a second time. A black screen. The murderer is hit again, and we see the look of agony on his face. A black screen. One shot has hit a window blind, loosening it. The daylight penetrating the cellar reveals a steel helmet and an American flag. The camera then cuts back to the cellar and there, lying on the floor, we see the fatally wounded murderer. With his night-vision device covering his eyes, he looks like a dead insect.

# Cinema, television and video

In the cinema, our perception of this sequence is reduced to the knowledge that, after the FBI agent has fired her shots, the murderer lies dead on the floor. It is only in the last few images of this sequence that we return to daylight and viewing at normal speed, whereas what we have just witnessed is for the most part below the perception threshold. It is not until Clarice loads her weapon that it becomes clear what we must have seen. She has actually used up all her ammunition of six cartridges. Although we haven't been able to perceive these six shots consciously, the final images make it possible to come to this conclusion. While the shots are being exchanged, the camera angle changes constantly; we see things alternately through the eyes of the murderer and of the FBI agent. The sequence described here is barely noticeable in the cinema. To see it at all, you really need to be able to break the picture sequence down into stills using a video recorder.

Clearly, as a means of reproducing scenes, the video recorder has an aesthetic potential comparable to that of a record player or CD player. It allows you to gain expert knowledge, whether you collect the films of a particular director or actor, or are interested in a particular genre.

With regard to video, Martin Scorsese is thoroughly optimistic, seeing in this technology the opportunity for engendering a new enthusiasm for the

cinema. In a short article called "The Second Screen", he writes of the new opportunities that the video recorder has opened up. There is now no problem showing films that are hardly known anymore but deserve to be studied, and it is finally possible to compare film scenes directly. He also welcomes the wider distribution it has brought for some of his own films, which now reach a larger audience through video.

The video recorder also enables formal and aesthetic analysis by creating stills. You can study the content and composition of a shot or look at a film sequence in the same way as you can listen again and again to a virtuoso performance of a passage of music, just for the sheer pleasure of it. The growth in the numbers of Hong Kong movie fans is in no small part due to the fact that video makes it possible to appreciate their technical brilliance. Of course, we have never been able to see many of these films in the cinema, viewing them only on video right from the start.

When a director like David Fincher now asks that his films be watched not once but four or five times, this need present no problem for the viewer. Video can never replace the cinema, of course, but it does enable different forms of perception. Lavish Hollywood productions are created with the aim of making them suitable not only for the one-off cinema experience, but also for repeated viewing on video. The more details intentionally concealed in a film, the more fun you will have in repeated viewings.

In that respect, most films nowadays have three premieres. First they appear in the cinema, then they are brought out on video, and finally they are shown on one of the many television channels. It is doubtful that any devel-

opment of the last few decades has had a greater influence on filmmaking than videotape. As its use has become more widespread, film and television have come closer together. The video recorder has become the mediating element between the two – and television is certainly no longer second best. With *Star Trek* (from 1979), *The X-Files* (1998), *Mission: Impossible* (1996, p. 164) and *The Fugitive* (1993), films for the cinema were modelled on famous television series. The same was true of David Lynch's cult series *Twin Peaks* (1989–91), which the director subsequently used as the basis for a film (1992). The barriers between the two media have become permeable. Helen Hunt and George Clooney were popular TV actors long before they became celebrated Hollywood stars, and several of today's prominent directors made music videos or worked for television before they were able to make a full-length feature film.

# Seeing and hearing

Technical developments also demonstrate how natural the connection between television and film is today. Televisions are now made with a screen format (16:9) that corresponds to the wide-screen format of the cinema. Larger and larger televisions are being produced and it is now a long time since the cinema screen was the only way of presenting a film. Dolby surround sound systems mean that even at home, the sound and music of a film can be perceived spatially. It is remarkable how far the TV experience has

been transformed through developments in technology. Video represents a kind of home movie, not to mention the further development in the form of DVD technology.

It must be acknowledged that such technical progress had its beginnings in cinemas. There too it was digital sound quality, particularly in the multiplex cinemas, that opened up a new cinematic age. You need think only of Steven Spielberg's war film *Saving Private Ryan* (1998, p. 292), winner of so many Oscars, which in the first 15 minutes gave us a sort of phenomenology of the sounds of war. We can hear how the bullets ricochet off metal, how they hiss into the water or whistle past the soldiers' ears. Whereas the film material at the beginning of *Saving Private Ryan* looks grainy and is reminiscent of the newsreels of the 1940s, the sound is extremely varied. It is as though the images portraying historical events gain authenticity through the soundtrack. We even experience Captain Miller's deafness, when, beside himself in horror at the many dead, for a moment he no longer hears any external noises. It has long been natural for the audience to see through the eyes of one of the characters in a film and to interpret a panning shot as the subjective view of a person. But in the 90s, we can even hear through the ears of a character in a film. The great success Spielberg enjoyed with *Jurassic Park* (1993, p. 68) was also due to the convincing use of sound, as we stand in the middle of a stampeding herd of small dinosaurs, or in the unforgettable scene in which a Jeep is pursued by a Tyrannosaurus Rex, whose powerful steps seem to make the whole cinema shake.

In the movies of the 90s, it is impossible to overestimate the importance of sound in making the images so convincing. David Fincher produced a winner in this regard with *Alien³* (1992). In the most gruesome scene of the film, a post-mortem has to be carried out on a young girl, as no one knows whether there is an alien in her body. We see the instruments that are needed to carry out the procedure. We don't see the actual post-mortem itself, but we do hear the child's ribcage being opened up. The scene is almost unbearable and is one of the coldest "images" that modern cinema has produced. Film scenes of this sort illustrate the power sound can exert and that it can be just as effective in its own right as the actual images of a film.

All the examples mentioned concern the reproduction technique of cinema and television as creators of illusion. But has the video also changed the aesthetics of film in the 90s? The example cited above from *The Silence of the Lambs* shows the extreme extent to which images can be accelerated. This becomes clearer when we think, for example, of the influence of music videos, which are largely characterised by brief shots and frequent cuts. Pictures are shown for only fractions of seconds, so that they are barely perceptible. In the battle scene at the beginning of Ridley Scott's *Gladiator* (2000), the cuts come so quickly that we get no intimation of the significance of a fragment of a second that decides between life and death. At the same time, we are aware of the sudden burst of speed in the sequence. First the legionaries are making meticulous preparations for the battle. Then on the command to attack, the film speeds up and takes us to the heart of the battle, where nothing is thought out in advance, and everything happens intui-

tively. Such scenes are an assault and a strain on the senses in equal measure. The viewer is all eyes, his intellect suspended.

# Remake?

The video recorder has long been viewed as the enemy of the cinema, as though it would corrupt the pure science of film. In an ironic twist, there is an echo of this criticism even in a successful 1990s film. Nora Ephron's *You've Got Mail* (1998) contains the caricature of an art critic who claims in a TV interview that, from a technological point of view, our world is out of kilter. Just think of the video recorder, he says: the idea of a video recorder is that you can record a TV programme if you're going out, but to his mind, the fact that you're going out shows that you don't want to watch the TV programme. As far as he is concerned, the only medium that can be justified is the radio. With his self-absorbed monologue, the critic tries to convince us that television and video are equally absurd. He maintains that both should be abolished. It becomes clear how serious his assessment is, however, when he casually asks his girlfriend whether she is actually recording the interview. Ephron's film may be dismissed as a romantic comedy, but even so the film poses the important question of the authenticity of the media. Can a love letter be taken seriously when it is sent as an e-mail? Do new technological means of communication make us lose our true personality? Are the contents only credible when they are written on paper? In a crucial

scene, the heroine of the film clutches her copy of Jane Austen's *Pride and Prejudice*, as though her identity might be concealed in this book. Thus the film not only tells a love story, but also constantly questions our relationship with the media. These are not just electronic devices that transmit or record specific information, and they are not neutral records of a technical nature. They are rather part of our identity, because we are not just what we stand for, but also what we like, read, listen to and watch.

Ephron's film bears a faint resemblance to Ernst Lubitsch's classic *The Shop Around the Corner* from 1940. Both films tell a love story where the couple get together only by a convoluted route. But fundamentally *You've Got Mail* does not have much in common with the classic film. In only one scene does the director clearly borrow from the original classic: when Meg Ryan and Tom Hanks meet for a blind date with disastrous consequences, you expect the original to outshine the modern version. Meg Ryan is disappointed because, instead of the e-mail friend she had hoped for, she meets only her professional adversary, who, moreover, conceals his e-mail identity. A heated argument ensues, at the end of which Tom Hanks leaves the bar. This scene makes it clear how mistaken ideals stop people from realising what they really are. In some respects, the film really ends here, and not with its happy ending. However, whereas Lubitsch leaves it up to the audience to judge, Ephron brings an added dimension to the touching closing scene of the film with the use of the song "Somewhere Over the Rainbow" on the soundtrack, thereby deliberately overdoing it and allowing for the possibility of an ironic reading.

# Quotation and Hollywood films

It's often said that the cinema of the 1990s is allusive. Video is clearly important here too, as it supports this trend. But others feel that the idea of allusive cinema is a figment of some critics' imagination. These critics are selective when choosing films to prove their hypothesis. People who claim that the cinema of the 1990s is postmodern and allusive cite Francis Ford Coppola's *Dracula* (1992), but not Steven Spielberg's *Schindler's List* (1993, p. 86). Whereas the first film can be related to many precursors and does actually represent a museum of film history, the second has to be seen in relation to real events of the past. We can also argue against the hypothesis of allusive cinema by saying that there have always been directors who have frequently displayed their knowledge of cinematic history. It was not only in the 1990s that Brian de Palma's works made reference to earlier films; they had been doing so for years. We need think only of the end of *The Untouchables* (1987), when the American director alludes to the famous scene from Eisenstein's *Battleship Potemkin* (1925), in which a pram clatters down a steep flight of steps. He quotes again but less obviously in *Mission: Impossible* (1995), a film which refers to *The Lady From Shanghai* (1948) and represents a homage to its creator, Orson Welles. Thus in de Palma's work, the desire to quote is in no way the exclusive preserve of the 1990s.

Whatever the objections to this idea of the cinema of quotation, it is true that the audience changed in the 1990s. The constant mass-media distribution of films means that there are more viewers who can recognise quotes and therefore know how to appreciate films. It is now much more a matter of course for films to be part of the cultural common knowledge. Without any jury having to rule on it, everybody knows today that *Psycho* (1960), *Ben Hur* (1959) and *Casablanca* (1942) belong to the canon of classic films on which film history is based and from which it continues to develop. In other words, for particular genres, these films set standards that demand quality and originality. Anyone who emphasises the desire to quote in present-day cinema is really only saying that the history of film is not over, but has always represented a starting point and point of reference for filmmakers.

# Film and personal reflection

Allusive cinema is a rather vague, general term for a highly creative association with originals, because quotes come in various forms: as remakes, as parodies or as homage. Usually they are allusions used by a director to express his admiration for a particular earlier film or film sequence. Such allusions can be clear, or less obvious. A master of the subtle allusion is the

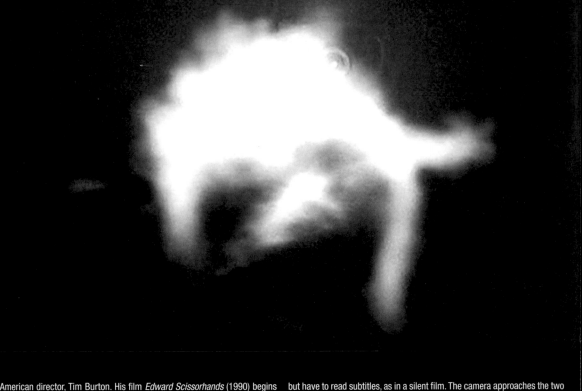

American director, Tim Burton. His film *Edward Scissorhands* (1990) begins with a young girl asking her grandmother where snow comes from. This paves the way for an allegorical trip through the history of film. When the camera leaves the room, we are led over the snow-covered houses of a suburb, until the view rises to a dark castle, in which a light burns. This is an allusion to Orson Welles' *Citizen Kane* (1941): the castle with the lit window recalls Charles Foster Kane's huge mansion, Xanadu, and the snow that falls over the artificial-looking suburb harks back to the glass snow-scene that falls from the hand of the dying tycoon. Burton's film quotations attest to his admiration for Welles, who even appears as a character in his film *Ed Wood* (1994, p. 104). With his reference to the snow-scene, he is also using one of the best cinematic metaphors: expressing in equal measure both childlike innocence and astonishment at the magic of the miniature world. Beyond the glass globe, you look towards a world of your own, dappled with dancing snowflakes, which comes to life in your imagination.

Burton's allusions underline the quality of Orson Welles' classics and make it possible to experience film history visually. The quotes in *Edward Scissorhands* are difficult to recognise precisely because they fit the new context so well. The better a quote is adapted to the new context, the more likely that it will be recognised only by a devotee of the original film.

Danny Boyle is much more direct with his quotes in his film *Trainspotting* (1996, p. 186). At an important point in the action, he refers to a famous earlier film. At a weekend disco, two boys are talking about their girlfriends. The music is so loud that we cannot hear what they are saying, but have to read subtitles, as in a silent film. The camera approaches the two in a single movement and, in the style of Pop Art, we recognise words such as "Vellozet" or "Synthomon" written on the walls, words which refer back to drinks from the Korova milk bar in Stanley Kubrick's *A Clockwork Orange* (1971). Whereas in his film Kubrick lets his camera focus on the face of the principal actor and then pans out, in Doyle's *Trainspotting* the camera gradually zooms in on the two people – an almost direct quote, in which only one element is reversed. This English director's film continues to allude to famous earlier films. The following sequence shows the principal actor of *Trainspotting*, arms folded, standing in front of a poster portraying Robert De Niro as Travis Bickle in the film *Taxi Driver* (1976), shooting with two pistols at once. It is not only the poster, but also even the defiant pose with the folded arms that recall Robert De Niro's interpretation of the role. A great many more allusions could be mentioned. In retrospect, the off-screen monologue at the start of the film seems to be a clear parallel with the opening monologue from *A Clockwork Orange*. The film also alludes to the record cover of the Beatles' "Abbey Road" LP, and there are shots that bring to mind Richard Lester's Beatles films. This is not merely an expression of Doyle's admiration for the films in question, for these references to "Swinging London" give added meaning to the film. They tell of the end of a particular form of pop culture that is being replaced by techno. What has changed is a youth culture that is defined by saying no. Unlike Tim Burton, the English director produces his allusions so that they are clearly recognisable, almost to the point of being literal re-enactments.

Quotations do not, however, necessarily have to refer to what are regarded as great film classics: we need think only of the *Scream* trilogy (1996, 1997, 1999), which contains constant allusions to successful horror films such as *Nightmare on Elm Street* (from 1984) or *Halloween* (from 1978). What links the audience and the film characters in this way is detailed knowledge of those horror thrillers. The attraction of the sequel lies precisely in the fact that games are constantly being played with the audience's sense of anticipation. We think we know how the plot will develop, and, as a result, we are fooled time and again, because nothing turns out quite as expected. In the 1990s, cinematic self-reflection is no longer the exclusive prerogative of the *auteur* film, but a component part of mainstream cinema.

# Non-linear narration

Along with speeding up pictures and the desire to quote, the third formal feature of the movies of the 90s was the exploration of non-linear narration. The directors happiest to experiment in this respect were Quentin Tarantino and Steven Soderbergh. But whereas Tarantino was more interested in the unexpected features of episodic narration and the resultant relativity of the contents, Soderbergh used this narrative device to develop a particularly eloquent film slang. What links both directors is that in their films they used ambitious sets with front and back lighting that could not be understood immediately, but became comprehensible only during the course of the film.

The significance of the individual film image no longer arose, as in linear narration, from any direct connection, but became apparent only when all the elements were brought together. The viewer was left with the task of reconstructing the story.

When, in Soderbergh's *The Limey* (1999), one of the first shots in the film shows the principal actor flying from England to America, we initially believe he is on his way to investigate the death of his daughter. When at the end of the film we see the same picture, it becomes clear that the story has for the most part taken place in the memory of the protagonist. In fact, the first picture was the last, but this in no way detracts from the suspense of the film. It is more the case that it is extremely logical, because, as a result of this narrative device, the theme now becomes the loneliness of this man who is left with only the images in his memory to cherish. *Out of Sight* (1998) by the same director and David Fincher's *Fight Club* (1999) are structured in a similarly artificial way.

There is no doubt that the most famous example from the 1990s in the art of non-linear narration is Quentin Tarantino's *Pulp Fiction* (1994, p. 118), the film that many saw as the greatest cult film of the last decade. It is remarkable in many respects, the first being its narrative form. The episodic representation method makes it difficult for the audience to differentiate between principal and secondary characters in any traditional sense. All the stories revolve around the gangster boss, Marsellus Wallace. So the film starts with the two killers, Jules and Vincent, who are doing a job for Marsellus, dealing with cheating business partners. An unpredictable story

11

now develops, full of suspicion, that will ultimately cost one of the two killers his life. *Pulp Fiction*, which one critic described as "a joyride through film history", contains numerous cinematic allusions, and its director may regard it as a virtuoso example of such allusive cinema, but it is not really the exceptional feature of the film. It is much more as though Tarantino wanted to make his films like a treacherous labyrinth, a place with no way out. Even his use of allusion serves more to confuse than to elucidate. Every conceivable form of allusion is used in his film. An obvious example is the ominous briefcase that glows when opened. This prop recalls Robert Aldrich's film *Kiss Me Deadly* (1955), which used the same motif as early as 1955. We never discover what is actually in the case, but know only what we hear when it is talked about, or see the ominous light shining from inside it.

Even the casting of the roles seems to have been inspired by cinematic history. In a dance scene with Uma Thurman, John Travolta recalls his past as an actor, reminding us of his success with *Saturday Night Fever* (1977); Christopher Walken plays a Vietnam War veteran when he gives the young Butch his father's watch, thereby alluding to his role in the *The Deer Hunter* (1978); and Bruce Willis, familiar to many as the amoral hero of numerous action films, plays a boxer with character who ultimately remains incorruptible. Such allusions and identification of the actors with their roles make any reality outside of the film disappear.

# In the labyrinth of images

The time structure of the film is even more radical. After Vincent Vega has been shot dead, he reappears in a subsequent scene. Of course, this is only possible because Tarantino muddies the chronology of his story. The film does not begin with the earliest scene chronologically, but jumps ahead, without the viewer being aware. This move is a stroke of genius, because it can highlight something that is a matter of principle: films take place not as a sequence starting from the present, but in a time called Future II. They run in the "past future". With *Pulp Fiction*, we find ourselves in a time warp that we can no longer leave. The killer, Vincent Vega, is shot dead when he is guarding the apartment of the boxer, Butch, who has betrayed their joint boss, Marsellus. When Vega reappears in the next but one scene, it can only be a flashback. The story has gone back to the beginning and we find out the macabre events that happened at the end of Jules' and Vincent's first job. Even if the audience can make out a logical connection between the individual episodes, it becomes clear during the film that even more things could have happened in the course of events that are initially assumed to represent the time line. Time seems infinitely divisible and another incident can always be revealed as having taken place between the episodes that are already known to the audience. It is like a person who rambles on in conversation, and always finds new pegs for more stories. In this anecdotal narrative device, the chronology of the episodes, which can be reconstructed

only in retrospect, occurs in the background. Instead, events both comical and macabre keep the viewer in suspense and make any questions about a narrative logic subordinate. The attraction of such a narrative device lies in solving the riddle that sends the viewer into a pictorial labyrinth. We have the impression of being led through different genres, almost like an ironic allusion to channel hopping on evening television.

# Dangerous fictions

There are many more buzz words that we could have chosen apart from those discussed, and the idea of genre is a case in point. Whereas at the beginning of the decade you might have had the impression that more and more films were mixing the genres in a new and interesting way, at the end of the decade, with *Titanic* (1997, p. 244) and *Saving Private Ryan (*1998, p. 292), single-varietal genre films of apparently long-outmoded types came back into being.

Another important trend, which has become increasingly apparent over the decade, is the growth in the use of digital images. *Toy Story* (1995, p. 140) was the first totally computer-generated full-length feature film. Whole lavish historic sets are now simulated using computers, like the Coliseum in Ridley Scott's *Gladiator* or the luxury liner surging through the sea in James Cameron's *Titanic*. The first example of this was George Lucas' *Star Wars: Episode 1 – The Phantom Menace* (1999), with its sensational

stunts. It is hard to predict further developments in this field, but they seem likely to affect the action film most.

The buzz words of acceleration, allusive cinema and non linear narration represent three paradigms that characterise, not cinema as a whole admittedly, but the important films of the 1990s. These are linked with the assertion that video is a prerequisite for all three phenomena. Acceleration throws up the question of the relationship between time and perception; allusions link the past with the present; and finally, non linear narration is a sort of mind-game, which makes it clear that television and cinema do not portray an image of reality, but have been re-creating it for years. Thus some films have explained this epistemological question at the end of the 1990s with a pessimistic perspective. Think of Peter Weir's media satire *The Truman Show* (1998, p. 262), or Terry Gilliam's *Twelve Monkeys* (1995), David Cronenberg's *eXistenZ* (1999) and Larry and Andy Wachowski's *The Matrix* (1999, p. 298) – all these films unsettle the viewer and ask whether people are not in fact deceived about the real character of the world. The relativity of perception, the reporting of events through the media and the displacement of the reality of this world combine to become the theme. It may be that the media give us the illusion of reality, that we only ever encounter it vicariously through duplicates, or a gigantic conspiracy is in progress. Such films bear witness to the uneasiness with which we have left the first millennium and entered the second. The extent to which such a feeling of unease and the concomitant apocalyptic ideas are due to the pessimism typical of the end of an era, remains to be seen.

Film, television and video are everywhere in the modern world. The more time we spend in front of cinema and television screens, the more critically we must examine the possibilities and limits of these media. In so doing, we will be forced to the conclusion that there will probably never be a natural or appropriate use of media, even if we knew what such a thing was. Voluntarily limiting oneself, say to only one film a week? One film a day might be more realistic. Everyone knows that good films are addictive. In this respect, the situation is no better for cinema than it is for the older media like the radio or the book. Criticism of the media has been around since before the advent of television. Centuries ago, reading too many novels led a Spaniard by the name of Don Quixote to do battle with windmills and think that he was a knight. A classic case of losing your grip on reality because of media consumption. In spite of any illusions, we can certainly neither dispute the good intentions of this sad-faced knight nor fail to admit that he experienced a thing or two.

*Jürgen Müller*

# DANCES WITH WOLVES

1990 - USA - 180 MIN. - WESTERN

**DIRECTOR** KEVIN COSTNER (*1955)
**SCREENPLAY** MICHAEL BLAKE, based on his novel of the same name **DIRECTOR OF PHOTOGRAPHY** DEAN SEMLER **EDITING** NEIL TRAVIS, STEPHEN POTTER, CHIP MASAMITSU, WILLIAM HOY **MUSIC** JOHN BARRY **PRODUCTION** JIM WILSON, KEVIN COSTNER for TIG PRODUCTIONS.

**STARRING** KEVIN COSTNER (Lt. Dunbar), MARY MCDONNELL (Stands With a Fist), GRAHAM GREENE (Kicking Bird), RODNEY A. GRANT (Wind in His Hair), FLOYD "RED CROW" WESTERMAN (Ten Bears), TANTOO CARDINAL (Black Shawl), ROBERT PASTORELLI (Timmons), CHARLES ROCKET (Lt. Elgin), MAURY CHAYKIN (Maj. Fambrough), JIMMY HERMAN (Stone Calf).

**ACADEMY AWARDS 1990** OSCARS for BEST PICTURE, BEST DIRECTOR (Kevin Costner), BEST ADAPTED SCREENPLAY (Michael Blake), BEST CINEMATOGRAPHY (Dean Semler), BEST FILM EDITING (Neil Travis, Stephen Potter, Chip Masamitsu, William Hoy), BEST MUSIC (John Barry) and BEST SOUND (Bill W. Benton, Jeffrey Perkins, Gregory H. Watkins, Russell Williams).

**IFF BERLIN 1991** SILVER BEAR for an OUTSTANDING SINGLE ACHIEVEMENT (Kevin Costner).

## "I was just thinking that of all the trails in this life there is one that matters most. It is the trail of a true human being."

1863, St. David's Field, Tennessee: for days, a regiment of Union soldiers has been trying to break through Confederate Army lines. The military stalemate comes to a close thanks to a suicidal ride by Lieutenant John W. Dunbar (Kevin Costner). Badly wounded, and fearing the loss of his leg, he decides he'd rather die, and arms outstretched like a crucified Christ, he shouts "Forgive me, father," and gallops through enemy lines towards what looks like certain death.

"How strange this life can be: I tried to kill myself, and they made a living hero out of me." *Dances with Wolves*, Kevin Costner's directorial debut, is the story of what happens after that unsuccessful suicide attempt. The result is a romantic version of the classical Western. Thanks to his heroic deed, Dunbar is allowed to decide where his next posting will be. He wants to ex-

perience the Wild West before it finally disappears, so he chooses Fort Hays, an isolated outpost on the edge of civilization. When he arrives at his destination, there's no sign of human life and the water has been poisoned. It takes him a few weeks to realize he's not alone in the seemingly endless prairie landscape, and slowly he begins to make tentative contact with the native Sioux Indians. Raw, naive and unprejudiced, he walks straight up to them.

As time goes by, he makes friends with a holy man named Kicking Bird (Graham Greene) and a warrior called Wind in His Hair (Rodney A. Grant), and he starts a love affair with Stands With a Fist (Mary McDonnell). Lieutenant John Dunbar gradually becomes "Dances with Wolves," a respected member of his Sioux tribe. The film tells the story of a man who

2

leaves everything behind and sets out to find the meaning of his life in harmony with nature.

In 1893, James Frederick Turner wrote: "The expansion westwards embodied all the strengths that made the American character," and this expansion played a decisive role in the formation of the American identity. It's the major theme of one of the oldest, most popular and also most thoroughly American film genres: the Western. The 1970s witnessed the deaths of many of the directors of the "frontier generation," whose vision and spirit had made a lasting mark on the Western – among them John Ford, Howard Hawks, King Vidor, Delmer Daves and Henry Hathaway. The classically narrated Western died with them. And after Michael Cimino's multi-million-dollar flop *Heaven's Gate* (1980) – a modern, and at the same time highly-idealized example of the genre – the Western came to be regarded as box-office poison.

Kevin Costner's *Dances with Wolves* briefly reanimated the Western in the early 90s, linking its familiar vocabulary and traditional imagery to modern, contemporary themes. The plot of the film is carried by Dunbar's diary entries, his observations serving as a voice-over, and it's through his eyes that

**PANAVISION**     In the credits at the end of a film, "Filmed on Panavision" refers to equipment produced by an American manufacturer of cameras and optical equipment. "Filmed *in* Panavision" signifies a recording- and copying-technique comparable to Cinemascope, and offering a higher resolution than other wide-screen techniques. Recording can take place on 70 mm or 35 mm film. In a 35 mm widescreen film, the image is first of all squeezed horizontally by means of an anamorphic lens, before being restored to its original form in the cinema through the use of a suitable projector. *Dances with Wolves* (1990) was filmed in anamorphic 35 mm material, from which a 70 mm copy was also made.

1   Raise the flag in victory for all! Dunbar wants to see the West before America destroys it for all time. He has not come to conquer, but to be one with nature.

2   Ambushed by images: The masterful camera work of Australian cinematographer Dean Semler rekindles the fire of a dying genre. The grand sweeping shots of the countryside, often filmed with a wide-angle lens, are reminiscent of director John Ford's legendary Hollywood westerns.

3   Looks are only skin deep: Dunbar and the Sioux soon discover that they have more in common than meets the eye.

4   Proceeding with caution: What starts out as bartering goods slowly grows into an exchange of knowledge and ways of living.

5   Jane of the Sioux: In film, western women are often kidnapped by Indians and taken into captivity. Here, the Sioux adopted "Stands With a Fist" (Mary McDonnell), who by no means sees her predicament as "a fate worse than death." In fact, she is initially scared that Dunbar will make her return to the white man's world.

3

we experience the Wild West. As in the Westerns of the 50s, a further "leading actor" is nature itself, its struggle with civilization here presented in highly impressive epic landscapes, filmed in Panavision with a wide-angle lens.

Kevin Costner uses a wide range of standard genre motifs – but only in order to disappoint our carefully-nurtured expectations. For Dunbar is a new version of the classical outsider, a man who listens to his inner voice and talks to the animals. Film historians see him as a distant relative of another character played by Costner: Ray Kinsella, in Phil Alden Robinson's baseball film *Field of Dreams* (1989).

Here the Civil War soldiers are not defenders of civilization, but violent and ignorant rednecks. Costner also exploits the conventions of the genre in order to create suspense: the audience's anticipation of a bloody massacre is maintained by the device of switching scenes constantly between the Indians breaking camp and the soldiers on their trail.

The film's enormous popularity was due not only to its unique images of the landscape, its thrilling scenes of battles and hunting, and its original treatment of Western conventions. What critics praised most was its exemplary "authenticity": i.e., the absence of famous faces (with the sole excep-

4

5

# "*Dances with Wolves* takes the stage like a rich anthology of cultural traditions. It gives us an almost ethnographic view of a disappearing civilization."

*Cahiers du cinéma*

tion of the leading actor) and the politically correct depiction of the Sioux. A third of the film had to be subtitled, as the Native American actors spoke in Lakota, their own language. Far from behaving like "savages," they invert the long-established image of the "Redskin" by proving considerably more civilized than the white soldiers. They are portrayed not as aggressors, but as victims; not as caricatures, but as human beings living in harmony with nature.

In 1970, *A Man Called Horse* had already gone well beyond the usual clichés of the genre to deliver a similar portrayal of Indian culture, with Richard Harris in the role of the white man, who (like Dunbar) is accepted into the community of a Native American tribe. He comes to recognize that one cannot understand Indian culture without becoming a part of it. Costner's film also borrows ideas from Arthur Penn's *Little Big Man* (1970), with Dustin Hoffman in the leading role. Penn's classic film didn't merely draw attention to the complexity of Indian culture and society, but was also a rich, multi-faceted and differentiated portrayal of America's original inhabitants.

The long history of the Western had produced only one Oscar-winner:

6  Earth, wind, fire and beyond: The four elements as well as clouds, sun and manifestations of light play a central role in *Dances with Wolves*. They dramatically change form with the progression of the story. Here we see dark clouds signaling an imminent Pawnee attack.

7  People like you and me: Costner goes to great lengths to provide his audience with a 3D picture of Native Americans. The noble and peace-loving "savages" give way to everyday, ordinary people, with human weaknesses. Rodney A. Grant as Wind in His Hair.

Wesley Ruggles's *Cimarron* (1931). Costner's romantic take on the unbroken world of the Indians was so popular with moviegoers (despite a playing-time of more than three hours) that *Dances With Wolves* was nominated for twelve Academy Awards, and won seven. It was followed by a number of Westerns by directors who deconstructed the conventions of the genre in a similar fashion to Costner. Examples include Sam Raimi's horror-spaghetti-Western, *The Quick and the Dead* (1995), Mario van Peeble's rap Western, *Posse* (1993), Lawrence Kasdan's documentary Western, *Wyatt Earp* (1994) – with Costner playing the lead – and Clint Eastwood's *Unforgiven* (1992), which also won an Oscar. Nowadays film-makers approach the Western without kowtowing to the classics of the genre, for its myths are as faded as its canonical images and thus have to be transposed into a more contemporary form.

APO

"With a few notable exceptions – Orson Welles and Charles Laughton among them – actors have not made great filmmakers. But with *Dances with Wolves*, Costner instantly steps up into that exalted front rank. He's got the moviemaker's fire in his gut."

*The Washington Post*

# WILD AT HEART

1990 - USA - 124 MIN. - ROAD MOVIE, LOVE FILM

DIRECTOR DAVID LYNCH (*1946)
SCREENPLAY DAVID LYNCH, based on the novel of the same name by BARRY GIFFORD DIRECTOR OF PHOTOGRAPHY FREDERICK ELMES
EDITING DUWAYNE DUNHAM MUSIC ANGELO BADALAMENTI PRODUCTION MONTY MONTGOMERY, STEVE GOLIN, SIGURJON SIGHVATSSON for POLYGRAM, PROPAGANDA FILMS.

STARRING NICOLAS CAGE (Sailor Ripley), LAURA DERN (Lula Pace), DIANE LADD (Marietta Pace), WILLEM DAFOE (Bobby Peru), ISABELLA ROSSELLINI (Perdita Durango), HARRY DEAN STANTON (Johnnie Farragut), CRISPIN GLOVER (Dell), GRACE ZABRISKIE (Juana), J. E. FREEMAN (Marselles Santos), MORGAN SHEPARD (Mr. Reindeer), SHERILYN FENN (Accident victim), JACK NANCE (00 Spool).

IFF CANNES 1990 GOLDEN PALM for BEST FILM (David Lynch).

## "This whole world is wild at heart and weird on top."

David Lynch's *Wild at Heart* starts with a bang, or more precisely, with ear-splitting music. Sailor Ripley, played by Nicolas Cage, repeatedly punches a man who provoked him, beating him almost to the point of death. Two years later, when Sailor is released from prison, Lula (Laura Dern) is there waiting for him. Sailor and Lula: the epitome of true love.

The two of them want nothing more than to head out to California and away from Lula's psychopathic mother Marietta (Diane Ladd). It was she who masterminded the fight, not just to keep Sailor away from her daughter, but also because Sailor happened to witness a crime that took place a few years back. Marietta now sends two men to follow their trail – one is private investigator Johnnie Farragut (Harry Dean Stanton) and the other is hired gun Marselles Santos (J. E. Freeman). Both happen to be ex-lovers of hers.

Things don't go according to plan, and Sailor and Lula never make it to California. After getting sidetracked for a while in New Orleans, the two wind up without a penny to their name in some rat hole in The Deep South. The place is called Big Tuna – no one knows why. The town's few buildings look like relics from the set of a Hollywood Western, and a desert wind blows through the town. The only motel is a run-down shack infested by roaches and other low-lifes: short-spoken rednecks, greasy hookers straight out of Fellini, and Bobby Peru (Willem Dafoe), who would be quite happy driving Lula mad and landing Sailor back in prison for another six years.

David Lynch supposedly took a mere six days to write the screenplay to *Wild at Heart*, which is based on a novel of the same name by Barry Gifford. The work blends elements of the road movie, soap opera and fractured fairy tale. Sailor, a modern day Elvis in a snakeskin jacket, and Lula, a sparkling bouquet of white trash that Sailor finds hotter than Georgia asphalt, are both too naive and too absorbed in their own love story to take much notice of the hell surrounding them. But it surrounds them like a dark cloud, together with

"The two romantic leads, like in Godard's *Breathless* and *Pierrot le Fou*, are totally isolated individuals. They have a lot to say, sometimes speaking directly to the camera, sometimes pointedly disregarding it. Yet each word rings as if the speakers were addressing themselves. Lula and Sailor wade in a bubble of joy surrounded by a hellish abyss, the real world." *Die Zeit*

Nicolas Kim Coppola was born in California on January 7, 1964. His father was a professor of literature, his mother a choreographer. He also has the distinction of being the nephew of director Francis Ford Coppola. His stage name was first credited in his on-screen debut, *Fast Times at Ridgemont High* (1982, Director: Amy Heckerling) so that he could establish himself in the business without using his famous name. As Nicolas Cage, he appeared in several films by his well-known uncle: *Rumble Fish* (1983), *The Cotton Club* (1984) and *Peggy Sue Got Married* (1986). Despite his wide range as an actor, which incidentally won him an Academy Award for his role as an alcoholic in *Leaving Las Vegas* (1995), Cage primarily makes action films. He and actress Patricia Arquette divorced in August 2001 and Cage is currently romantically involved with Lisa Marie Presley, daughter of Elvis and ex-wife of Michael Jackson.

the disgusting, distorted image of the face of Lula's mother. The film turns punk whenever the couple are seen lying in bed and making love (which is a frequent occurrence); the movements are filtered by a bright strobe effect and accompanied by reverberating heavy metal. The match that strikes for the obligatory cigarette after the act of carnal pleasure resounds like a detonation. Fire is the film's dominating motif, and it is intricately woven into the narrative. In flashback, we see a man burning alive, a house going up in flames, and a car falling off a cliff and exploding. Lula's mother Marietta (played by Laura Dern's real life mother Diane Ladd) serves as the mistress of fire, and torments Lula like a menacing witch throughout the journey. In fact it was Marietta who was responsible for pouring gasoline on Lula's father and burning him alive. She also made sure that her wrath was felt by other members of the family, including Uncle Pooch, who raped and impreg-

nated Lula when she was just a young girl. One night on their trip, Sailor and Lula pass by a car wreck. They watch helplessly as a girl dies as a result of serious injuries. As an audience member, one experiences a similar paralysis all throughout this film – although you may not always want to watch, you just can't turn away.

*Wild at Heart,* with its gruesome and surreal story line, unusual montages of images and camera angles, and its insistent music is a consummate Lynch film. In retrospect, the film also seems like a forerunner to the newer school of *auteur* cinema that directors like Quentin Tarantino ushered in to mass audiences: it is a self-referential form of cinema that breaks down the boundaries between popular taste and subculture, allowing for a colorful blend of original ideas, bits of racy trash and Hollywood memorabilia.

APO

1 There's no place like home: David Lynch's *Wild at Heart* is a candy-coated, surreal wad of white trash that's more than just weird on top. Click your heels three times and Oz just might come to Kansas. Here, Sheryl Lee as "Glinda" the Good Witch.

2 Love me tender: Sailor Ripley (Nicolas Cage) plays an all right kind of guy who's gotten a bum rap. Following in the footsteps of his idol Elvis Presley, he's on a roadtrip to his own private Graceland with sweetheart Lula.

3 A little ol' buttercup, but you'd never suspect it: Lula (Laura Dern) is hotter than Georgia asphalt.

3

4

**"Lynch films what might be described as the essence of intangible, imminent danger. He doesn't capture a concrete object, but the atmosphere surrounding it, perhaps even its aura. Willem Dafoe and Isabella Rossellini are not meant to be the personification of mindless evil, but rather the passion that steams its wickedness."**

*Süddeutsche Zeitung*

5

4  Cat Ballou: Perdita Durango (Isabella Rossellini) is mean and evil through and through.

5  Wild women do and they don't regret it: Lula's mother Marietta Pace (Diane Ladd) has multiple personalities and lovers. Here pictured with part-time beau Marselles Santos (J.E. Freeman).

6  Friend or Da-Foe? Godforsaken Big Tuna is home to Sailor's nemesis Bobby Peru (Willem Dafoe).

7  A wham, bam, traffic jam: Tied at the hip, Sailor and Lula run from the past until thoughts of getting stuck in a rut almost send Sailor packing altogether.

# GOODFELLAS

1990 - USA - 145 MIN. - GANGSTER FILM, DRAMA

DIRECTOR MARTIN SCORSESE (*1942)
SCREENPLAY NICHOLAS PILEGGI, MARTIN SCORSESE DIRECTOR OF PHOTOGRAPHY MICHAEL BALLHAUS EDITING THELMA SCHOONMAKER
MUSIC TONY BENNETT, ARETHA FRANKLIN, BOBBY DARIN, MUDDY WATERS PRODUCTION IRWIN WINKLER for IRWIN WINKLER PRODUCTIONS, WARNER BROS.

STARRING ROBERT DE NIRO (Jimmy "The Gent" Conway), RAY LIOTTA (Henry Hill), JOE PESCI (Tommy DeVito), LORRAINE BRACCO (Karen Hill), PAUL SORVINO (Don Paul Cicero), FRANK SIVERO (Frankie Carbone), TONY DARROW (Sonny Bunz), MIKE STARR (Frenchy), FRANK VINCENT (Billy Batts), CHUCK LOW (Morris Kessler).

ACADEMY AWARDS 1990 OSCAR for BEST SUPPORTING ACTOR (Joe Pesci).

IFF VENICE 1990 SILVER LION for BEST DIRECTOR (Martin Scorsese).

## "As far back as I remember, I always wanted to be a gangster..."

In 1972 Francis Ford Coppola directed his masterpiece *The Godfather*, which glorified the Mafia as an institution founded on laudable virtues such as loyalty, honor and solidarity. Just one year later, Martin Scorsese, another Italian-American filmmaker, created the first counter argument to Coppola's film. His low budget production *Mean Streets* (1973), featuring actors who were virtual unknowns at the time (i.e. Robert De Niro and Harvey Keitel), provided the audience with authentic and believable portraits of the daily lives of less glamorous Mafia thugs in Brooklyn's Little Italy. These were the blue-collar men of organized crime who didn't atone for their sins at the rectory, but rather out on the streets with their lives.

Francis Ford Coppola brought the final installment of his *Godfather Trilogy – The Godfather – Part III* (1990) – to theaters 17 years after the first, and Martin Scorsese was again right there with him presenting the antithesis. After interludes in other genres, Scorsese filmed his second mobster film, this time as a large-scale studio production. *GoodFellas* spans three decades in the life of Henry Hill, a New York gangster of Irish-Italian descent. The film is based on the 1985 bestseller *Wiseguy – Life in a Mafia Family* by Nicholas Pileggi, who also co-wrote the screenplay.

The film begins with a scene that scrapes right at the grit of the plot. The year is 1970. Three men are riding in a car at night on a New York highway. All of a sudden, Henry (Ray Liotta), Tommy (Joe Pesci) and Jimmy (Robert De Niro) hear a peculiar thumping noise and pull over to the side of the road. Henry opens the trunk, revealing a man's body covered in bloody rags. Tony Bennett's lively brass tune *From Rags To Riches* plays in the background as Tommy repeatedly stabs the helpless man. Jimmy takes over, shooting him repeatedly even after he stops moving. This display of overkill is followed by a voiceover of Henry saying "As far back as I remember, I always wanted to be a gangster."

The film then flashes back to Henry's childhood. Interspersed with Henry's own narration and later that of his wife Karen (Lorraine Bracco), the film proceeds to tell the tale of a guy who wanted nothing more in life than to be a criminal. The story begins in Brooklyn in the late 1950s. Henry is 13 years old and watches from the window of his parents' apartment as the Italian big shots with their fancy and expensive zoot suits run their taxi dispatch. These men are not nobodies like Henry's parents or neighbors, and the little boy wants more than anything to be a part of their world. Instead of at-

1   Put it here, Pal: Hundreds of people pay Paulie Cicero (Paul Sorvino) and his cronies for protection. Henry sees them as a sort of police squadron that upholds neighborhood law and order.

2   Dreaming of Elvis's pink caddy: Young Henry (Christopher Serrone) likes what he sees. Day after day, he watches the local guidos in their designer Italian suits driving the slickest wheels in town.

3   Membership has its privileges: Even if not being Italian means Henry (Ray Liotta) will never get to be a fully-fledged Mafioso, being a Goodfella is enough to keep his Irish eyes a smilin'.

2

...ending school, he plays "lackey" to Mafia boss and taxi company owner Paul Cicero (Paul Sorvino). Little by little he works his way up the ranks, finally being taken on as an "apprentice" like Tommy DeVito (Pesci) in Jimmy Conway's (De Niro) band of hoods. He eventually achieves the status of "Wiseguy," a "Goodfella" – as the Mafiosi refer to themselves. These guys' number one commandment reads: "Never betray a friend and always keep your mouth shot."

Over the course of the years, their business relationship matures into a genuinely binding friendship. The three are a truly unstoppable team. Their criminal endeavors prove immensely profitable and Henry gets accustomed ...o his swanky new threads and, despite his numerous affairs, to Karen's

undying devotion. Unfortunately, wealth also prompts him to cultivate a... expensive drug habit.

Those who venture too close to the sun are bound to fall from the skie... sooner or later. There are early signs that the seemingly perfect façade of thi... gangster lifestyle is deteriorating. After spending time in the slammer, Henr... realizes that the only way he can save his life is by breaking the unwritte... laws of the Mafia. Joining the FBI's witness protection program, he come... face to face with his worst nightmare: he is condemned to live out the rest o... his days in anonymity in the bourgeois suburbs of middle America. In hi... meticulous attention to detail, Scorsese follows the tradition of the grea... 19th-century novels, painstakingly showing us the clothes, cars, wives an...

"It is almost possible to think, sometimes, of the characters as really being good fellows. Their camaraderie is so strong, their loyalty so unquestioned. But the laughter is strained and forced at times, and sometimes it's an effort to enjoy the party, and

mistresses of the mob. Most impressive is the care he takes in conveying how a meal is prepared and consumed. Whether it's a signature pasta sauce or cooking a lobster from behind bars, food and the manner of its preparation seem to be almost as much a priority as money: it is the symbol for a well-ordered life.

German cinematographer Michael Ballhaus, who also collaborated with Scorsese on *After Hours* (1985), *The Last Temptation of Christ* (1988) and *The Age of Innocence* (1993), translates Scorsese's visions into striking images with his no-holds-barred style. The three-minute long shot, in which the camera follows Henry and Karen on their first date, remains ingrained in the memory. While crowds queue outside the Copacabana Club, Henry leads Karen past the bouncers and waiters, through a long hallway and then the kitchen, winding up at a table, which appears as if by magic directly in front of the stage.

4  The three musketeers: One crime leads to another and before they know it, Goodfellas Joe Pesci, Ray Liotta and Robert De Niro have pockets full of dough. One for all and all for one... for now.

5  What she doesn't know won't hurt her: At first, Henry's girlfriend Karen (Lorraine Bracco) is in the dark about his line of work. Nevertheless, she lets him wine and dine her at the "Bamboo Club."

6  Codes etched in stone: After Henry breaks the Goodfellas' first commandment by squealing on his friends, he is left with no choice other than to join the witness protection program.

5

eventually, the whole mythology comes crashing down, and then the guilt – the real guilt, the guilt a Catholic like Scorsese understands intimately – is not that they did sinful things, but that they want to do them again." *Chicago Sun-Times*

The *GoodFellas* soundtrack, as in so many Scorsese pictures, serves not only as a musical underscoring of the action, but also as an elevated plain, documenting Henry's metamorphosis from wannabe crook in his early years up until the point where drug addiction practically turns his life into a paranoid labyrinth of despair. Chronologically sequenced pop songs take us on a jukebox tour of 25 years of American history, providing a knowing commentary on the action. Tear-jerkers from the 50s represent the protagonists' longing for the good old days, whereas the rock of the 60s and early 70s convey Henry's mounting paranoia. The soundtrack is most effective when it is ironic, as in the opening sequence when it juxtaposes brutal scenes with easy listening tunes.

Like Scorsese, the cast are also in prime form. Robert De Niro, Ray Liotta, Joe Pesci, Lorraine Bracco and Paul Sorvino form a dream team transforming a gangster movie into a fine display of ensemble acting. For his performance as the unbelievably charming mobster Tommy DeVito, constantly on the verge of a nervous breakdown, Pesci was awarded the 199 Oscar for best supporting actor.

*GoodFellas* is rightly considered one of the best films of the tail end of the 80s and is in every respect a typical Scorsese movie. It is full of contradictions, it is uncompromisingly brutal, at times it is hysterical and jarring, but it remains all the while infallibly seductive.                    APC

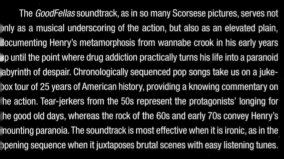

7   A part that fit like a glove: The part of charismatic killer Jimmy was practically tailor-made for Robert De Niro.

8   Seated at the table of honor: In almost all Scorsese films, morality and guilt are dynamically central themes. Here, Henry makes a Judas of himself by contravening Goodfella ethics.

9   A loose cannon: Tommy (Joe Pesci) is eternally on the brink of a nervous breakdown, spazzing out at the very thought of weakness. Time has taught Henry that it is best to ignore these outbursts.

**JOE PESCI**   When he began his career, Joe Pesci was still in his baby booties. Born in 1943 in Newark, New Jersey, the American actor got his start doing radio gigs at the age of four and at ten was already making television appearances. He then changed professional tracks for awhile, trying his hand at music (under the name Joe Ritchie, Pesci recorded the LP "Little Joe Sure Can Sing" and went on to play guitar with the band Joey D and the Starliters). His first film stints flopped and a frustrated Pesci headed back to New York, leaving Hollywood to open up a restaurant. In 1980, Martin Scorsese cast Pesci as Joey La Motta in his masterpiece *Raging Bull* (1980) – a role, which garnered Pesci his first Oscar nomination. Pesci's commercial and critical breaks came in 1990 with the blockbuster films *Home Alone* and Scorsese's *GoodFellas*, respectively; his performance of a psychotic gangster won him an Oscar in 1991. Recently, Pesci appeared in Richard Donner's film *Lethal Weapon 4* (1998).

# CAPE FEAR

1991 - USA - 128 MIN. - THRILLER, REMAKE

DIRECTOR MARTIN SCORSESE (*1942)
SCREENPLAY WESLEY STRICK, based on the script of the same name by JAMES R. WEBB and the novel *THE EXECUTIONERS* by JOHN D. MACDONALD DIRECTOR OF PHOTOGRAPHY FREDDIE FRANCIS MUSIC BERNARD HERRMANN, adapted and arranged by ELMER BERNSTEIN PRODUCTION BARBARA DE FINA for AMBLIN ENTERTAINMENT, CAPPA FILMS, TRIBECA PRODUCTIONS (for UNIVERSAL, GEFFEN).

STARRING ROBERT DE NIRO (Max Cady), NICK NOLTE (Sam Bowden), JESSICA LANGE (Leigh Bowden), JULIETTE LEWIS (Danielle Bowden), JOE DON BAKER (Claude Kersek), ROBERT MITCHUM (Lt. Elgart), GREGORY PECK (Lee Heller), MARTIN BALSAM (Judge), ILLEANA DOUGLAS (Lori Davis), FRED DALTON THOMPSON (Tom Broadbent), ZULLY MONTERO (Graciella).

## "Justice is mine!"

Rapist Max Cady (Robert De Niro) has been waiting fourteen years for this moment: after his release from prison, he can finally take revenge on his lawyer. During his trial, his defence attorney Sam Bowden (Nick Nolte) was so revolted by his crimes that he held back evidence that could have meant a more lenient sentence for the brutal criminal. During his time in prison, Cady has not only learned to read and write and studied American law, but has also created for himself a bizarre fantasy world to which his tattooed body bears witness. One of the many tattoos reads "The Lord shall revenge me" and his back is emblazoned with a gigantic cross on which the scales of "Truth" and "Justice" hang. Until now, the Bowdens, a small family on the verge of breaking up, have managed to create their own hell, but now they are threatened and tyrannised by Cady as well. Cady is particularly interested in Bowden's wife Leigh (Jessica Lange) and his underage daughter Danielle (Juliette Lewis). In desperation, Bowden turns to smarmy private detective Claude Kersek (Joe Don Baker) but rather than improving the situation, this merely puts the lawyer himself beyond the law. Bowden realises that he alone can save his family from a terrible fate. Martin Scorsese's movie is a remake of J. Lee Thompson's thriller *Cape Fear* (1962), in which

Robert Mitchum played the part of Max Cady and Gregory Peck played the panic-stricken lawyer. In the Scorsese version, both of these actors appear in supporting roles.

The basic plot follows a Spielberg theme: as in *Jaws* (1974), a small town idyll is suddenly destroyed with horrific violence for no apparent reason. Unsurprisingly, Spielberg himself originally wanted to film *Cape Fear*. Scorsese was working on the screenplay for *Schindler's List* (1993) at the time, which was also originally an idea of Spielberg's. Eventually the directors decided to swap projects.

Early drafts of the screenplay ran into problems as the element that had attracted Spielberg most wasn't right for Scorsese. Rather than taking an innocent American family struck down out of the blue, Scorsese and scriptwriter Wesley Strick wrote and re-wrote the screenplay, so that the faithful husband became a notorious serial adulterer with an argumentative wife and a rebellious daughter going through a difficult puberty.

From a moral point of view, the Bowdens' dishonesty gives Cady yet another motive for his crazy revenge campaign. Some critics disapproved of this and Scorsese's *Cape Fear* was even compared to Adrian Lyne's *Fatal*

2

3

"*Cape Fear* is the most story-driven film he (Scorsese) has ever made, as well as the one most rooted in genre." *Variety*

4

> ## "It is De Niro – his body covered with tattoos and the tackiest wardrobe in the New South – who dominates the film with his lip-smacking, blackly comic, and terrifying portrayal of psychopathic self-righteousness."
>
> *Newsweek*

*Attraction* (1988), a movie which illustrates the dire consequences of immorality in the family.

*Cape Fear*, however, is most definitely not an appeal for marital faithfulness. It is much closer to *Taxi Driver* (1975), Scorsese's early masterpiece, especially in its portrayal of extreme violence: like Cady, Travis Bickle (also played by Robert De Niro) sets off on a righteous crusade and the bigotry of those around him seems to justify his actions. However, whereas Travis gradually becomes divorced from reality, Max Cady is already living in his own world at the very beginning of the film. His Old Testament wrath gives him an almost supernatural strength, and transforms him into a figure like the angel of death. This exaggeration has an almost surreal effect and makes Cady a symbol of the repressed fears and unconscious desires of the average American family – a demon which the head of the family, the father, must exorcise in the dramatic finale.

This earthly purgatory, which Scorsese later laconically described as "a concession to the genre", is reminiscent of the dramatic showdowns of several Hitchcock films. Hitchcock's influence also shows in the atmosphere of panic and the victims' feelings of guilt which make them more vulnerable to their attacker. There's another good reason why Hitchcock seems ubiquitous in *Cape Fear*: the original screenplay from the 1960s was initially supposed to have been filmed by him.

SH

1 The time for revenge has come: Max Cady (Robert De Niro), disfigured by the symbols of his hatred.

2 The wolf has cast off his sheep's clothing: Danielle Bowden (Juliette Lewis) realises, far too late, that what she thought was a game has become deadly serious.

3 A sick mind in a sound body: Cady's cynicism is surpassed only by his brutality.

4 Even Leigh Bowden (Jessica Lange) is no longer able to keep up the façade of happy families.

5 Modelled on Hitchcock: in the spectacular showdown, Sam Bowden (Nick Nolte) has to face up to his past.

---

**HITCHCOCK** Director (London 1899 – Los Angeles 1980). No other director has had such a lasting influence on the thriller genre as Alfred Hitchcock. Nothing happened to change this in the 90s. His powerful style influenced numerous successors and imitators, as did his pessimistic view of the world and the often extreme representation of violence in his movies. This is particularly true for Scorsese's generation, and directors like Brian de Palma, who can be considered the most consistent Hitchcock admirer, true to his role-model throughout the last decade, as in *Raising Cain* (1991). Younger filmmakers like Quentin Tarantino (*Reservoir Dogs*, 1991/92, *Pulp Fiction*, 1993/94), who are in revolt against the conventional narrative modes of the 90s, are also unthinkable without Hitchcock.

# JFK

1991 - USA - 187 MIN. - POLITICAL THRILLER, DRAMA

DIRECTOR OLIVER STONE (*1946)
SCREENPLAY OLIVER STONE, ZACHARY SKLAR, based on the books *ON THE TRAIL OF THE ASSASSINS* by JIM GARRISON and *CROSSFIRE: THE PLOT THAT KILLED KENNEDY* by JIM MARS DIRECTOR OF PHOTOGRAPHY ROBERT RICHARDSON
MUSIC JOHN WILLIAMS PRODUCTION A. KITMAN HO, OLIVER STONE for IXTLAN CORPORATION, KITMAN HO PRODUCTIONS.

STARRING KEVIN COSTNER (Jim Garrison), TOMMY LEE JONES (Clay Shaw), GARY OLDMAN (Lee Harvey Oswald), JAY O. SANDERS (Lou Ivon), SISSY SPACEK (Liz Garrison), JOE PESCI (David Ferrie), MICHAEL ROOKER (Bill Broussard), LAURIE METCALF (Susie Cox), JOHN CANDY (Dean Andrews), WALTER MATTHAU (Senator Long), DONALD SUTHERLAND (Colonel X), JIM GARRISON (Earl Warren).

ACADEMY AWARDS 1992 OSCARS for BEST CINEMATOGRAPHY (Robert Richardson) and BEST FILM EDITING (Joe Hutshing, Pietro Scalia).

## "Just because you're paranoid, that doesn't mean that they're not out to get you."

Can two men be hit by the same bullet several times in a row? Can one man, an average shot to boot, fatally wound a man in a moving car with a low quality gun from a great distance and in bad visibility? Jim Garrison (Kevin Costner), state attorney of New Orleans, is convinced that all of that is impossible. That means however that Lee Harvey Oswald (Gary Oldman), the solitary assassin of American president John F. Kennedy, could not have committed the crime alone. "I'm just the scapegoat", Oswald asserted before he fell victim to an assassin's bullet in his turn. Three years after the fatal shots were fired at the President on November 22, 1963, in Dallas, Garrison decides to start searching for the real killers. By chance, the assassination does come under his jurisdiction, as it was suspected that Oswald had spent some time in New Orleans. After an initial investigation, Garrison finds so many inconsistencies and contradictions in the Warren Report, the official version of the murder as represented in the US government's enquiry, that he re-opens the whole case. The conclusions reached by the incorrupt-

ible state attorney seem even less credible than the "magic bullet" thesis in the Warren report itself. Could it really be the case that the military, the CIA and high-ranking government officials including Vice President Lyndon B. Johnson himself were involved in a vast conspiracy to get rid of a President considered too much of a peace-monger by the mighty arms industry?

Director Oliver Stone obviously has no doubts. The masters of war conspiracy theory is based on two accounts of the event: Jim Mars' *Crossfire: The Plot That Killed Kennedy* (1989) and Jim Garrison's *On the Trail of the Assassins*, written a year earlier by the real-life model for Stone's main character. Although it is suspected that in reality the controversial attorney entertained Mafia contacts, Stone transforms him into a shining example of American justice to make his re-telling of the case into a general appeal for unreserved critical reappraisal of the past.

When *JFK* was released it became clear that many Americans simply didn't care: "There are conspiracy theories about all sorts of things. There are

1   A day that shook America. The assassination of
    John F. Kennedy on November, 22, 1963, in Dallas
    ranks among the nation's greatest traumas.

2   District Attorney Jim Garrison (Kevin Costner) is
    becoming increasingly estranged from his wife Liz
    (Sissy Spacek).

3   Garrison meticulously pieces the clues together.
    Finally one thing is clear: the American President
    was the victim of a conspiracy.

4   The President in the assassin's sights. It is still a
    mystery how many weapons were fired at
    Kennedy.

5   To track down the truth, director Oliver Stone
    mixes fact and rumour, footage from historic
    archives and reconstructed scenes.

## "I don't know much about the film. I haven't seen it and at the end of the day there are conspiracy theories circulating about all sorts of things. Hey, there are some people who think Elvis is still alive..."

George Bush, Head of the CIA 1976–1977, US President 1989–1993

even rumours that Elvis Presley is still alive…". So spoke the then US President George Bush senior, and statements like that were all grist to Stone's mill. The real strength of the film is the meticulous presentation of the evidence showing that the idea of Oswald as solitary killer is no longer tenable. One of his most effective weapons is to ask why the results of the investigation on President John F. Kennedy's murder must remain secret until 2029 if there is really nothing to hide.

Stone is less interested in the psychology of his characters, and some areas are thinly sketched, like the marital problems of Garrison and his wife Liz (Sissy Spacek). An excellent cast ensures that the characters nonetheless manage to remain convincing and the plot never becomes boring. Joe Pesci plays a manic Communist-hater and Tommy Lee Jones a smoothy conspirator – political explosiveness aside, it is the supporting actors rather than the stars which make *JFK* a cinematic event.

Stone finds no definitive proof for his version of the Kennedy murder. The audience are overwhelmed rather than persuaded by the swift succession of staccato scenes and flashbacks, and by the montage of authentic material and staged sequences. Techniques like that moved some critics to describe the film as propaganda. Stone and his supporters do not dispute this charge: *JFK* is propaganda, but above all it is an important lesson in history, justified by a universal lack of critical historical awareness – a problem not limited to America alone.

SH

**FACTION**   Faction combines facts and fiction without claiming to be historical truth. In this very American way of reappraising the past, people and events are mostly presented as symbolic figures or as key happenings in American history. The faction phenomenon is not limited to film, but is also found in literature like Norman Mailer's fictional autobiography of Marilyn Monroe (*Marilyn, a Biography*, 1973). The foremost factional filmmaker is Oliver Stone, whose numerous films develop a historical panorama of the USA: movies such as *Salvador* (1985), *Platoon* (1986) and *The Doors* (1990) appeal to the historical consciousness of his people and show the USA as a land divided within itself. *JFK* triggered off a whole series of documentary-style biographies in the USA, many of which were also about conspiracy theories.

4

# RAISE THE RED LANTERN
## Dahong Denglong Gaogao Gua

1991 - HONGKONG / PEOPLE'S REPUBLIC OF CHINA - 125 MIN. - LITERATURE ADAPTATION, DRAMA

DIRECTOR ZHANG YIMOU (*1950)
SCREENPLAY NI ZHEN, based on a novel by SU TONG  DIRECTOR OF PHOTOGRAPHY ZHAO FEI  MUSIC ZHAO JIPING  PRODUCTION CHIU FU-SHENG for ERA INTERNATIONAL, CHINA FILM.

STARRING GONG LI (Songlian), MA JINGWU (the Master), HE CAIFEI (Meishan), CAO CUIFENG (Zhuoyun), KONG LIN (Yan'er), JIN SHUYUAN (Yuru), DING WEIMIN (Mother Song), CUI ZHIHGANG (Doctor Gao), CHU XIAO (Feipu), CAO ZHENGYIN (old servant woman).

IFF VENICE 1991 SILVER LION for BEST DIRECTOR (ZHANG YIMOU).

## "People are spirits, spirits are people: breath is the only difference."

"What else is there for women to do?" After the death of her father, Songlian (Gong Li), a young Chinese woman is married off by her stepmother. Rather than becoming the only wife of a poor man, Songlian chooses to live as one of the many wives of a rich man. As "fourth mistress" in the house of her husband (Ma Jingwu), she is subject to a strict regime. Cared for and guarded by servants and housekeepers round the clock, Songlian and her three "sisters" are condemned to complete inactivity, and the age-old family traditions weigh on them like a curse. It soon becomes clear that the strict morals and tradition are nothing but a façade that conceals suffering and decadence. The "first sister", an older woman who is merely tolerated, finds the arrival of the new, girlish wife disgraceful. Songlian is shocked to learn that her lord and master regularly abuses the under-age maid-servant. It doesn't take Songlian long to realise that the real mistress of the house is the wife with red lanterns in her courtyard in the evening, a sign that the master will visit her that night. At first she tries to build up a relationship with her "sisters", but she soon abandons her efforts. Competitiveness, envy and intrigue rule their day-to-day life. Songlian initially attempts to fight against the ossified family rituals, but she gradually learns to use them as a weapon against her rivals. She joins in the power games of the wives that nip any feelings of solidarity in the bud. The chosen wife enjoys certain privileges, but these are not as important as the favour of the master, the only possible form of self-assertion and human contact that remains in their introverted and isolated world. Instead of joining forces against the inhuman system, the wives begin a merciless war against each other.

1    A bird in a gilded cage. The "Fourth Wife",
     Songlian (Gong Li), is a captive in her husband's
     house. It's not long before the rival wives start
     messing each other around.

2    Songlian is married off to a wealthy Chinese man.
     She has to give up her university course after her
     father dies.

**3** "What else can you do as a woman?" Isolated and forced into a totally regimented daily routine, Songlian doesn't recognize herself anymore.

**4** You rub my back... – whoever is the "master's" current favourite is granted certain privileges.

Although the movie is sober and uncompromising, Zhang Yimou's images of 1920s China are breathtakingly beautiful. They can be interpreted both as a psychological study and as a social parable of China oppressed by its communist rulers. The director himself described the movie as a "microcosm of human existence".

*Raise the Red Lantern* impresses not just with the nuances of its acting, but above all through its highly effective use of cinematic stylistic devices. The camera concentrates on the wives and the servants and never focuses directly on the master of the house, making him seem both unapproachable and threatening. The plot takes an almost mechanical course that follows the cycle of the seasons and reflects the way in which the wives' lives are ruled by others. Visually the film is dominated by repeated takes of the estate's rigorously symmetrical architecture. This gives an impression of the inevitable, the inescapable, strengthened by the fact that the camera never leaves the compound where the wives' houses are grouped around the main house. Even the "nights of love" are announced with a military shout: "lanterns in courtyard number four!"

Towards the end of the film, the whole compound is covered in snow and the material world seems almost to dissolve into a timeless, abstract sphere. The architecture becomes a compact and oppressive embodiment of life in captivity, devoid of human warmth, amounting to nothing more than a foreshadowing of inevitable death. Sadly, even the final victory over a competitor cannot put an end to the self-destructive rivalry between the oppressed women: the following summer, a new wife, "sister number five" moves into the vacant house.

SH

**CINEMATIC ARCHITECTURE** Architecture provides both stage and scenery for a movie plot, and makes a major contribution to its atmospheric texture and believability. It is one of the cinema's main means of expression. This is particularly true for genres such as Horror and Science Fiction. Buildings can also be used to structure a plot (*Raise the Red Lantern*) and to generate symbolic meaning, as for example in the some of the films of the British director Peter Greenaway (*The Baby of Mâcon*, 1993). Architecture is the unacknowledged star of many movies.

"In China, *Raise the Red Lantern* is regarded as a symbol of the present situation; the fact that the film has so far not been allowed to be shown in Chinese cinemas is evidence of this." epd Film

# THE SILENCE OF THE LAMBS

1991 - USA - 118 MIN. - THRILLER

DIRECTOR JONATHAN DEMME (*1944)
SCREENPLAY TED TALLY, based on the novel of the same name by THOMAS HARRIS DIRECTOR OF PHOTOGRAPHY TAK FUJIMOTO
MUSIC HOWARD SHORE PRODUCTION GARY GOETZMAN, EDWARD SAXON, KENNETH UTT, RON BOZMAN for STRONG HEART
PRODUCTIONS (for ORION).

STARRING JODIE FOSTER (Clarice Starling), ANTHONY HOPKINS (Dr Hannibal Lecter), SCOTT GLENN (Jack Crawford),
TED LEVINE (Jame Gumb), ANTHONY HEALD (Dr Frederick Chilton), BROOKE SMITH (Catherine Martin), DIANE BAKER
(Senator Ruth Martin), KASI LEMMONS (Ardelia Mapp), ROGER CORMAN (FBI Director Hayden Burke), GEORGE A.
ROMERO (FBI Agent in Memphis).

ACADEMY AWARDS 1992 OSCARS for BEST PICTURE, BEST SCREENPLAY based on material previously produced or published
(Ted Tally), BEST DIRECTOR (Jonathan Demme), BEST ACTOR (Anthony Hopkins) and BEST ACTRESS (Jodie Foster).

## *"I'm having a friend for dinner."*

Clarice Starling (Jodie Foster), daughter of a policeman shot in the line of duty, wants to join the FBI. At the FBI Academy in Woods, Virginia, she races over training courses, pushing herself to the limit. Wooden signs bear the legend "HURT-AGONY-PAIN: LOVE IT" – they're not just there to exhort the rookies to excel, they also reveal the masochism involved. The movie goes through the whole range of this theme, from heroic selflessness to destructive self-hate. Jack Crawford (Scott Glenn), who is Starling's boss and the head of the FBI's psychiatric department, sends her to Baltimore to carry out a routine interview with an imprisoned murderer who is resisting questioning. As well as being a psychiatrist, the prisoner is also an extreme pathological case who attacked people and ate their organs. For eight years

Dr Hannibal "The Cannibal" Lecter (Anthony Hopkins) has lived in the window-less cellar of a high security mental hospital. Crawford hopes the interview will provide clues to the behaviour of a second monster, a killer known as "Buffalo Bill" who skins his female victims and has so far skilfully evaded the FBI. Crawford's plan works, and the professorial cannibal agrees to discuss the pathology of mass murderers with his visitor Clarice – on one condition. Lecter will give her expert advice on Buffalo Bill in exchange for the tale of her childhood trauma. "Quid pro quo" – she lays bare her psyche, he gives her a psychological profile of her suspect. The gripping dialogue that develops between the ill-matched couple can be understood on many levels. On one hand, we see a psychoanalyst talking to his patient, on the

> ## "It has been a good long while since I have felt the presence of Evil so manifestly demonstrated..."
>
> *Chicago Sun-Times*

2

3

1   The naked man and the dead: "Buffalo Bill" (Ted Levine) uses a sewing machine to make himself a new identity from the skin of his victims; above him are butterflies, a symbol of that metamorphosis.

2   The staring matches between Starling (Jodie Foster) and Lecter (Anthony Hopkins) are a battle for knowledge: Lecter is to help the FBI build a profile of the killer; Starling is to surrender the secret of her childhood.

3   The pair meet in the lowest part of the prison system, a basement dungeon from the underworld.

4   The eyes have it: in the serial killer genre, eyes become a tool for appropriation, destruction and penetration.

other, a young detective interrogating an unpredictable serial killer, and that ambiguity is the determining quality in Lecter and Starling's relationship. Both follow their own aims unerringly, refusing to give way, and the struggle that results is one of the most brilliant and sophisticated duels in cinema history. The daughter of a US senator falls into the hands of Buffalo Bill, and suddenly the FBI is under increasing pressure to find the murderer. Lecter's chance has come. In return for his help in capturing Jame Gumb alias Buffalo Bill (Ted Levine), he asks for better conditions and is transferred to a temporary prison in Memphis. He kills the warders and escapes in the uniform of a policeman, whose face he has also removed and placed over his own. His last exchange with Starling takes place over the telephone, when he rings from a Caribbean island to congratulate her on her promotion to FBI agent and bids her farewell with the words: "I'm having a friend for dinner". After hanging up, Lecter follows a group of tourists in which the audience recognise the hated Dr Chilton (Anthony Heald), director of the secure mental hospital in Baltimore, who clearly will be Lecter's unsuspecting dinner "guest".

The Silence of the Lambs marked a cinematic high point at the beginning of the 90s. It is impossible to categorise in any one genre as it combines

several. There are elements from police movies (where crime does not pay), but it's also a thriller that borrows much from real historical figures: the model for both Gumb and Lecter is Edward Gein (1906–1984), who was wearing braces made from his victims' skin when arrested in 1957.

But The Silence of the Lambs is also a movie about psychiatry. Both murderers are presented as psychopaths whose "relation" to one another forms the basis for criminological research, even though their cases are not strictly comparable. The movie was so successful that it became one of the most influential models for the decade that followed, enriching cinema history to the point of plot plagiarism and quotation.

## Suspense and Deception

Hannibal Lecter had already appeared on the silver screen before The Silence of the Lambs. In 1986, Michael Mann filmed Thomas Harris' 1981 novel Red Dragon under the title Manhunter. Five years later, Jonathan Demme refined the material, and the changing perspectives of his camera work give what is fundamentally a cinematic re-telling of Beauty and the

# "*The Silence of the Lambs* is just plain scary – from its doomed and woozy camera angles to its creepy Freudian context."

*The Wahington Post*

*Beast* a new twist. Demme films his characters from both within and with-out.

The director plays with the fluid border between external and internal reality, between memory and the present, as when we see Clarice's childhood in two flashbacks for which we are completely unprepared. Jodie Foster's eyes remain fixed on the here and now while the camera zooms beyond her into the past, probing her psychological wounds. During the final confrontation between Clarice and Jame Gumb, the perspective changes repeatedly. We see the murderer through Clarice's eyes but we also see the young FBI agent through the eyes of Jame, who seeks out his victims in the dark using infrared glasses.

This changing perspective in the movie's final scenes emphasises the extreme danger that Clarice is in. Other sequences are straightforward trickery, like the changing perspectives in the sequence which builds up to the finale. A police contingent has surrounded the house where they expect to find Jame Gumb, and black police officer disguised as a deliveryman rings the bell. On the other side of the door, we hear the bell ring. Jame dresses and answers the door. The police break into the house, whilst we see the murderer open the door to find Clarice standing before him – alone. In the next take, the police storm an empty house. This parallel montage combines two places that are far apart, two actions with the same aim, two houses, of which one is only seen from outside, the other from inside. We are made to

5    6

**5** The cannibal clasps his hands. Cage and pose are reminiscent of Francis Bacon's portraits of the pope.

**6** Lecter overpowers the guards with their own weapons: one policeman is given a taste of his own pepper spray.

**7** The monster is restrained with straitjacket and muzzle; the powers of the state have the monopoly on violence for the time being.

**8** A policeman is disembowelled and crucified on the cage. With his outstretched arms, he looks like a butterfly.

7

think that both actions are happening in the same place. The parallel montage is revealed as a trick and increases the tension: we suddenly realise that Clarice must face the murderer alone.

More than one film critic assumed that this ploy meant that even Hollywood films had moved into an era of self-reflexivity. Instead of consciously revealing a cinematic device, however, the parallel montage serves primarily to heighten the movie's atmosphere of danger and uncertainty. Nevertheless, *The Silence of the Lambs* works on both levels, both as exciting entertainment and as a virtuoso game with key cultural figures and situations. Some critics went so far as to interpret the perverted killer Buffalo Bill as Hades, god of the underworld, and although analyses like that may be interesting, they are not essential to an understanding of the film or its success.

At the 1992 Oscar awards, *The Silence of the Lambs* carried off the so-called Big Five in the five main categories, something which only two films (*It Happened One Night* (1934) and *One Flew Over the Cuckoo's Nest* (1975) had managed previously. Ten years after his escape, Hannibal Lecter appeared again on the silver screen (*Hannibal*, 2001). Jodie Foster refused to play the role of Clarice for a second time and was replaced by Julianne Moore (*Magnolia*) and Ridley Scott took over from Jonathan Demme as director.                                                                                                      RV

8

# "I go to the cinema because I feel like being shocked." *Jonathan Demme*

10

**9** In "Buffalo Bill's" basement lair, Starling is just about to be plunged into total darkness …

**10** … where she has to feel her way blindly, straining to hear, while "Buffalo Bill" watches her through infra-red goggles.

---

**PARALLEL MONTAGE**   A process developed early in the history of cinema. Editing enables two or more events happening in different places to be told and experienced at the same time. The best-known kind of parallel montage in movies is the "last-minute rescue", where images of an endangered or besieged character are juxtaposed in rapid succession with those of the rescuers who are on their way. Action movies use such sequences over and over as a means of increasing the tension, and the device has remained basically the same from David Griffith's 1916 film *Intolerance* to today's thrillers. Parallel montage allows us to be a step ahead of the figures in a film. We are allowed to know things that the characters do not themselves realise, and we are also in several places at the same time, an experience which is only possible in fiction.

# THELMA & LOUISE

1991 - USA - 129 MIN. - ROAD MOVIE, DRAMA

DIRECTOR RIDLEY SCOTT (*1937)
SCREENPLAY CALLIE KHOURI DIRECTOR OF PHOTOGRAPHY ADRIAN BIDDLE MUSIC HANS ZIMMER PRODUCTION PERCY MAIN, MIMI POLK, RIDLEY SCOTT for PERCY MAIN PRODUCTIONS.

STARRING SUSAN SARANDON (Louise Sawyer), GEENA DAVIS (Thelma Dickinson), HARVEY KEITEL (Hal Slocumb), MICHAEL MADSEN (Jimmy), CHRISTOPHER MCDONALD (Darryl), BRAD PITT (J. D.), STEPHEN TOBOLOWSKY (Max), TIMOTHY CARHART (Harlan), LUCINDA JENNY (Lena the waitress), MARCO ST. JOHN (truck driver).

ACADEMY AWARDS 1992 OSCAR for BEST ORIGINAL SCREENPLAY (Callie Khouri).

## "You've always been crazy, this is just the first chance you've had to express yourself."

The movie's first image is of a broad landscape that slowly brightens and then immediately sinks back into darkness. Two friends, Thelma (Geena Davis) and Louise (Susan Sarandon) are treating themselves to a weekend away. Thelma has to get ready in secret, as her helpless husband would never let her out of the house if he knew, as he needs her to make his coffee and fasten his gold bracelet every morning. The unfamiliar freedom is a revelation to her, and at the first stop she orders a drink and takes up a cowboy's invitation to dance. Things turn nasty and he tries to rape her, only giving up when Louise holds a pistol to his head. The crisis seems to have passed when the cowboy starts shouting unbearable obscenities after the two women. Louise turns round and shoots him dead with the words "You watch your mouth, buddy". Horrified at their own actions, the friends flee, convinced that no one would believe their version of events. Thelma's self-confidence has been sapped by long years of marriage and she reacts at first with childish despair, whereas Louise coolly organises their escape to Mexico.

The film then develops a double perspective. The first follows the two women, who become more daring, more independent and less tolerant with every obstacle that crosses their path. Thelma begins to get the hang of being free and getting her own way. She locks a policeman into his own trunk at gunpoint when he tries to arrest them, and then blows up a petrol tanker when the driver directs a stream of sexist comments at them as he drives by. The second perspective shows us the police investigations. Detective Hal Slocumb (Harvey Keitel) is a sensitive cop who suspects the

MS

**ROAD MOVIE**

From the earliest days of the movies, train travel was a popular motif, due to cinema's fascination with movement. When cars and motorbikes became more widespread, movement could be intimately connected with a character's individual development, and from the 40s onwards, outsiders and dropouts were continually portrayed as motorised nomads. The enormous success of Dennis Hopper's *Easy Rider* (1969) helped turn the Road Movie into a recognisable genre.

Similar to the Western, the Road Movie genre generally concentrates on solitary men who only feel free if they are in constant and restless movement. Alongside *Thelma & Louise*, other 90s movies which depict social conflict in the form of epic journeys through the country include David Lynch's *Wild at Heart* (1990) and Oliver Stone's *Natural Born Killers* (1994).

truth about the murder and tries to mediate, but he is powerless to stop the machinery of the FBI once it begins to roll. Thelma spends a night with con man and playboy J. D. (Brad Pitt), who puts the detectives on the trail of the two women. Eventually, an entire flotilla of screeching police cars catches up with Thelma and Louise at the brink of a canyon. A standoff develops and the policemen cock their guns. In a moment of high emotion, Thelma urges Louise to drive on. Louise puts the car in gear and floors the pedal, and they roar off over the edge of the abyss to certain death. The picture freezes as the car hovers high over the canyon and gets brighter and brighter until all we see is pure white light.

*Thelma & Louise* is the story of a liberation. As the journey progresses, the frightened and helpless Thelma develops into a smart, strong woman. The more critical the friends' situation gets, the more assertive she

becomes. Looking back on her married life, she realises how her husband tyrannised her, and the tragedy of her seemingly normal life becomes clear.

*Thelma & Louise* is also a story about a journey into the light. In the course of the movie, the exterior scenes get brighter and brighter until they are almost over-exposed. In jarring contrast, the interiors where the police carry out their interrogations are filmed in cold blue and green. Scott's movie doesn't map out an exclusively female pattern of behaviour for the two friends, but rather lets them take on roles that are usually reserved for men. Reviewers in the US criticised the movie for its man-hating attitudes and glorification of violence, but in fact *Thelma & Louise* makes no generalisations about the sexes. It is one of the few movies where lines and actions were applauded or booed aloud during cinema screenings. Seldom does cinema tread so provocatively on society's fault-lines.

# "These great 'heroines' bring Callie Khouri's furious screenplay to life with totally infectious energy."

*Cinema*

5

4

6

1   Farewell domesticity: Thelma (Geena Davis) forces a policeman into the boot of his car.

2   Pursued by hundreds of policemen, Thelma and Louise (Susan Sarandon) stare resolutely towards the future.

3   A sensational moment from the film: a tanker, the symbol of masculine power, is blown sky-high.

4   Brad Pitt came fresh from the world of advertising to star as a sex symbol in this film.

5   Composed and resolute, Louise reaches for her gun, having no other option.

6   The film repeatedly offers the two women a fleeting respite in the still of the night.

# THE LOVERS ON THE BRIDGE
## Les Amants du Pont-Neuf

1991 - FRANCE - 126 MIN. - DRAMA

DIRECTOR LÉOS CARAX (*1960)

SCREENPLAY LÉOS CARAX DIRECTOR OF PHOTOGRAPHY JEAN-YVES ESCOFFIER MUSIC VARIOUS, including LES RITA MITSOUKO, DAVID BOWIE, IGGY POP, ARVO PÄRT, GILLES TINAYRE PRODUCTION CHRISTIAN FECHNER, ALBERT PRÉVOST, HERVÉ TRUFFAUT, ALAIN DAHAN for FILMS CHRISTIAN FECHNER, FILM A2.

STARRING JULIETTE BINOCHE (Michèle), DENIS LAVANT (Alex), KLAUS-MICHAEL GRÜBER (Hans), DANIEL BUAIN (Alex's Freund), MARION STALENS (Marion), CHRICHAN LARSSON (Julien).

## "I want to be drunk with you, so I can see you laugh."

The first scenes of Léos Carax's movie *The Lovers on the Bridge* are like a documentary shot in cinéma vérité style: a young man staggers along on the central reservation of a road, oblivious to the cars which roar past him. One of the cars knocks him over. A young woman, with a lost air, observes how he is finally picked up by a bus that takes homeless people to a night shelter. Later that night the two meet again on the Pont-Neuf, the oldest bridge in Paris, which is closed for renovation. And there begins Carax's love story, a tale of two outsiders whom life has not treated well.

The young woman is called Michèle (Juliette Binoche) and is a painter who is almost blind in one eye. She is haunted by her bourgeois origins and by an unhappy relationship that forces her to keep a pistol in her paint box. Alex, the young man (Denis Lavant), is hyperactive, antisocial and permanently under the influence of drugs. He occasionally works as a fire-eater. One other memorable character is the old vagabond Hans (Klaus-Michael Grüber), the man who has lived on the bridge for longest. Alex falls in love

with Michèle but has no words to express his love. In order to discover something about the woman he loves, he breaks into her apartment and reads her letters.

Léos Carax went to great lengths for the production of his movie and the recreation of the homeless milieu in which it is set. He had the bridge copied and built almost in an almost life-size replica near Montpellier, complete with sham house fronts on the banks of an artificial Seine. The filming of the movie was dogged by misfortune. First the producer died and then the relationship between Léos Carax and his long-time partner and leading actress Juliette Binoche broke down. The movie took three years to finish and by the time it reached the movie theatres it was three times over budget. Its 160 million francs production costs made it the most expensive French movie ever made up. Although strictly speaking it was not a box office success, the critics loved it, perhaps because its strengths lie in its opulent images rather than in its sparing dialogues. Visually, the movie is

3

1 Painter Michèle (Juliette Binoche) looks more intently at the world inside than she does at the real world.

2 Home as crossover and in-between world: the famous Pont-Neuf bridge in Paris.

3 Michèle asleep.

immensely stylised, but at the same time it also gives a strong impression of realism, so that the audience is never sure whether what it is watching is the product of a fertile imagination or simply an intelligent and realistic film. There are two murders in the movie, which may be real or may just have taken place in Michèle's mind. The empty eye socket, which Alex sees when he lifts Michèle's eyelid, is probably only a figment of his imagination. *The overs on the Bridge* is an uncomfortable movie, compellingly filmed and open to many different interpretations.

Léos Carax has never been one for conventional cinematic idioms. The movie is a kind of cinematic litmus test which shows a great number of dif-

ferent visual layers and shades of emotion and mood. Some of its more exciting scenes have an almost hypnotic quality, as when Michèle and Alex dance wildly during the firework display commemorating the 200th anniversary of the French Revolution or when Michèle waterskis behind a stolen police boat.

The source of Carax's inspiration becomes clear in one of the last shots in the movie. The two lovers are shown in a pose which reminds us of the figurehead of a ship, a homage to Jean Vigo's film *L'Atalante* (1934), a masterpiece which combines a dream-like atmosphere with the realities of Parisian life.                                                                                          APO

4

5

4　The people who live on the bridge have the fireworks celebrating the bicentenary of the French Revolution in their front room.

5　A love without words: Alex (Denis Levant) and Michèle on their bridge.

## "This wounded tarantella of a film is unique. The emotion wells from its form not its core, and is as pure and direct as the great never-to-be-forgotten pre-war melodramas. Few words, music of every denomination, and so many breathtaking images that one drowns in them." *Le Monde*

**JULIETTE BINOCHE** Juliette Binoche won her first Academy Award in 1997 for her supporting role as the nurse in *The English Patient*. The daughter of an actress and a sculptor, her career as an actress began in the mid-80s in her native land with movies such as Jean-Luc Godard's *Hail Mary* (*Je vous salue, Marie*, 1983) and Léos Carax's *Bad Blood* (*Mauvais Sang*, 1986). She and Carax were partners for many years until their relationship broke up during the filming of *The Lovers on the Bridge*. Her roles in Philip Kaufman's film of Kundera's novel *The Unbearable Lightness of Being* (1987), Louis Malle's *Damage* (1992) and Krysztof Kieslowski's *Three Colours: Blue* (*Trois Couleurs: Bleu*, 1993) won her an international reputation as the archetypal French actress. She has recently consolidated her position at the forefront of European cinema with roles in Michael Haneke's cool, distanced *Code Unknown* (*Code: Inconnu*, 1999) and in Lasse Hallström's sugary romance about confectionery, *Chocolat* (2000).

# TWIN PEAKS: FIRE WALK WITH ME

1992 - USA - 134 MIN. - MYSTERY DRAMA

DIRECTOR DAVID LYNCH (*1946)
SCREENPLAY DAVID LYNCH, ROBERT ENGELS DIRECTOR OF PHOTOGRAPHY RON GARCIA MUSIC ANGELO BADALAMENTI
PRODUCTION GREGG FIENBERG for LYNCH-FROST PRODUCTIONS, CIBY PICTURES.

STARRING SHERYL LEE (Laura Palmer), RAY WISE (Leland Palmer), KYLE MACLACHLAN (Dale Cooper),
MOIRA KELLY (Donna Hayward), CHRIS ISAAK (Chester Desmond), DANA ASHBROOK (Bobby Briggs),
KIEFER SUTHERLAND (Sam Stanley), DAVID BOWIE (Phillip Jeffries), HARRY DEAN STANTON (Carl Rodd),
PEGGY LIPTON (Norma Jennings).

## "A freaky accident."

When Laura Palmer is murdered in Portland, Oregon, FBI Agent Chester Desmond (Chris Isaak) and his young colleague Sam Stanley (Kiefer Sutherland) are not sent to investigate. But the case (a young girl wrapped in a plastic tarpaulin found murdered on a riverbank) bears a clear resemblance to the murder which happens months later in the small town of Twin Peaks. In the course of the investigation Agent Desmond disappears without trace and Agent Dale Cooper (Kyle MacLachlan) is sent to replace him. Several inauspicious signs, including a letter of the alphabet found under a fingernail of the victim, convince Dale Cooper that the murderer will strike again. But who knows where and when …

The film of the television series begins appropriately with an imploding television set, followed by the famous place name sign from the series' opening credits and Angelo Badalamenti's atmospheric film music – we're back in Twin Peaks alright. Laura Palmer is still alive, and what we see are her last days, in the hope of finding out what the series left unclear.

Lynch claimed that his main reason for developing the TV series Twin Peaks (1990–1991) into a lengthy feature film was the feeling that he had

not yet finished with the material. The series' creators, David Lynch and Mark Frost, had originally hoped that the crime story of Twin Peaks would gradually fade into the background and eventually become completely unimportant. The unexpected success of the series meant that they were eventually forced to present their audiences and producers with a murderer. As Lynch had warned, viewer numbers then fell and he ended up suffering for a mistake that was not his own.

However the bizarre, imaginary world of Twin Peaks and the inconsistencies of its main characters continued to haunt Lynch, and before long he began work on the movie Twin Peaks: Fire Walk With Me. Accusations that he was trying to cash in on the success of the TV series are unfair. The movie brings together some of the plot strands which had been lost in the increasingly complex weave of the story. The incest theme, which only emerged slowly in the series, is one of the main elements in this process, and Lynch was also able to give more space to the sexual aspects of the story in general, as he no longer had to worry about TV regulations in the many countries where Twin Peaks was broadcast. Numerous hints and questions left

open in the series are explained, and in the movie Lynch does his characters more justice by working on their psychic conflicts and making them more convincing. As obscure hints and contradictions were the lifeblood of the series, clarifying matters in the movie was a risk. In the final edit, a number of scenes were omitted, some off-beat marginal figures were cut to fit the material to film length and a more clearly defined plot framework was provided. Many ironic allusions fell by the wayside, and so for instance regular viewers of the TV series were disappointed to see that the frequent references to doughnuts and cherry pie had disappeared. Much of what was cut were the elements that served to lighten the mood of the series, and so the movie turned out much darker than its TV model. The bizarre atmosphere of Twin Peaks and the threatening presence of the forest condense into a claustrophobic nightmare. Audiences unfamiliar with Lynch's earlier work are unsure how to react, but, the movie remains a monument to Lynch's single-mindedness and versatility. He did more than continue the series: he fitted his material to the demands of a different medium. The message makes uncomfortable viewing, but his treatment of it is clear.

SH

---

**FILM AND TV**    The wide distribution of video and DVD players means that movies are no longer viewed solely on the wide screen, but often at home on a television screen. The two different media and picture formats are therefore easily compared and discussed. Television's means of expression often influence movie making, as is the case for the aesthetic of the video clip and the quick editing techniques used by directors such as Oliver Stone (*Natural Born Killers*, 1994). Other directors like Britain's Peter Greenaway have experimented with new technical possibilities such as high definition TV (*Prospero's Books*, 1991). A further example is David Lynch's *Twin Peaks* (1990–91), a TV series which also complies to the more sophisticated requirements of cinematic art. Despite subsequent efforts to reconcile TV and cinema – for example Oliver Stone's three-part TV series *Wild Palms* (1993) – such ambitious projects remain the exception rather than the rule.

1    During his investigation, Agent Dale Cooper (Kyle MacLachlan) visits a bizarre dream world, where he is given puzzling tip-offs by a dwarf.

2    Beautiful but flawed: before her murder Laura Palmer (Sheryl Lee) did not lead the completely blameless life she would have had people believe.

3    *Twin Peaks: Fire Walk With Me* is a prequel to the TV series. The viewer is given insights into Laura Palmer's double life and in the end finds out who the real killer was.

4    There can't always be cherry cake: many ironic allusions fell victim to editorial cuts, including Dale Cooper's fondness for local specialities.

5    The cryptic dream symbolism has a clearer role to play in the much darker film version.

3

"People want to forget the world around them, but at the same time they're scared of it. Watching a film at home is much safer. There are worlds I'd rather not experience — but if I go to the cinema, I want to be right in the middle of the action." *David Lynch*

4

5

# JURASSIC PARK

♦♦♦

1993 - USA - 126 MIN. - ACTION FILM

DIRECTOR STEVEN SPIELBERG (*1947)
SCREENPLAY MICHAEL CRICHTON, DAVID KOEPP, based on the novel *DINOPARK* by MICHAEL CRICHTON
DIRECTOR OF PHOTOGRAPHY DEAN CUNDEY MUSIC JOHN WILLIAMS PRODUCTION KATHLEEN KENNEDY, GERALD R. MOLEN
for AMBLIN ENTERTAINMENT.

STARRING SAM NEILL (Dr Alan Grant), LAURA DERN (Ellie Sattler), JEFF GOLDBLUM (Dr Ian Malcolm),
RICHARD ATTENBOROUGH (John Hammond), SAMUEL L. JACKSON (Arnold), BOB PECK (Robert Muldoon),
MARTIN FERRERO (Donald Gennaro), B. D. WONG (Dr Wu), JOSEPH MAZZELLO (Tim), ARIANA RICHARDS (Lex).

ACADEMY AWARDS 1994 OSCARS for BEST VISUAL EFFECTS (Dennis Muren, Stan Winston, Phil Tippett, Michael Lantieri),
BEST SOUND (Ronald Judkins, Shawn Murphy, Gary Rydstrom, Gary Summers), BEST SOUND EFFECTS EDITING
(Richard Hymns, Gary Rydstrom).

## "You should have more respect."

John Hammond (Richard Attenborough) has a vision: he wants to build the biggest and most unusual theme park in the world. As is so often the case in mainstream cinema, his vision compensates for a personal shortcoming – he has a pronounced limp. On a secluded island off the coast of Costa Rica, his idea is to present the public with the most extraordinary thing imaginable: living dinosaurs. Thanks to advances in genetics, such a thing is now possible, and by reactivating the DNA of dinosaur blood from mosquitos trapped in fossilised tree resin, Jurassic Park's scientists clone dinosaurs back into existence after millions of years of extinction.

Unfortunately, the plan begins to go wrong when a park employee is fatally injured by particularly dangerous species of dinosaur as it is being unloaded. His family claims for compensation and the park's insurers and investors commission a safety report. To carry out the investigation, Hammond invites a group of experts to the park including palaeontologist Alan Grant (Sam Neill), his girlfriend Ellie Sattler (Laura Dern) a biologist who specialises in extinct plants of the dinosaur age, an insurance expert, and chaos theoretician Ian Malcolm (Jeff Goldblum). Hammond hopes that the giant lizards will impress the scientists so much that they will abandon their critical attitudes and leave filled with enthusiasm for his project. When the helicopter with the scientists approaches the island and the movie's memorable theme tune is heard for the first time, the audience is also convinced that they are about to see something really amazing. Grant and Sattler are only used to dealing with

# "Spielberg plays like a virtuoso on the keys of the visual arts industry. He takes our longing for the miraculous, and then makes the miraculous accessible to people like you and me."

*epd Film*

the dinosaurs' excavated skeletons and they fall in love with the prehistoric creatures at first sight. The insurance expert is positively bursting with enthusiasm and greed. Only Ian Malcolm takes a pessimistic view of the park and predicts that messing around with nature can only bring catastrophe.

It's hard not to be impressed with the computer animated dinosaurs of *Jurassic Park*, which stride majestically across the screen. Spielberg knows how to make the most of them and builds an exciting plot around them.

Before *Jurassic Park*, dinosaurs had only ever been seen on the screen when scientists took a trip back in time or discovered lost continents in the earth's interior where primitive nature survived. But when Steven Spielberg came to make his movie, advances in genetics had added a new motif to the dinosaur story. If it's possible to decipher the human DNA code, why not the genes of an animal which lived on the earth many millions of years ago? The explosive potential of such experiments when combined with human greed soon become all too clear to the protagonists of the movie.

Disaster strikes on the island when Robert Muldoon (Bob Peck, a greedy Park employee), decides to sell embryos to the competition and deactivates the security system for a few minutes to carry out the theft.

Muldoon chooses a weekend when the security staff are on the mainland. As in a traditional horror film, all the prerequisites are prepared, and preparation for a night of spectacular terror, the weather forecast predicts violent storms. The nightmare begins: fences are ripped up, high-voltage cables tear and flail, bridges are flooded, mudslides sweep away the sides of the mountains, there's thunder and lightning, the heavens send forth fire and brimstone and there's also a tyrannosaurus rex, one or two velociraptors, a poisonous dilophosaurus and a herd of brachiosauri. The electricity fails and the visitors' computerised jeeps come to a standstill. Alan Grant, Ian Malcolm, Hammond's two grandchildren and the insurance expert are in extreme danger. The latter falls victim to a tyrannosaurus attack. The chaos theoretician survives, but is wounded and has to be left behind. Grant escapes with the two children.

One of the movie's most memorable scenes is the second attack by the tyrannosaurus. We see vibrations in a puddle of water which become stronger and stronger until it is filled with small waves and the earth trembles under the creature's claws. The hunted visitors try to escape in the jeep, but it can't get up enough speed on the swampy ground.

1  "What used to fascinate me even as a child was King Kong." *Steven Spielberg*

2  Man playing God. Their eyes (Richard Attenborough, Laura Dern, Sam Neill) may be shining, but they are blinded by their enthusiasm.

3  Nature unleashed. Rarely a recipe for success.

4  What looks like a hermetically sealed world turns out to have a few loopholes.

Most impressive of all is the precarious balance that Spielberg maintains on the knife-edge between horror film and family entertainment. He carefully avoids showing the dinosaur's brutal and horrific behaviour in any great detail, while still managing to keep up the tension to please the horror and animation fans. *Jurassic Park* once again proves the cinematic truism that it is more effective to show the consequences of horrific happenings than to show the events themselves. Rather than seeing the blood spurt when a cow is devoured by a velociraptor, we see the waving grass and then hear ear-piercing bellows of fear followed by slurping noises and the sound of bones.

In the morning after the night of terror it seems as if nothing has happened: Alan Grant has found a safe haven in the tree tops with the children. A brachiosaur peacefully grazes under their feet and even allows itself to be stroked. It shows its appreciation by grunting like a walrus and the children feel they could befriend this extinct giant.

But the peace does not last. A small group fights its way into the command bunker of the park. In the meantime the others have managed to re-boot the park's computer and have telephoned for a helicopter to come and take them off the island. They await their rescue in the Jurassic Park museum, where fossilized dinosaurs are exhibited to whet the visitors' appetite for the real thing. Finally, past and present clash for one last time. Two murderous velociraptors attack the group, but a tyrannosaur appears which fights back and saves the survivors. The dream ends, and once again humans and dinosaurs are separated by a distance of millions of years.

SL

**SOUND DESIGN** The simulated dinosaurs seem so overwhelmingly convincing because they are the result of a combination of many different hi-tech techniques. The model animators worked closely with computer animators, blue screen experts and animal trainers. Spielberg often uses sound to reinforce the impression of terror and danger, so boffins and sound engineers were kept particularly busy on this movie, where they found themselves on completely new acoustic territory. The dinosaurs had to sound life-like, but no one could say what an enraged dinosaur attacking two children in a kitchen might have sounded like: the solution they finally arrived at was to mix dolphin noises with walrus grunts until the whole thing sounded sufficiently aggressive. Another challenge was to produce an acoustic effect to mirror the optical effect of dinosaur's footsteps making rings in a water glass. Sound engineers solved that problem by placing the glass on a guitar and plucking the strings. Effects like that provided plenty of acoustic thrills for the new sound systems of the multiplex cinemas.

5   Sceptics (Jeff Goldblum) may not be heroes, but in the end they are usually right.

6   The hunt for the kill in a shiny chrome kitchen. The boy (Joseph Mazzello), rigid with fear, is trying to hide from the dinosaurs.

7   An American nightmare: the monster doesn't even respect the cars.

5

# FOUR WEDDINGS AND A FUNERAL

1993/1994 - GREAT BRITAIN - 117 MIN. - COMEDY

**DIRECTOR** MIKE NEWELL (*1942)
**SCREENPLAY** RICHARD CURTIS **DIRECTOR OF PHOTOGRAPHY** PHILIP SINDALL **MUSIC** RICHARD RODNEY BENNETT
**PRODUCTION** DUNCAN KENWORTHY for WORKING TITLE (for POLYGRAM, CHANNEL FOUR).

**STARRING** HUGH GRANT (Charles), ANDIE MACDOWELL (Carrie), KRISTIN SCOTT THOMAS (Fiona), SIMON CALLOW (Gareth), JAMES FLEET (Tom), ANNA CHANCELLOR (Henrietta), CHARLOTTE COLEMAN (Scarlett), CHARLES BOWER (David), SARA CROWE (Laura), TIMOTHY WALKER (Angus).

## "Marriage is just a way of getting out of an embarrassing pause in conversation."

It's just another normal Saturday morning. At a shrill ring from the alarm clock, Charles (Hugh Grant) falls out of bed, staggers into his tailcoat and rushes off to church. Hardly a weekend goes by when he and his friends are not invited to some wedding or other. Charles is always late. He may be invited to lots of weddings, but he has no intention of marrying himself. As his friends get hitched one by one, the shy and chaotic bachelor remains a "serial monogamist" as he says himself, apparently unable to sustain any serious relationship. But at this particular wedding reception he meets Carrie (Andie MacDowell) – the woman of his dreams, and it's a classic case of love at first sight. Carrie seduces him and they spend the night together. The next morning, Charles hesitates a moment too long and suddenly the American beauty has disappeared from his life – if not from his thoughts.

Of course they meet again – at the next wedding. Before Charles can pluck up the courage to speak, Carrie introduces him to her future husband, who she marries at the movie's third wedding. The fourth, which is only stopped at the last minute by the courageous intervention of Charles' deaf brother, is Charles' own – but the bride's name isn't Carrie.

The succession of wedding celebrations is interrupted by a burial: one of Charles' friends, the bon-vivant and cynic Gareth (Simon Callow), dies of a heart attack at Carrie's wedding. When his friend Matthew holds the funeral speech, Charles suddenly realises that despite the absence of a wedding certificate and the accompanying celebrations, Matthew and Gareth had also made a real commitment for life.

These four weddings and one funeral are the main events of Mike Newell's light-hearted satire on the fossilized code of conduct and behaviour of the British upper classes. The only couples held together by true love are those who will never marry. If Gareth is to be believed, marriage is simply a way of dealing with the embarrassing pauses in conversation which become more frequent as a relationship progresses. Charles' other friend Tom (James Fleet) is equally pragmatic: he hopes to find a nice girl who won't feel nauseous when she looks at him and with whom he can simply be happy.

The script of *Four Weddings and a Funeral* was written by Richard Curtis, one of Britain's most productive film writers and the creator of many successful television series and feature films. He wrote the series

"Mike Newell's film finds its premise in one of modern life's minor truths: if you are a sociable specimen of the yuppie breed, you spend much of your spare income suiting yourself up for friends' weddings." *Time Magazine*

3

4

5

6

Blackadder and Mr. Bean together with Rowan Atkinson, who plays a small but hilarious role in this movie as a stuttering priest. Four Weddings and a Funeral was a small budget production, but it became Britain's s most successful movie to date and was only knocked off the number one spot when Roger Michell's romantic comedy Notting Hill came along in 1999, also starring Hugh Grant and written by Richard Curtis. Mike Newell's movie shows as little of the everyday life of its characters as it shows of the real social conditions in Britain. His protagonists all come from "good" families and we only see them in their Sunday best, either at weddings or on their way there. The audience's gaze sweeps through the party like that of a curious guest. Interesting people catch the eye, and the witty dialogue catches the ear. From the very first ring of the alarm clock to the last kiss, the timing of this brilliant farce is perfect, and it combines all the best elements of comedy and melodrama. APO

---

**BAFTA AWARD**    The British Academy of Film was founded in 1947 by a committee of 14 people under the director David Lean. Its aim was to promote excellence in the British movie industry. In 1958 it fused with the professional body of television producers and directors and in 1978 it was renamed the British Academy of Film and Television Arts (BAFTA). The BAFTA award is the most important film and television prize in Britain and is awarded yearly in various categories. The golden mask that commemorates each award was designed by the artist Mitzi Cunliffe.

---

1  The role of the shy young bachelor who attends wedding after wedding turned British actor Hugh Grant into a super-star.

2  David (Charles Bower, centre), the speech- and hearing-impaired brother of Charles, saves him at the last minute from making the biggest mistake of his life.

3  Hats off: the role of the independent and self-assured American lady Carrie could have been tailor-made for Andie MacDowell.

4  Suffering in silence: Fiona (Kristin Scott Thomas), who's been in love with Charles for years, is just a "good friend" as far as he's concerned.

5  Last minute rush: Charles and his flat-mate Scarlett (Charlotte Coleman) dash from one wedding to the next.

6  An arch commentator: the long drawn out parties wouldn't be half so much fun without Gareth's (Simon Callow, left) witty observations.

# PHILADELPHIA                                              ♟♟

1993 - USA - 125 MIN. - DRAMA, COURTROOM DRAMA

DIRECTOR JONATHAN DEMME (*1944)
SCREENPLAY RON NYSWANER DIRECTOR OF PHOTOGRAPHY TAK FUJIMOTO MUSIC HOWARD SHORE PRODUCTION EDWARD SAXON,
JONATHAN DEMME for COLUMBIA TRISTAR, CLINICA ESTETICO.

STARRING TOM HANKS (Andrew Becket), DENZEL WASHINGTON (Joe Miller), JASON ROBARDS (Charles Wheeler),
MARY STEENBURGEN (Belinda Conine), JOANNE WOODWARD (Sarah Becket), ANTONIO BANDERAS (Miguel Alvarez),
RON VAWTER (Bob Seidman), JEFFREY WILLIAMSON (Tyrone), CHARLES NAPIER (Richter Garnett), LISA SUMMEROUR
(Lisa Miller).

ACADEMY AWARDS 1994 OSCARS for BEST ACTOR (Tom Hanks) and BEST SONG (Bruce Springsteen, "The Streets of Philadelphia").

IFF BERLIN 1994 SILVER BEAR for BEST ACTOR (Tom Hanks).

# "Forget everything you've seen
# on television and in the movies."

Andrew Becket (Tom Hanks) and Joe Miller (Denzel Washington) are two ambitious young lawyers. They have just presented opposing sides of a civil law case; afterwards in the elevator they simultaneously tear their dictaphones out of their pockets to record the case results; somewhere a cell phone rings and without interrupting their dictation, both search for their phones. Youth, ambition and lots of energy – that's what they have in common, but nothing more: Joe Miller is black, a legal eagle who advertises his work in local TV commercials; Andrew Becket is a WASP, graduate of an elite university and employed by one of Philadelphia's most prestigious law firms. He is also gay. A few days later things start to happen: Becket is made a senior partner of the firm by his mentor Charles Wheeler (Jason Robards) and is entrusted with a very important case. A blood test shows that he has AIDS. No one in the firm is supposed to know about his illness. But when a vital document disappears under mysterious circumstances and he is fired for

incompetence, he suspects his disease is the real reason for the dismissal and decides to sue his former employers for discrimination. Unfortunately, there is not a single lawyer in the city who is prepared to take on his case – apart from Joe Miller, who as a black man knows what it's like to be discriminated against. After a long period of hesitation he decides to help Becket, above all because the case will bring both money and publicity.

1993/94 seemed to herald a new trend in Hollywood. Two films were released which confronted audiences with historical and social reality. Hard on the heels of Steven Spielberg's Holocaust movie *Schindler's List* came Jonathan Demme's *Philadelphia*, and more than ten years after "gay cancer" first became public knowledge, the first big budget movie about AIDS had appeared.

The interesting thing about *Philadelphia* is that it is not what it claims to be. It is a complete failure as a film about gays and AIDS. It succeeds how-

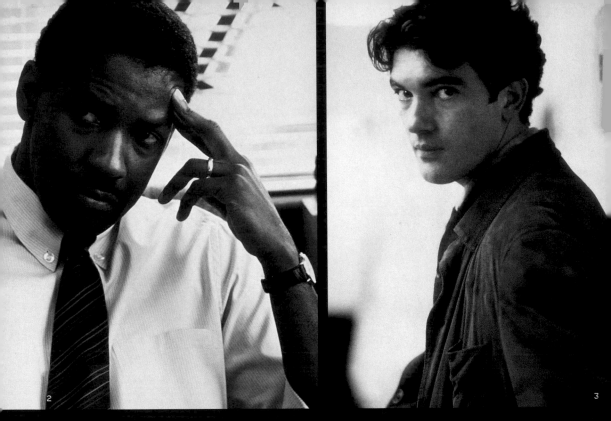

2   3

"It is, at the very least, a giant step forward for Hollywood, which tends to portray homosexuals as either psychopathic cross-dressers or the giddy fruitcakes who live next door." *The Washington Post*

4   5

6

ever as a tension-filled and exciting courtroom drama about deep-seated social prejudices against those who think, look and love differently. In this respect it resembles Stanley Kramer's movie *Guess Who's Coming to Dinner?* (1967) where parents Spencer Tracy and Katharine Hepburn have to get used to the idea of a black son-in-law. Becket's lawyer Joe Miller, convincingly portrayed by Denzel Washington, is the prototypical normal person. His hatred of gays is deep-rooted and his ignorance of the disease astonishing. When Becket goes to visit him for the first time in his office, they shake hands. A few moments later, Miller discovers that Becket has AIDS. The camera reveals his fear, it follows his eyes to the objects Andrew has touched like the cigars Miller keeps for his clients and a photo of his new-

born daughter. When Andrew has left, he immediately makes a doctor's appointment. But the irony is that Becket could not wish for a better lawyer: Miller forces the jury to examine its own prejudices, just as the cinema audience is forced to do.

*Philadelphia* was classified as suitable for children. No bodily fluids are exchanged between gay men, and there is nothing more explicit than a peck on the cheek. The same fears demonstrated by Joe Miller's dealings with gays are mirrored in the movie's treatment of what is supposed to be its main theme. Despite, or perhaps because of this, Demme's attempt to make contact was rewarded with a clutch of international film prizes, including two Oscars. APO

**HOMOSEXUALITY IN THE MOVIES**
Homosexuality hardly appeared at all in the movies from the very beginning of cinema to recent years. Social acceptance was extremely limited and pressure from the industry was too great. One of the very first movies ever made is called *The Gay Brothers* (William Dickson, 1895) and shows two men dancing a waltz. From the mid1930s onwards, the portrayal of homosexuality in film became virtually impossible in the USA thanks to the industry's self-imposed production code. If homosexuals appeared at all, they were presented as ridiculous camp characters. Homosexuality in movies has only ceased to be an issue since the 1980s.

1 The courage to play an outsider: the role of the attorney (Andrew Becket) suffering from AIDS presented a real challenge for Hollywood star Tom Hanks.

2 Worried he might catch something: homophobic attorney Joe Miller (Denzel Washington) knows all about discrimination.

3 Faithful unto death: Andrew's partner Miguel Alvarez (Antonio Banderas) knows he caught the disease by playing around.

4 A plausible façade: as long as Andrew can keep up appearances, the partners in his chambers still think he's the best.

5 Overstepping the mark: Denzel Washington is outraged when someone in a supermarket thinks he's gay.

6 Andrew's mentor Charles Wheeler (Jason Robards, left) holds the ambitious young attorney in high esteem – perhaps because he recognizes in him something of himself. He is inconsolable when he learns the truth about his protégé.

# IN THE LINE OF FIRE

1993 - USA - 128 MIN. - POLITICAL THRILLER

DIRECTOR WOLFGANG PETERSEN (*1941)
SCREENPLAY JEFF MAGUIRE DIRECTOR OF PHOTOGRAPHY JOHN BAILEY MUSIC ENNIO MORRICONE PRODUCTION JEFF APPLE for CASTLE ROCK ENTERTAINMENT, COLUMBIA PICTURES.

STARRING CLINT EASTWOOD (Frank Horrigan), JOHN MALKOVICH (Mitch Leary/John Booth/James Carney), RENE RUSSO (Lilly Raines), DYLAN MCDERMOTT (Al D'Andrea), GARY COLE (Bill Watts), FRED DALTON THOMPSON (Harry Sargent), JOHN MAHONEY (Sam Campagna), GREG ALAN-WILLIAMS (Matt Wilder), JIM CURLEY (President), SALLY HUGHES (First Lady).

## "Why not call me Booth?"

America is traumatized by its dead Presidents, from Abraham Lincoln, murdered by J. W. Booth in 1865 while watching a play from a box at the theatre, right up to JFK, whose death became one of the most disturbing and macabre events in the history of television. The amateur film of Kennedy's murder in 1963 is probably the most minutely analysed pieces of celluloid of all time, and the pictures were broadcast repeatedly in a constant re-examination of the murder, an early example of reality TV.

In the Line of Fire uses that idea as a plot mechanism, but Petersen's movie is really about the ancient duel between good and evil. At first glance the divide seems simple enough: undercover cop Frank Horrigan (Clint Eastwood) is tough and hands-on, his evil opponent Mitch Leary (John Malkovich) thoughtful and intellectual. They are both cynics. But at a second glance another perspective begins to appear. We see Frank play beautiful ballads on the piano and tenderly court his colleague Lilly (Rene Russo), whereas Leary murders two women in their apartment and kills two hunters in cold blood while practising his aim.

Clint Eastwood plays ageing bodyguard Frank Horrigan, a man who feels he failed President Kennedy. The role goes against his image as an

unscrupulous supporter of lynch justice, which he owes above all to the "Dirty Harry" movies. The impatient individualist of In the Line of Fire also hates bureaucrats but he has a kindly side too. Eastwood's Frank Horrigan doesn't hide the signs of age or the unhealed wounds on his soul. Leary, his diabolic opponent, also suffers; the system that taught him the art of perfect killing suddenly no longer wants him. Once part of a special unit that planned and carried out assassinations on the government's orders, he has now been discharged. Malkovich's Leary is an intellectual killer who carries out his plan to revenge his dismissal by assassinating the President of the USA with super-cool precision. His sudden outbreak of rage when Frank manages to talk with him on the telephone only makes him seem even more dangerous and unpredictable. Eastwood's stony face contrasts with Malkovich's changing disguises, from eccentric hippy to smart software manager.

Combined with Petersen's fine sense for the right dose of suspense, this constellation carries the movie throughout its length despite occasional narrative shallows. Leary sometimes calls himself Booth after Lincoln's murderer, and plays a gripping cat and mouse game with Frank who sees the case as a chance to make good his previous failure. Booth's real concern is

2

1   Frank Horrigan (Clint Eastwood): patriotism is
    a question of honour.

2   The horrors of the past keep catching up with
    Officer Horrigan, who is as uncompromising as he
    is fearless.

3   Loss of honour to be avenged: John Malkovich
    as the demonic adversary Mitch Leary.

4   If Frank Horrigan ever smiles …

5   … it's only because of his good-looking
    colleague Lilly (Rene Russo).

not the President's personal safety. The movie distances itself from politics and reveals a clear satirical undertone when it presents an election campaign as a carnivalesque parade, and when the President is removed from the line of fire of a presumed assassin during a public appearance there are strong overtones of slapstick.

The movie concentrates instead on the duel between Leary and Horrigan and plays with the closeness between criminal and victim. Whenever Frank and his colleagues try to locate him, Leary is constantly one step ahead. Leary is a brilliant strategist, and can even manipulate the telephone wires to cover his tracks.

Thanks to the extreme economy of John Bailey's camera work (*Silverado*, 1985) and Anne Coates' (*Lawrence of Arabia*, 1962) masterful editing, Petersen manages to balance and combine the two diverging halves of the movie, its hectic action scenes and the romance between Frank and Lilly. He constantly inserts ironic breaks, as when the CIA and the FBI attack each other in Leary's empty apartment as they have no idea that the other would be there. In the end, however, after a last minute showdown where Frank throws himself in front of the President and saves his life, there can only be one winner.

BR

**WOLFGANG PETERSEN**   *Das Boot* (*The Boat*) is Petersen's best-known project, made in 1979–1981 as a television series and as a feature film which was eventually nominated for an Oscar. He began his career in 1960 as a director's assistant at the Ernst-Deutsch Theater in Hamburg. After his studies at the Berlin Film and Television Academy, he made a name for himself with television productions, particularly with *Reifezeugnis* ("High School Graduation", 1977), a feature-length episode of a crime series. In his first English-language movie *The NeverEnding Story* (1984) Petersen made a surprising departure from his usual direct style. Since *Enemy Mine* (1985) Petersen has worked in Hollywood, where *In the Line of Fire* was an important breakthrough for him. His latest work is the largely computer animated shipwreck spectacle *The Perfect Storm* (2000), starring George Clooney in the leading role.

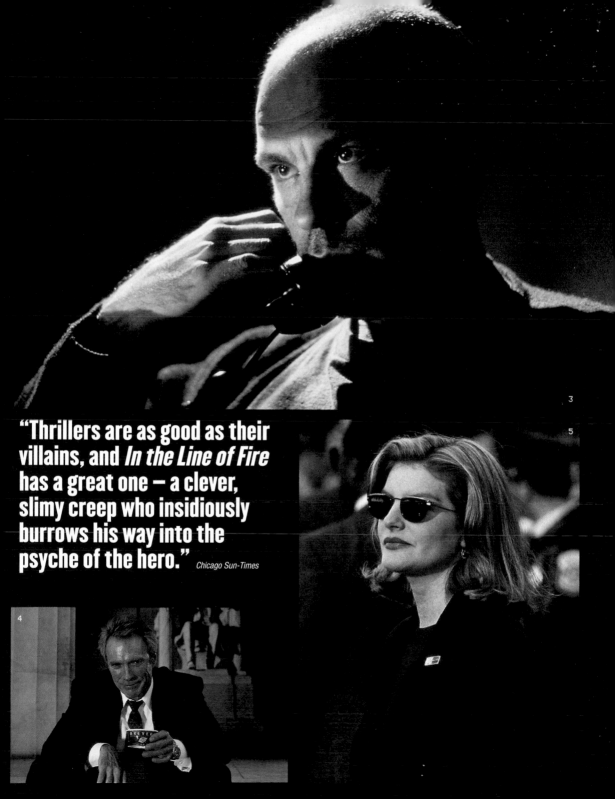

3

5

"Thrillers are as good as their villains, and *In the Line of Fire* has a great one – a clever, slimy creep who insidiously burrows his way into the psyche of the hero." *Chicago Sun-Times*

4

# SCHINDLER'S LIST

1993 - USA - 195 MIN. - HISTORICAL FILM, DRAMA

**DIRECTOR** STEVEN SPIELBERG (*1947)
**SCREENPLAY** STEVEN ZAILLIAN, based on the novel of the same name by THOMAS KENEALLY **DIRECTOR OF PHOTOGRAPHY** JANUSZ KAMINSKI **MUSIC** JOHN WILLIAMS **PRODUCTION** STEVEN SPIELBERG, GERALD R. MOLEN, BRANKO LUSTIG for AMBLIN ENTERTAINMENT, UNIVERSAL PICTURES.

**STARRING** LIAM NEESON (Oskar Schindler), BEN KINGSLEY (Itzhak Stern), RALPH FIENNES (Amon Goeth), CAROLINE GOODALL (Emilie Schindler), JONATHAN SAGALL (Poldek Pfefferberg), EMBETH DAVIDTZ (Helen Hirsch), MALGOSCHA GEBEL (Victoria Klonowska), SHMULIK LEVY (Wilek Chilowicz), MARK IVANIR (Marcel Goldberg), BÉATRICE MACOLA (Ingrid).

**ACADEMY AWARDS 1994** OSCARS for BEST PICTURE, BEST DIRECTOR (Steven Spielberg), BEST ADAPTED SCREENPLAY (Steven Zaillian), BEST CINEMATOGRAPHY (Janusz Kaminski), BEST FILM EDITING (Michael Kahn), BEST ART DIRECTION – SET DECORATION (Allan Starsky, Ewa Braun) and BEST MUSIC (John Williams).

## "It is said that he's a good man."

Can the horrors of the Holocaust be filmed without trivialising them? Can life under fascism be filmed without showing images which everybody has seen before? Steven Spielberg came up with one solution in his film about the German industrialist Oskar Schindler. The story he tells is unique, eccentric even, but the message is crystal clear: responsibility cannot be passed on to someone else, but is always a matter for the individual.

When the film starts, the German army has occupied Poland. The occupiers make a ghetto for the Jews in Krakow, and force them to register. We see their faces, one by one, individual people in great distress, many of whom are later tortured and murdered. This is no anonymous mass.

When we see Oskar Schindler (Liam Neeson) for the first time our eyes are drawn irresistibly to his Nazi party badge. He is an opportunist woman-

iser, and is building an enamel factory in Poland for the German army. Jewish workers are cheaper than Polish ones, so he takes Jews. His accountant Itzhak Stern (Ben Kingsley) turns out to be an organisational genius and becomes the real director of the factory. Schindler's job is to bribe the Nazi officials. He is more hard-bitten businessman than hero, and at first his humanity is a more a question economics than it is of morals: happy workers, he reasons, produce more than discontented ones.

In 1942, the ghetto is destroyed and all the Jews are deported to a work camp in Plaszow. Schindler observes the harrowing events. A little girl wanders silently through the chaos, seemingly oblivious to events around her. Her red coat is the only spot of colour in this film, which is shot almost exclusively in documentary black and white. We later see her corpse in Auschwitz.

Through a bizarre friendship with sadistic Lager commandant Amon Goeth (Ralph Fiennes), Schindler manages to keep his workers although they are forced to live in the detention centre. This protects them from being tortured by the guards and means that they can trade on the black market, without which it is impossible to survive. Eventually Plaszow is dissolved and all its inmates are transported to Auschwitz, so Schindler has to make a decision. He uses his entire capital to bribe the Nazis and buy the lives of his workers. He saves over 1100 people, who he transports with two trains, one for men, one for women, to his hometown of Brünnlitz to open a munitions factory. Since the factory produces goods for the war effort, his workers are considered indispensable and their lives are saved. Even when the women's train arrives in Auschwitz by mistake, through fearlessness and bribery

Schindler manages to get the women out again. His strengths are his stubbornness and deviousness. He pretends to be a money-grabbing businessman long after his motivation has changed and he has a real desire to help as many Jews as possible to survive. His weaknesses for drink, women, pleasure and luxury lead the Nazis to think of him as one of their own, but his factory in Brünnlitz produces munitions of such poor quality that the army has no use for them. With the rest of his money, he bankrupts himself making sure that all of "his" Jews survive until the end of the war. As he is listed as a collaborator and Nazi Party member, he is forced to flee to Argentina before the Allies arrive. Today, the descendants of his Jewish workers outnumber the total population of Jews living in Poland.

1   An inscrutable face (Liam Neeson as Oskar
    Schindler) – is this scepticism or self-assurance?

2   Camp commander Amon Goeth's (Ralph Fiennes)
    uniform matches his facial expression. His lips
    are pinched and his gaze is haughty.

3   Horrific pictures, like snapshots in some satanic
    photo album.

4   Hands cannot type as fast as they would like to
    in the attempt to prevent disaster.

# "I just want to tell an interesting and true story." *Steven Spielberg*

**STEVEN SPIELBERG**    When Spielberg announced that he wanted to make a movie about the Holocaust, everyone was appalled. The Jewish World Congress forbade him to film on the Auschwitz site. Spielberg's image as a maker of successful entertainment movies was too strong (*Jaws*, 1975, *Raiders of the Lost Ark*, 1981, *E.T. – The Extra-Terrestrial*, 1982 and *Jurassic Park*, 1992), and he was considered too lightweight. Today his Holocaust Foundation is the biggest archive of materials on Holocaust survivors in the world. And his second 'serious' film *Saving Private Ryan* (1998) is considered a prime example of how to make a moving and yet commercially successful movie about war. Not only has he managed to bridge the gap between entertainment and intellectually demanding cinema with extraordinary success, but he is now also considered to be the most successful director of all time, as he has managed to get serious without losing his audience.

'The film deals with survival, where it ought to be talking about death,' is an objection raised by Claude Lanzmann against Spielberg. 'But the Jewish people and Jewish culture survived Hitler,' is Spielberg's response." *epd Film*

5 The broken and traumatized prisoners are momentarily disorientated after their liberation.

6 Itzhak Stern (Ben Kingsley) is an organisational genius. Many Jews owe him and Schindler their lives.

5

# THE PIANO

ḭḭḭ

1993 - AUSTRALIA / FRANCE / NEW ZEALAND - 120 MIN. - DRAMA, HISTORICAL FILM

DIRECTOR JANE CAMPION (*1954)
SCREENPLAY JANE CAMPION DIRECTOR OF PHOTOGRAPHY STUART DRYBURGH MUSIC MICHAEL NYMAN PRODUCTION JAN CHAPMAN for MIRAMAX, CIBY 2000.

STARRING HOLLY HUNTER (Ada McGrath), HARVEY KEITEL (George Baines), SAM NEILL (Stewart), ANNA PAQUIN (Flora McGrath), KERRY WALKER (Aunt Morag), GENEVIÈVE LEMON (Nessie), TUNGIA BAKER (Hira), IAN MUNE (Reverend), PETER DENNETT (sailor), PETE SMITH (Hone).

ACADEMY AWARDS 1994 OSCARS for BEST ACTRESS (Holly Hunter), BEST SUPPORTING ACTRESS (Anna Paquin), BEST ORIGINAL SCREENPLAY (Jane Campion).

IFF CANNES 1993 GOLDEN PALM, SILVER PALM for BEST ACTRESS (Holly Hunter).

# "The voice you hear is not my speaking voice but my mind's voice"

A woman's fate around 1850, at the other end of the world and on the edge of civilization. In the days when fathers were still able to decide what was to become of their daughters, Ada McGrath (Holly Hunter) is married off in New Zealand. There is a chronic lack of womenfolk on the island, and her husband, settler Stewart (Sam Neill), has never clapped eyes on her before the wedding. But doesn't seem to mind her nine-year-old daughter, and nor does he care about the fact that Ada has not spoken at all for six years. The good Lord loves mute creatures as well as those who speak, as he writes to her father in Scotland. But he is more puzzled by the piano that she brings with her, and it remains on the beach where she lands as he doesn't have enough men to carry all her luggage. The instrument is Ada's real voice, and Stewart fails to understand how much it means to her. Her playing has an intensity which expresses the whole force of her personality. Stewart is not a cruel man, but for him Ada represents a level of civilization which is a different

realm to the wild nature he hopes to tame and cultivate, worlds apart from the forest fires and land clearing which are the settlers' main concerns. Mother and daughter, clad entirely in black with bonnets and crinolines, appear to have arrived from another planet as they wade through the mud of the impenetrable New Zealand bush.

In her despair at the loss of her piano, Ada turns to George Baines (Harvey Keitel) who lives a little way outside the settlement in a forest hut. We discover nothing about the illiterate Baines other than the fact that he has abandoned his British roots and gone native. He is covered with tattoos and speaks the Maori's language, and is therefore useful to the settlers as a negotiator and translator. Baines is what Fenimore Cooper would have called a frontiersman. He bridges the gap between two cultures; and despite his familiarity with the wilderness he also transmits his native culture. Ada comes to trust Baines because like her he is an outsider. Unlike Stewart, he

...stantly realises what the piano means to her. Stewart accepts immediately when Baines offers him a stretch of forest in exchange for the instrument. He doesn't ask Ada.

Outraged, she rushes to Baines, who has had the piano carried to his house. "The piano belongs to me!" she scrawls in desperation on a page of the notebook which hangs around her neck. Holly Hunter won an Oscar for her portrayal of the role of Ada, and it is extraordinary how much aggression she manages to inject into the diminutive person of the unbending, contrary, small-lipped mute.

Ada demands that Baines return the instrument, but he suggests a deal: she can earn it back key by key with piano lessons. Ada beats him down to just the black keys, but George doesn't want to learn to play; he wants to listen to Ada, watch her and "do certain things" to her as she plays.

They agree on a rate of exchange. The closer he gets to her, the more keys he has to let her have. Finally she agrees to lie naked next to him for the last ten keys, and the piano is hers once more. But she still returns to Baines.

Ada is strengthened by her feelings for Baines and excited by the sensuality of their erotic meetings, which gradually free her from the fear of her own body that her Victorian upbringing has given her. She attempts to win her husband's affection and one night even tries to seduce him. Up until then, she had always remained distant when Stewart tried to claim his marital rights, but now it is he who pushes her away. Ada belongs to him, but now she wants him as a sexual object.

Stewart is annoyed. The movie's audience was also unsettled, accustomed above all to the primacy of male desire in American cinema and the male gaze on the female body. Jane Campion sees her story with the dis-

# "*The Piano* is a miracle of violence and repose, refinement and cruelty, passion and restraint." *Positif*

1 A surreal moment: washed up on a deserted beach in the wilderness with only music as a comfort.

2 People take familiar cultural objects with them to foreign lands – but why? (Holly Hunter and Anna Paquin).

3 For contact between different cultures to be successful, it must be gentle (Harvey Keitel as George Baines).

3

tance of 20<sup>th</sup> century eyes. Her literary inspirations, like the love triangle in Emily Brontë's *Wuthering Heights*, are not just set in an atmosphere of Victorian narrow-mindedness, they are also products of it. A story like *The Piano* in which the reality of society's sexual drives is revealed would have been absolutely unthinkable at the time in which it is set.

When Ada's daughter Flora (Anna Paquin) tells her step-father about her mother's secret meetings with Baines, Stewart is beside himself with jealousy and rage. He follows his wife to Baines' house and tries to rape her. Stewart cannot help himself, he is a man of his times whose mental limitations "border on the tragic" as critics were keen to point out. He hacks off one of her fingers, so that she can no longer play the piano. He has finally understood her, or at least has realised how he can hurt her most. He sends Baines the finger – and gives up.

Ada leaves the island together with George on the boat in which she arrived. The piano is now nothing but ballast to her, and she wants it thrown overboard. As the rope holding it unwinds, she puts her foot in one of the loops and is nearly dragged down into the depths: She manages to break free, and at the end is shown sitting at the piano again with a metal finger which Baines has forged for her. The clacking of the artificial finger on the keys lends an ironic distance to the emotions of the music. And she begins to learn to speak again.

SL

# "These characters don't have our 20<sup>th</sup> century sensitivity as far as sexuality is concerned. They aren't prepared for its intensity and power."

*Neue Zürcher Zeitung*

**HOLLY HUNTER**  Holly Hunter's collaboration with Ethan and Joel Coen began unusually for an actress. In their debut movie *Blood Simple* (1984) she doesn't appear at all – we only hear her voice on an answering machine. Her break-through as a film actress came in one of the Coen brothers' wild, anarchic comedies. Alongside Nicolas Cage, she played the charming police woman who yearns for a child in *Raising Arizona* (1987). A year later she appeared as a bubbly journalist in *Broadcast News* and was nominated for an Oscar for the first time. At only 1.57 meters with thin lips and a some-times pinched facial expression, Holly Hunter doesn't fulfil Hollywood's conventional expectations where female beauty is concerned. She was so keen to have the role of Ada in Jane Campion's movie *The Piano* (1993) that she applied for it unbidden with a stream of faxes.
Holly Hunter was born in Georgia in 1958 and grew up on a farm, the youngest of seven children. Her career began on Broadway in 1980, and today she still alternates theatre and film roles. In the comedy *O Brother, Where Art Thou?* (2000) she plays the faithless Penelope who has long stopped waiting for her husband George Clooney to return from his crazy odyssey.

4  Love finds its voice first and foremost in music.    5  A picture beautiful enough to be a painting by an Old Master.

# FORREST GUMP

1994 - USA - 142 MIN. - COMEDY

DIRECTOR ROBERT ZEMECKIS (*1952)

SCREENPLAY ERIC ROTH, based on the novel of the same name by WINSTON GROOM  DIRECTOR OF PHOTOGRAPHY DON BURGESS
MUSIC ALAN SILVESTRI PRODUCTION WENDY FINERMAN, STEVE TISCH, STEVE STARKEY, CHARLES NEWIRTH for PARAMOUNT.

STARRING TOM HANKS (Forrest Gump), ROBIN WRIGHT (Jenny Curran), GARY SINISE (Lt. Dan Taylor), SALLY FIELD (Mrs Gump), MYKELTI WILLIAMSON (Benjamin Buford "Bubba" Blue), MICHAEL CONNER HUMPHREYS (Forrest as a boy), HANNA HALL (Jenny as a girl), TIFFANY SALERNO (Carla), MARLA SUCHARETZA (Lenore), HALEY JOEL OSMENT (Forrest Junior).

ACADEMY AWARDS 1995 OSCARS for BEST PICTURE, BEST ACTOR (Tom Hanks), BEST DIRECTOR (Robert Zemeckis), BEST VISUAL EFFECTS (Allen Hall, George Murphy, Ken Ralston, Stephen Rosenbaum), BEST FILM EDITING (Arthur Schmidt), and BEST ADAPTED SCREENPLAY (Eric Roth).

## "Shit happens!"

A bus stop in Savannah, Georgia. A man with the facial expression of a child sits on the bench, a small suitcase next to him and a box of chocolates in his hand. While he is waiting for the bus, he tells the story of his life to the others sitting around him.

The story begins sometime in the 1950s in a place called Greenbow in Alabama. Here Forrest Gump (Michael Conner Humphreys), a young boy named after a hero from the Civil War, is growing up without a father. He is different from the other children: his IQ of 75 is way below average, and as his mother (Sally Field) says, his spine is as bent as a politician's morals. But his mother is a strong-willed woman, and she manages to balance out these defects. She makes her boy wear leg braces and although she's prepared to

use her body to convince the headmaster that Forrest doesn't need to go to a special school, she teaches her son morals: "Dumb folks are folks who act dumb", being one of the many pearls of wisdom from her rich repertoire.

Forrest, who is friendly and unsuspecting, doesn't have an easy life. No one wants to sit next to him on the school bus, apart from Jenny (Hanna Hall), who soon becomes his only friend. When Forrest is being teased by his school mates for the thousandth time, she tells him to run away. Forrest always does what people tell him, and suddenly he discovers hidden gifts like speed and endurance. The leg braces shatter, and with them the limitations of his simple mind fall away. Swifter than the wind, Forrest runs and runs and runs through his youth.

Years later, when he's almost an adult, Forrest is running away from his schoolmates again and by mistake ends up on a football field. Simple-minded Forrest is offered a college scholarship and a place on an All-American football team.

"Life is like a box of chocolates. You never know what you're gonna get" – another gem from Mrs Gump's treasury. There's a lot in this for Forrest. Thanks to his knack for being in the right place at the right time, his football career is followed by military service and the Vietnam War, where he becomes not only a war hero but also a first-class table tennis player. After the war he fulfils a promise he made to Bubba (Mykelti Williamson), his friend and comrade in arms, and he makes his fortune as the captain of a

shrimping boat. He becomes even richer when he invests his millions in what he believes to be a fruit firm by the name of "Apple".

Forrest Gump's life is a 40-year, long-distance run through American post-war history. He shakes hands with Presidents Kennedy and Nixon, shows Elvis Presley the hip thrust and inspires John Lennon's song "Imagine". He invents the Smiley as well as the "Shit happens" sticker. By pure chance his finger is always on the pulse of the times. He gets mixed up in a protest action for racial integration, in a demonstration against the Vietnam War and accidentally witnesses the Watergate Affair.

Just as Forrest's career and his experiences of American history are unintentional, his meetings with the love of his life, Jenny (Robin Wright), are

**Hanks is a kid again in director Robert Zemeckis' *Forrest Gump*. Slow-witted and likeable, Forrest races through the rubble of the 50s, 60s and 70s."** *Time Magazine*

1 As simple as they come: Forrest Gump (Tom Hanks) fulfils the American dream in his own way.

2 A safe seat: one of his mother's sayings was "Dumb folks are folks who act dumb" and this stays with him all his life.

3 Jenny (Hanna Hall) is Forrest's (Michael Conner Humphreys) only friend. She sticks by him, even though everybody teases him because he is so slow physically and mentally.

4 A woman's wiles: Forrest's single mother (Sally Field) uses everything in her power, even her own body, to ensure that her son leads a normal life.

3

4

ilso unplanned. Instead of fulfilling her dream and becoming a folksinger she has ended up a junkie hanging round the hippie scene, singing in a third-rate night club. When his mother dies, Forrest moves back to Greenbow, where he has a short but unsuccessful affair with Jenny. Once more, Forrest tries to run away from his destiny and he runs through America for three years without a concrete destination, accompanied by a growing band of follow-ers.

Director Robert Zemeckis is known for being a specialist in technically demanding entertainment movies. He literally turned Meryl Streep's head in *Death Becomes Her* (1992) and his *Back to the Future* trilogy suggests that he has a weakness for time travel (*Back to the Future I, II*, 1985, 1989,

1990). *Forrest Gump*, adapted by Eric Roth from the novel of the same name by Winston Groom, is also a strange journey into the past.

With the help of George Lucas' special effects firm Industrial Light & Magic (ILM), Zemeckis uses sophisticated visual tricks and original film footage to create the illusion that Forrest was actually present at various historical occasions. For the scene where Forrest shakes hands with President Kennedy in the Oval Office, the digital technicians of ILM used archive material with the real people cut out and a superimposed image of Forrest Gump. Tom Hanks was filmed in front of a blue screen and this was combined with the archive film by computer. Computer technology is present throughout *Forrest Gump*, though audiences are unlikely to notice it. With its help, a

"Throughout, Forrest carries a flame for Jenny, a childhood sweetheart who was raised by a sexually abusive father and is doomed to a troubled life. The character's a bit obvious: Jenny is clearly Forrest's shadow – darkness and self destruction played against his lightness and simplicity." *San Francisco Chronicle*

thousand real extras were transformed into a hundred thousand simulated demonstrators.

The naive boy-next-door image which Tom Hanks had developed elsewhere made him the ideal actor for this part, which one critic described as "Charlie Chaplin meets Lawrence of Arabia". His Forrest Gump is the counterpart of Josh Baskin, the twelve-year-old who grows into the body of a man overnight in Penny Marshall's comedy *Big* (1988).

*Forrest Gump* is not a direct reflection of contemporary history, but it does reflect a distinctly American mentality. History is personalised and shown as a series of coincidences. The moral of the movie is as simple as

7

5   Love, Peace and Happiness? Jenny (Robin Wright) resorts to drugs while running away from herself.

6   An inspired move. *Forrest Gump* owes a large part of its authentic feel to the special effects of Industrial Light & Magic. These lead the viewer to think that Forrest really did meet President Nixon.

7   A promise with consequences: Forrest promises his dying friend Bubba (Mykelti Williamson) that he will fulfil their shared dream of going shrimp fishing.

the sayings of Forrest's mother. Everything is possible – you just have to want something to happen, or be at the right place at the right time, even if you hardly realise what is going on and don't take an active part in events. International movie-goers loved the unique and entertaining worldview of this simple soul from Alabama, underscored by a sound track which is a musical cross section of the whole century. The movie made 330 million dollars in the USA, and almost doubled that sum worldwide. It was awarded six Oscars in 1995, and suddenly Smileys were in fashion again and everyone went around saying "Shit happens!". Winston Groom's novel and Bubba's shrimp cookbook stood on many bookshelves. *Forrest Gump* is somewhat reminiscent of Hal Ashby's comedy *Being there* (1979), where Peter Sellers plays a simple gardener who only knows the world from his television. Ashby's movie is an intelligent and sometimes highly comic satire, but *Forrest Gump* didn't take that opportunity, or didn't want it: it's pure entertainment which only pretends to reflect on modern history. That combination of historical reproduction and conventional Hollywood plot links *Forrest Gump* to Steven Spielberg's *Schindler's List* (1993): the audience flick through the movie like a photo album, reassure themselves about their own past and leave the movie theatre two hours later, satisfied and by no means unpleasantly moved.    APO

# ED WOOD

⬆⬆

1994 - USA - 126 MIN. - COMEDY

DIRECTOR TIM BURTON (\*1960)
SCREENPLAY SCOTT ALEXANDER, LARRY KARASZEWSKI, based on the biographical novel *NIGHTMARE OF ECSTASY: THE LIFE AND ART OF EDWARD D. WOOD JR.* by RUDOLPH GREY DIRECTOR OF PHOTOGRAPHY STEFAN CZAPSKY
MUSIC HOWARD SHORE PRODUCTION DENISE DINOVI, TIM BURTON for BURTON/DINOVI PRODUCTIONS (for TOUCHSTONE).

STARRING JOHNNY DEPP (Ed Wood), MARTIN LANDAU (Bela Lugosi), SARAH JESSICA PARKER (Dolores Fuller), PATRICIA ARQUETTE (Kathy O'Hara), JEFFREY JONES (Criswell), BILL MURRAY (Bunny Breckinridge), G. D. SPRADLIN (Reverend Lemon), VINCENT D'ONOFRIO (Orson Welles), LISA MARIE (Vampira), MIKE STARR (Georgie Weiss).

ACADEMY AWARDS 1995 OSCARS for BEST SUPPORTING ACTOR (Martin Landau), and FOR BEST MAKE-UP (Ve Neill, Rick Baker, Yolanda Toussieng).

## *"Cut!!! Perfect!!!"*

Ed Wood enjoys the doubtful but wonderfully marketable reputation of being the worst director of all time. Tim Burton's movie is a monument to a colleague who more than deserves it. Burton may have immeasurably more talent as a filmmaker, but he still feels that there is a spiritual link between his work and that of Wood, who was a tireless maker of cheap movies in the 50s. Accordingly, his homage always maintains a certain level of respect: even at his funniest and most absurd moments, Ed Wood is never made to look ridiculous.

Hollywood has always perpetuated its own myth by celebrating its heroes and legends. This movie is something of an exception as it turns its attention to one of tinsel town's hopeless losers. To prevent Ed Wood (Johnny Depp) from appearing an amiable but hopelessly incompetent idiot, Burton almost overdoes the thematic links between his career and that of Orson Welles (Vincent D'Onofrio). Like Wood, Welles was the epitome of the all-American filmmaker, who tried to realise his cinematic vision by being a

writer, producer, director and leading actor all rolled into one. He is now considered to be the embodiment of the uncompromising artist doomed to failure by a refusal to bow to the production conditions of a capitalist film industry.

The dimensions of their failures may have been different, but in a key scene of the movie, Ed and Orson are shown drowning their sorrows together as victims of the same system. Ironically, Burton himself was not free from the constraints of the industry, despite enjoying a wunderkind reputation in the mid 90s: as he wanted to give the movie the flatness of a 50s B movie and make it in black and white, he had to do without Columbia's financial backing and make *Ed Wood* as an independent production.

What Wood as director lacked in artistic talent and financial resources, he made up for with boundless enthusiasm and the noble art of improvisation. His absolute lack of (self) irony gives his movies their unmistakable touch. Everything was meant absolutely seriously, and one of Wood's great-

st problems was that he was even more naive than the audience he hoped to bring flooding to the movie theatres. Johnny Depp plays Wood like a child who, even with the most unlikely-looking toys, is able to simply ignore reality and disappear into the fairytale world of his own imagination.

Plots are so crude they seem out of this world, dialogue is unintentionally comic, a colour-blind cameraman uses the same light for every scene regardless of whether it is day or night, special effects look as if they were made in a kindergarten and staggeringly untalented actors, all friends of the director, are constantly falling over the scenery. As one of Wood's actresses said, "His carelessness in technical matters is only surpassed by his com-

plete lack of concern in showing his amateurism". But Wood was far too wrapped up in himself and his work to be bothered with such details. He wasn't careless out of disrespect for his audience, it was just that his thoughts were always way ahead of the scene he was working on.

His problem was that he always saw things as a whole, as a complete vision, just like his great colleague Orson Welles. After every first take, Depp shouts "Cut!!! That was perfect!!!" and opens his eyes as wide as they'll go to demonstrate his absolute abandonment to his own crazy ideas: this is Burton biting back any suggestion of cynicism, and it is exactly the attitude that gives the movie its human integrity.                    UE

1   Look at me: Ed Wood (Johnny Depp) and Bela Lugosi (Martin Landau) try their hand at long-distance hypnosis.

2   Strange passion: is Wood in love with his wife Dolores (Sarah Jessica Parker) or just with her angora jumper?

3   The director in discussion with his hero. On the wall are posters of films he used as models.

4   Wood's *Plan 9 From Outer Space* is considered to be one of the worst films of all time.

5   Wood's working principle: the first take is always the best.

# "A moving, dream-like homage to a monstrous, childish form, *Ed Wood* is also a paean to the way love of film gets passed down." *Cahiers du cinéma*

**ED WOOD**

Edward D. Wood jr. (1924–1978) belonged to a long-gone age when Hollywood directors were not mass-produced in film schools, but came from all walks of life and based their work on their own experiences. He was both a veteran of the war in the Pacific and a self-confessed transvestite (something which took great courage at the time) with a particular weakness for cuddly angora pullovers. He exposed his personal obsessions to the outside world without any regard for their effect in his very first movie, *Glen or Glenda?* (1952), a pseudo-religious, superficial horror film about a sex change. Audiences were outraged, alienated and way out of their depth. Later he preferred to indulge himself primarily in the genres of horror and science fiction. *Plan 9 From Outer Space* (1959), his most infamous movie, was a tale of alien grave robbers. Around that time Wood met Bela Lugosi, the original movie Dracula, who had long been cast off by official Hollywood and left for dead. With his practically non-existent means, Wood tried to save the great actor from oblivion and give him the sort of send-off that he deserved. This touching act of humanity makes the quality of the movies they made together seem almost irrelevant. The fact that the only Oscar *Ed Wood* won was best supporting actor for Martin Landau as Lugosi speaks volumes about the treatment of men and myths in Hollywood.

# NATURAL BORN KILLERS

1994 - USA - 119 MIN. - ROAD MOVIE, SATIRE

DIRECTOR OLIVER STONE (*1946)
SCREENPLAY DAVID VELOZ, RICHARD RUTOWSKI, OLIVER STONE, based on a story by QUENTIN TARANTINO
DIRECTOR OF PHOTOGRAPHY ROBERT RICHARDSON MUSIC VARIOUS SONGS PRODUCTION JANE HAMSHER, DON MURPHY,
CLAYTON TOWNSEND for IXTLAN, NEW REGENCY, J. D. PRODUCTIONS.

STARRING WOODY HARRELSON (Mickey Knox), JULIETTE LEWIS (Mallory Knox), ROBERT DOWNEY JR. (Wayne Gale),
TOMMY LEE JONES (Dwight McCluskey), TOM SIZEMORE (Jack Scagnetti), EDIE MCCLURG (Mallory's mother),
RODNEY DANGERFIELD (Mallory's father), BALTHAZAR GETTY (gas station attendant), RICHARD LINEBACK (Sonny),
LANNY FLAHERTY (Earl).

IFF VENICE 1994 SPECIAL JURY PRIZE (Oliver Stone).

## "We got the road to hell in front of us."

Natural Born Killers begins on a desert highway with a close up of a hissing snake, accompanied by Leonard Cohen singing "Waiting for a Miracle" – a hypnotic introduction, which makes the scenes that follow all the more shocking. Mickey and Mallory (Woody Harrelson and Juliette Lewis) are letting off steam in a diner. Whilst Mickey calmly finishes his piece of cake, his ethereal girlfriend brutally beats up a young redneck. A blues song floats out from the jukebox. Later, the pair of them kill almost all the other diners. Mickey and Mallory are a nightmare couple: they are Bonnie and Clyde or Sid and Nancy, but most of all they are the natural born killers of Oliver Stone's title. During their odyssey through South West America they randomly kill 52 people and only spare witnesses who will report deeds.

Mickey and Mallory are a gift for the TV nation which quickly styles the two serial killers as TV superstars. They are pursued not only by the police but by the media too, who hope to profit from their fame. In many of his films, from Salvador (1986) and The Doors (1991) to Any Given Sunday (1999), Oliver Stone has worked on the contradictions and myths of modern America. Natural Born Killers, based on a story written by Quentin Tarantino, combines Stone's favourite themes – violence, capitalism, the media, pop culture – in a dark, satirical tour-de-force about the obsessions of the American media. The movie breaks the bounds of classic narrative cinema, polarising and disturbing its audiences, disappointing their expectations before leaving them in a state of breathless astonishment. To do that Stone makes use of practi-

**DIRECTOR'S CUT**  Directors' contracts which are made according to the conditions of the Hollywood Directors' Guild contain a clause which gives the director a peri-od of six weeks to edit and synchronise a film as he or she wishes without any studio interruption or involvement. Generally however, director's cut is used to describe a version of the film made after its release in cinemas according to the director's own artistic criteria.

cally all of the cinema's technical possibilities, changing the cameras and the film and video formats, using all the colour and effect filters imaginable, and blending in back projections and archive material. He underscores Robert Richardson's hyperactive camera work and the occasionally hysterical edit-ing with an eclectic sound track including everything from Orff's "Carmina Burana", Bob Dylan and Patsy Cline to Nine Inch Nails and Dr. Dre. Stone claimed to have used over 100 different pieces of music in the movie. The music often acts as a counterpoint to the action on screen, as in "I love Mallory", a scene filmed in the style of an American sitcom, where instead of wholesome family life the opposite is shown. Stone adds canned laughter and applause to the verbal and physical beating which Mallory's vile father deals out to his wife and daughter.

Stone knows full well that he is throwing a stone at the media glass house where he himself lives. When Mickey and Mallory have sex in front of a hostage, the window of their motel shows some explosive archive materi-al: in between the reptiles and insects and the images of Hitler and Mussolini are scenes from *The Wild Bunch* (1969) and *Midnight Express*, the movie whose screenplay won Stone his first Oscar in 1978.

Does art imitate life or life art? Can images cause real violence? Stone's fiction was certainly overtaken by reality. One of Mickey and Mallory's admirers in the movie remarks that if he were a mass murderer he'd want to be just like them. Years later, Stone was still answering charges that his movie had inspired countless copy-cat crimes.

APO

1  Totally cracked up: Mickey Knox (Woody Harrelson) doesn't let anything stand in his way on his deadly journey towards media stardom.

2  Director Oliver Stone uses unusual visual devices like super-imposition and colour effects to convey his message to the general public.

3  Look back in anger: Mallory's past is like a soap opera of brutality where the laughter of the band drowned out her father's physical and verbal beatings.

"Visually, the film is a sensation, resembling a demonically clever light show at a late '60s rock concert. The narrative is related in color 35mm, black-and-white, 8mm and video, and at different speeds." *Variety*

4 Prison director Dwight McCluskey (Tommy Lee Jones) is as fanatical as he is hungry for media attention. He later falls victim to the hell that he himself has created.

5 Messianic: in prison Mickey provokes a riot when he tells his interviewer about the cleansing power of killing.

# INTERVIEW WITH THE VAMPIRE: THE VAMPIRE CHRONICLES

1994 - USA - 122 MIN. - HORROR FILM, DRAMA

DIRECTOR NEIL JORDAN (*1950)
SCREENPLAY ANNE RICE, based on her novel of the same name DIRECTOR OF PHOTOGRAPHY PHILIPPE ROUSSELOT
MUSIC ELLIOT GOLDENTHAL PRODUCTION DAVID GEFFEN, STEPHEN WOOLEY for GEFFEN PICTURES
(for WARNER BROS.).

STARRING BRAD PITT (Louis), TOM CRUISE (Lestat), KIRSTEN DUNST (Claudia), CHRISTIAN SLATER (Malloy),
STEPHEN REA (Santiago), ANTONIO BANDERAS (Armand), VIRGINIA MCCOLLAM (Prostitute on the riverbank),
MIKE SEELIG (Pimp), SARA STOCKBRIDGE (Estelle), THANDIE NEWTON (Yvette).

## "The world changes, we do not, and there lies the irony that finally kills us."

San Francisco. Two men sit in a hotel room high over the gloomy streets. One of them, Malloy (Christian Slater), is a journalist and he is here to take down the life story of the other. It's a fascinating, incredible story that begins two hundred years previously in New Orleans in 1791, when Louis (Brad Pitt) first became a vampire. When his wife dies in childbirth, the young widower is beside himself with grief and no longer capable of looking after his plantation. Searching for oblivion and death he spends his nights in the town's dives, and his sorrow drives him into the arms of prostitutes and to the gambling table – and he is constantly on the lookout for a fatal fight to end his torment. But however much he longs for death, his wishes are never granted. One night Louis meets the vampire Lestat (Tom Cruise), who tells him of eternal youth and an existence without grief. Louis then makes a fateful decision that he will later regret.

Neil Jordan's vampires have very little to do with the traditional mythology presented in innumerable movies and books. Rather, they are descended in a direct line from Friedrich Wilhelm Murnau's *Nosferatu* (1921), although they are considerably better looking. Being a vampire is no fun, and there is no escape except through crucifixes or silver bullets. Vampires are people – but they are forced to live as outcasts.

After his transformation into a vampire, Louis' grief is replaced by melancholy and solitude when he learns about the less appetising sides of a vampire's existence. He doesn't want to kill anybody and instead feeds on rats and other small animals. Lestat on the other hand is a bloodsucker who goes by the book. In haunts of low repute and at intoxicating balls he searches for his victims, handsome young men and women mostly, killing them and drinking their blood with the same carelessness with which he indulges his passion for the hunt.

One night Louis kill a little girl called Claudia (Kirsten Dunst), and to bind Louis to himself, Lestat turns her into a vampire. At first, the relationship between Louis, Lestat and their adopted daughter seems a happy menage à trois, but before long things turn sour and it becomes a living hell for all three of them. Only Lestat seems to enjoy being undead. Louis longs for the life which Lestat has taken from him, and the child-woman Claudia dreams of a life which she will never know.

The movie is based on Anne Rice's best-selling novel *Interview With the Vampire* and is Neil Jordan's second adaptation of fantasy literature. In 1984 he made the Red Riding Hood story *The Company of Wolves* based on a book by Angela Carter. In both movies there is a similar mixture of sensuality and

"The initial meeting between Louis and Lestat takes the form of a seduction; the vampire seems to be courting the young man, and there is a strong element of homoeroticism in the way the neck is bared and the blood is engorged." *Chicago Sun-Times*

the supernatural, and hints of homoeroticism, incest and paedophilia, although these elements are mostly latent in *Interview With the Vampire*, where they are concealed in looks and fatal embraces.

The opulent images of the film and the emotions they inspire are far more impressive than with the coherency of the plot. Dante Ferretti, the set designer, creates a visually overwhelming and uncanny vampire world that reaches from the swamps of Louisiana all the way to the catacombs of Paris. Cameraman Philippe Rousselot (*Diva*, 1981) uses colours which seem overlain with black velvet, as though to illustrate what Louis has lost: Louis has to wait a hundred years before he can see a glorious dawn again like the one he saw before his transformation: and when he sees it, it's in a black and white movie, in Murnau's silent classic *Sunrise* from 1927. **APO**

**VAMPIRE FILMS**   The first known vampire movie was called *Le Manoir du Diable* (*The Devil's Manor*) and was produced by Georges Méliès in 1896. Vampire films are all about the ways in which plants, aliens, or beings either living or dead rob victims of their vital juices, mostly blood. Many vampire films, including F. W. Murnau's classic *Nosferatu* (1921), take their themes from Bram Stoker's novel *Dracula*. Vampire movies have been made in a wide variety of genres, including comedies, thrillers and westerns.

"When he's on the prowl, Cruise likes to seduce young women before exacting his dark red sustenance. With alarming swiftness, the victims swift from sexual excitement to outright horror, as Cruise's purpose becomes clear."

*The Washington Post*

5  The picture of haughtiness. Lestat relishes his life as a vampire, and he is completely devoid of scruples.

6  The vampire Armand (Antonio Banderas) satisfies his blood lust on the stage.

7  Neither wife nor daughter: Claudia (Kirsten Dunst) becomes Louis' companion.

6

7

# PULP FICTION

1994 - USA - 154 MIN. - GANGSTER FILM

DIRECTOR  QUENTIN TARANTINO (*1963)
SCREENPLAY  QUENTIN TARANTINO, ROGER ROBERTS AVARY  DIRECTOR OF PHOTOGRAPHY  ANDRZEJ SEKULA  MUSIC  VARIOUS SONGS
PRODUCTION  LAWRENCE BENDER for JERSEY FILMS, A BAND APART (for MIRAMAX).

STARRING  JOHN TRAVOLTA (Vincent Vega), SAMUEL L. JACKSON (Jules Winnfield), UMA THURMAN (Mia Wallace), HARVEY KEITEL (Winston Wolf), VING RHAMES (Marsellus Wallace), ROSANNA ARQUETTE (Jody), ERIC STOLTZ (Lance), QUENTIN TARANTINO (Jimmie), BRUCE WILLIS (Butch Coolidge), MARIA DE MEDEIROS (Fabienne), CHRISTOPHER WALKEN (Koons), TIM ROTH (Ringo/Pumpkin), AMANDA PLUMMER (Yolanda/Honeybunny).

IFF CANNES 1994  GOLDEN PALM.

ACADEMY AWARDS 1995  OSCAR for BEST ORIGINAL SCREENPLAY (Quentin Tarantino, Roger Roberts Avary).

## "Zed's dead, baby. Zed's dead."

After his amazing directorial debut *Reservoir Dogs* (1991), Quentin Tarantino had a lot to live up to. The bloody studio piece was essentially a purely cinematic challenge, and such an unusual movie seemed difficult to beat. But Tarantino surpassed himself with *Pulp Fiction*, a deeply black gangster comedy. Tarantino had previously written the screenplay for Tony Scott's uninspired gangster movie *True Romance* (1993) and the original script to Oliver Stone's *Natural Born Killers* (1994). At the beginning of his own movie, he presents us with another potential killer couple. Ringo and Yolanda (Tim Roth and Amanda Plummer), who lovingly call each other Pumpkin and Honeybunny, are sitting having breakfast in a diner and making plans for their future together. They are fed up with robbing whisky stores whose multi-cultural owners don't even understand simple orders like "Hand over the cash!" The next step in their career plan is to expand into diners – why not start straight away with this one? This sequence, which opens and concludes *Pulp Fiction* serves a framework for the movie's other three interwoven stories, which overlap and move in and out of chronological sequence. One of the protagonists is killed in the middle of the movie, only to appear alive and well in the final scene, and we only understand how the stories hang together at the very end.

The first story is "Vincent Vega and Marsellus Wallace's Wife". Vincent and Jules (John Travolta and Samuel L. Jackson), are professional assassins on their way to carry out an order. Their boss Marsellus Wallace (Ving Rhames) wants them to bring him back a mysterious briefcase. A routine job, as we can tell from their nonchalant chit-chat. Their black suits make them look as if they have stepped out of a 40s *film noir*. Vince is not entirely happy, as he has been given the job of looking after Marsellus' wife Mia (Uma Thurman) when the boss is away. In gangster circles, rumour has it that Vincent's predecessor was thrown out of a window on the fourth floor – apparently for doing nothing more than massaging Mia's feet.

"The Golden Watch", the second story in the film, is the story of has-been boxer Butch Coolidge (Bruce Willis). He too is one of Marsellus' "niggers" as the gangster boss calls all those who depend on him. Butch has accepted a bribe and agreed to take a dive in after the fifth round in his next fight. At the last minute, he decides to win instead and to run away with the money and his French girlfriend Fabienne (Maria de Medeiros).

In the third story, "The Bonnie Situation", a couple of loose narrative strands are tied together. Jules and Vincent have done their job. However, on the way back, Vincent accidentally shoots his informer who is sitting in the

"Hoodlums Travolta and Jackson – like modern-day Beckett characters – discuss foot massages, cunnilingus and cheese-burgers on their way to a routine killing job.
The recently traveled Travolta informs Jackson that at the McDonald's in Paris, the Quarter Pounder is known as 'Le Royal'. However a Big Mac's a Big Mac, but they call it 'Le Big Mac'."

*The Washington Post*

back of the car. The bloody car and its occupants have to get off the street as soon as possible. The two killers hide at Jim's (Quentin Tarantino), although his wife Bonnie is about to get back from work at any moment, so they have to get rid of the evidence as quickly as possible. Luckily they can call upon the services of Mr Wolf (Harvey Keitel), the quickest and most efficient cleaner there is.

To like *Pulp Fiction*, you have to have a weakness for pop culture, which this film constantly uses and parodies, although it never simply ridicules the source of its inspiration. Quentin Tarantino must have seen enormous quantities of movies before he became a director. The inside of his head must be

like the restaurant where Vincent takes Mia: the tables are like 50s Cabrios, the waiters and waitresses are pop icon doubles: Marilyn Monroe, James Dean, Mamie van Doren and Buddy Holly (Steve Buscemi in a cameo appearance). Vincent and Mia take part in a Twist competition. The way the saggy-cheeked, ageing John Travolta dances is a brilliant homage to his early career and *Saturday Night Fever* (1977).

With his tongue-in-cheek allusions to pop and film culture, Tarantino often verges on bad taste: in one scene from "The Golden Watch", a former prisoner of war and Vietnam veteran (Christopher Walken) arrives at a children's home to give the little Butch his father's golden watch. The scene begins like a kitsch scene from any Vietnam movie, but quickly deteriorates into the scatological and absurd when Walken tells the boy in great detail about the dark place where his father hid the watch in the prison camp for so many years.

Tarantino has an excellent feel for dialogue. His protagonists' conversations are as banal as in real life, they talk about everything and nothing, about potbellies, embarrassing silences or piercings. He also lays great value on those little details which really make the stories, for example the toaster, which together with Vincent's habit of long sessions in the bathroom will cost him his life – as he prefers to take a detective story rather than a pistol into the lavatory.

Tarantino's treatment of violence is a theme unto itself. It is constantly present in the movie, but is seldomly explicitly shown. The weapon is more important than the victim. In a conventional action movie, the scene where Jules and Vincent go down a long corridor to the apartment where they will kill several people would have been used to build up the suspense, but in Tarantino's film Vincent and Jules talk about trivial things instead, like two office colleagues on the way to the canteen.

One of the movie's most brutal scenes comes after Vincent and Mia's restaurant visit. The pair of them are in Mia's apartment, Vincent as ever in the bathroom, where he is meditating on loyalty and his desire to massage Mia's feet. In the meantime Mia discovers his supply of heroin, thinks it is cocaine and snorts an overdose. Vincent is then forced to get physical with her, but not in the way he imagined. To bring her back to life, he has to plant an enormous adrenaline jab in her heart.

*Pulp Fiction* also shows Tarantino to be a master of casting. All the roles are carried by their actors' larger-than-life presence. They are all "cool": Samuel L. Jackson as an Old-Testament-quoting killer, and Uma Thurman in a black wig as an enchanting, dippy gangster's moll. Bruce Willis drops his habitual grin and is totally convincing as an ageing boxer who refuses to give up. Craggy, jowly John Travolta plays the most harmless and good-natured assassin imaginable. If *Pulp Fiction* has a central theme running through it, then it's the "moral" which is present in each of the three stories. Butch doesn't run away when he has the opportunity but stays and saves his boss's life. Vincent and Jules live according to strict rules and principles and are very moral in their immoral actions. Vincent is so loyal that it finally costs him his life. Jule's moment of revelation comes when the bullets aimed at him miraculously miss. Coincidence or fate? Jules, who misquotes a Bible passage from Ezekiel before each of the murders he commits, decides that henceforth he will walk the path of righteousness. In the last scene when Ringo and Honeybunny rob the diner, Ringo tries to take the mysterious shiny briefcase. He fails to spot Jules draw his gun and under normal circumstances he would be a dead man. But Jules, who has decided to turn over a new leaf, has mercy on both of them –and that's not normal circumstances.  APO

4

> **"Tarantino's guilty secret is that his films are cultural hybrids. The blood and gore, the cheeky patter, the taunting mise-en-scene are all very American — the old studios at their snazziest."** *Time Magazine*

1 Do Mia's (Uma Thurman) foot massages turn into an erotic experience?

2 The Lord moves in mysterious ways: Jules (Samuel L. Jackson) is a killer who knows his Bible by heart.

3 Completely covered in blood: Vincent (John Travolta) after his little accident.

4 Everything's under control: as the "Cleaner" Mister Wolf (Harvey Keitel) takes care of any dirty work that comes up.

5 Echoes of *Saturday Night Fever*: Mia and Vincent risk a little dance.

6 In his role as Major Koons Christopher Walken plays an ex-Vietnam prisoner-of-war as he did in *The Deer Hunter*.

7

"Split into three distinct sections, the tale zips back and forth in time and space, meaning that the final shot is of a character we've seen being killed 50 minutes ago."

*Empire*

**PULP**      Cheap novels in magazine format, especially popular in the 30s and 40s, owing their name to the cheap, soft paper they were printed on. The themes and genres of these mostly illustrated serial novels and short stories ranged from comics to science fiction to detective stories. The first pulp stories appeared in the 1880s in the magazine *The Argosy*. In the 1930s there were several hundred pulp titles available, but by 1954 they had all disappeared – pulp was replaced by the cinema, the radio and above all, the new paperback book.

7   Will his pride desert him? Boxer Butch (Bruce Willis) gets paid every time he loses in the ring.

8   You gotta change your life! Jules and Vincent talk about chance and predestiny.

9   Hand over the cash! Yolanda (Amanda Plummer) carries out ...

10   ... the plan that she and Ringo (Tim Roth) hatched a few moments before.

8

# SPEED

1994 - USA - 116 MIN. - ACTION FILM

DIRECTOR JAN DE BONT (*1943)
SCREENPLAY GRAHAM YOST DIRECTOR OF PHOTOGRAPHY ANDRZEJ BARTKOWIAK MUSIC MARK MANCINA PRODUCTION MARK GORDON for 20TH CENTURY FOX.

STARRING KEANU REEVES (Jack Traven), DENNIS HOPPER (Howard Payne), SANDRA BULLOCK (Annie), JOE MORTON (Captain McMahon), JEFF DANIELS (Harry Temple), ALAN RUCK (Stephens), GLENN PLUMMER (Jaguar driver), RICHARD LINEBACK (Norwood), BETH GRANT (Helen), JAMES HAWTHORNE (Sam).

ACADEMY AWARDS 1995 OSCARS for BEST SOUND (Bob Beemer, Gregg Landaker, David MacMillan, Steve Maslow) and BEST EFFECTS, SOUND EFFECTS EDITING (Stephen Hunter Flick).

## "Miss, can you handle this bus?" – "Oh sure. It's just like driving a really big Pinto."

Jack Traven (Keanu Reeves) and his partner Harry Temple (Jeff Daniels) work in the Anti-Terrorist Unit of the Los Angeles Police Department. When the film opens, they are trying to free some hostages who are trapped in an elevator in one of the city's skyscrapers. The kidnapper is demanding a ransom of three million dollars, without which a bomb will explode killing all the hostages. In the last second, Jack and Harry manage to get the captives to safety. In a normal movie, a moment's relaxation would follow. But in Jan de Bont's action spectacle *Speed*, what would normally be enough material for a whole evening's entertainment is merely the curtain-raiser to a racing roller coaster ride in three acts which grips the audience from beginning to end.

The next morning, while Harry Temple is still sleeping off his hangover after the celebrations, Jack sets off for work. Suddenly a bus explodes a few metres away, and a public telephone rings at the same moment. It is Howard Payne (Dennis Hopper), the bomber they had believed dead. This time he wants 3.7 million dollars – but the personal revenge is more important than the money. He sets Jack the task of finding a bus which is driving through Los Angeles full of passengers. On board is a bomb that will explode as soon as

the bus goes faster than 50 miles an hour. However, the bomb will also explode should the bus drop its speed below 50 miles an hour. Jack manages to find the bus, and to clamber on board. While he feverishly attempts to defuse the bomb, the bus driver is shot by one of the passengers. Annie (Sandra Bullock), another passenger, takes the wheel – and isn't about to let go of it again in a hurry. During the hellish ride that follows she steers the heavy bus at break-neck speed along congested freeways and through red lights.

At the last moment Jack manages to get all the passengers out of the exploding bus, which they have driven onto the runway of a nearby airport. Jack and Annie fall into each other's arms. In a normal film, we might expect that to be the end of the story. But Jan de Bont has yet another surprise in store: in the third act he has Annie covered in dynamite like a gift-wrapped present, racing towards certain death in an out-of-control subway train, accompanied by Payne and Jack.

Before his debut as a director with *Speed*, Dutchman Jan de Bont was a cameraman on many big-budget action films. He obviously paid great attention to the directing on the sets of movies like *Die Hard* (1987), *The Hun*

3

4

_or Red October_ (1990) or _Lethal Weapon 3_ (1992). _Speed,_ his first movie, is the condensed essence of all action films, freed from all unnecessary ballast: with one exception, there are no senselessly violent scenes or mindless destruction. Minor figures are kept in the background, and we learn nothing about their previous lives. The terse dialogue isn't used for reasoning or moralising, it simply advances the plot or gives the audience a split-second pause to draw breath. De Bont tells his story almost exclusively with pictures, and the racing images alone create an almost unbearable tension. The focal point of _Speed_ really is speed; and like the bus, the movie maintains its tempo without flagging from the first to the last. Its timing is as precise as the clockwork mechanism of Payne's bomb. APO

---

**TYPECASTING**      If actors play several similar roles in quick succession, their future career is often determined by this stereotype. A particular type of character, like a villain, becomes identified with an actor's face, and thereafter they may only be offered roles that correspond to that image. One of the most famous examples is Edward G. Robinson who played many different roles, but will always be remembered as a gangster.

---

1   Fasten your seatbelts: police officer Jack (Keanu Reeves) next to reluctant bus driver Annie (Sandra Bullock).

2   Other directors make cars fly, with action specialist Jan de Bont it's buses.

3   Yet another psychopath: Dennis Hopper plays the part of terrorist bomber Howard Payne.

4   Mind the gap: a dangerous initiative to save lives.

5   The psychopath means business: the explosion at the start of the film shows how dangerous an opponent he is.

6   Like Annie, viewers are held captive right up to the very last minute.

# APOLLO 13

1995 - USA - 139 MIN. - ADVENTURE FILM

DIRECTOR RON HOWARD (*1954)
SCREENPLAY WILLIAM BROYLES JR., AL REINERT, based on the book *LOST MOON* by JIM LOVELL, JEFFREY KLUGER
DIRECTOR OF PHOTOGRAPHY DEAN CUNDEY MUSIC JAMES HORNER PRODUCTION BRIAN GRAZER, TODD HALLOWELL for IMAGINE ENTERTAINMENT.

STARRING TOM HANKS (Jim Lovell), BILL PAXTON (Fred Haise), KEVIN BACON (Jack Swigert), GARY SINISE (Ken Mattingly), ED HARRIS (Gene Kranz), KATHLEEN QUINLAN (Marilyn Lovell), MARY KATE SCHELLHARDT (Barbara Lovell), EMILY ANN LLOYD (Susan Lovell), MIKO HUGHES (Jeffrey Lovell), MAX ELLIOTT SLADE (Jay Lovell).

ACADEMY AWARDS 1996 OSCARS for BEST SOUND (Rick Dior, Steve Pederson, Scott Millan, David MacMillan) and BEST FILM EDITING (Daniel P. Hanley, Mike Hill).

## "Houston, we have a problem."

In May 1961, President Kennedy promised that an American would land on the moon before the decade was out. This was his answer to Russia's head start in the space race, which had been an unpleasant surprise for America. The first spacecraft to orbit the earth was a Russian Sputnik and a Russian cosmonaut was the first man to travel in space. Although the official reason for the space race was scientific research, in actual fact it was a prestige duel between the super powers. The astronauts were old fashioned explorers rather than servants of science.

However, after only two successful moon landings, mankind's final heroic chapter came to a shuddering halt. The third lunar mission Apollo 13 started on 11 April 1970. It seemed routine until five words uttered by Commander Jim Lovell (Tom Hanks) instantly entered everyday speech and

tore the nation and the watching world out of its complacency: "Houston, we have a problem." What Lovell meant by this heroic understatement worthy of Hemingway was that the oxygen tank vital to the astronauts' survival had exploded. Apollo 13 then suffered a whole series of related problems and there followed dramatic, drawn-out rescue attempts to bring back the three astronauts adrift in space. Like every modern American fairytale, the crisis brought together the potent combination of highly developed technology and the tried and tested virtues of a pioneer nation: inventiveness, pragmatism and selfless teamwork.

*Apollo 13*'s dramatic handicap is that virtually every viewer knows from the very beginning that the story has a happy ending. However, Ron Howard set out to write a simple heroic epic – and succeeded in being just

2

1  On the way to the moon. Apollo 13's journey gets off to an encouraging start.

2  The astronauts' wives watch the rocket take off.

3  A legendary place: in the Houston control room engineers work together to save the astronauts' lives.

4  Fear eats the soul (Kevin Bacon, centre): several systems aboard the space module have failed, making the return journey extremely hazardous.

as cool, laconic and unsentimental as Lovell's report of the near fatal disaster from 200,000 miles away. All the characters are in the same boat, they all put their personal problems aside and do their bit for the happy ending. That goes for the three astronauts themselves as much as for the colleague dropped from the mission shortly before the start with suspected measles, who goes over and over the most incredible rescue manoeuvres in the flight simulator. It also includes national hero Neil Armstrong, who reassures Lovell's mother in a nursing home, and goes right down to the most insignificant employee of the Texas mission control centre.

Movies that exalt supposed national virtues and claim as American the capacity to make impossible things possible by sheer force of will may seem naive or even dangerous. Manned space travel also has its critics, and the genre ingredients used here to create emotional effect have all been seen once too often. Nevertheless, as Apollo 13 approaches splashdown at the end of the movie and the entire mission control centre breaks out in shouts and cheers, it's a hard-baked and cynical viewer who begrudges them some sort of approving remark.

UE

3

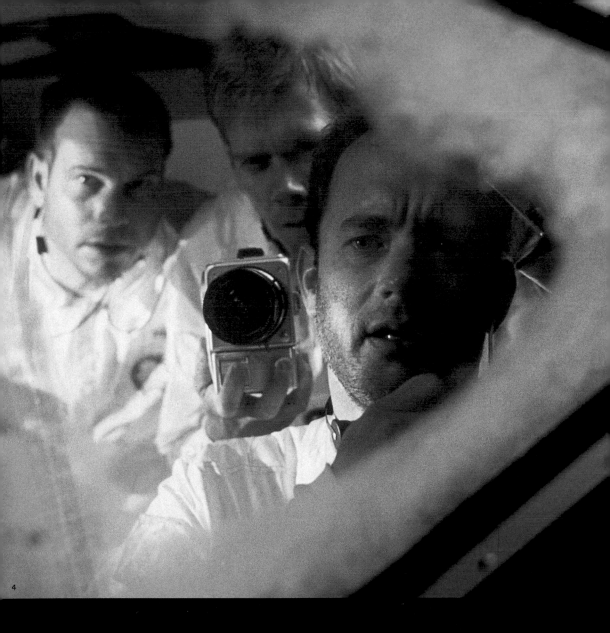

4

Manned space travel was promoted in the 60s as mankind's last great adventure. The crude fantasies of armies of SF authors aside, the real space race for the moon and stars features astonishingly seldom in Hollywood feature films. Strictly speaking, there are only two movies on the subject that can be considered anything like a masterpiece. The first is *The Right Stuff* (1983), Philip Kaufman's partly mythical, partly tongue-in-cheek adaptation of Tom Wolfe's reportage novel of the same name, describing the transition period when the first astronauts took over from the old test pilots and proclaimed themselves to be the true heroes of the modern-day Wild West. Clint Eastwood's late work *Space Cowboys* (2000), whose brilliant title says it all, would have to be the second: a laconic yet wry movie with a touch of melancholy, it tells the story of the forgotten pioneers of the first hour who are called upon to get Houston out of a tight spot. An old-fashioned satellite is out of control and the old-timers are the only ones who still know how it works. Their mission is a success and they finally receive the fame that is their due.

5

6

"In the summer *Apollo 13* shot like a rocket to the top of the US box office. President Clinton had it shown to him at the White House, and the Speaker of the House and science fiction writer Newt Gingrich declared the film quite simply 'brilliant'." *Frankfurter Rundschau*

5   Jim Lovell (Tom Hanks) during preparations for the flight.

6   Fred Haise (Bill Paxton) gives the other two astronauts a worried look.

7   Flight director Gene Kranz (Ed Harris) tries to keep a cool head.

8   Ken Mattingly (Gary Sinise), the astronaut who stayed behind, does everything he can to ensure his friends can come home.

9   Worrying images on TV: the Apollo 13 space module is just about to re-enter the earth's atmosphere.

# DEAD MAN WALKING

1995 - USA - 122 MIN. - MELODRAMA

DIRECTOR TIM ROBBINS (*1958)

SCREENPLAY TIM ROBBINS, based on SISTER HELEN PREJEAN'S autobiography of the same name DIRECTOR OF PHOTOGRAPHY ROGER A. DEAKINS MUSIC DAVID ROBBINS PRODUCTION JON KILIK, TIM ROBBINS, RUDD SIMMONS for WORKING TITLE FILMS, HAVOC PRODUCTIONS.

STARRING SEAN PENN (Matthew Poncelet), SUSAN SARANDON (Sister Helen Prejean), ROBERT PROSKY (Hilton Barber), RAYMOND J. BARRY (Earl Delacroix), R. LEE ERMEY (Clyde Percy), CELIA WESTON (Mary Beth Percy), LOIS SMITH (Helen's mother), SCOTT WILSON (Farley), ROBERTA MAXWELL (Lucille Poncelet), MARGO MARTINDALE (Sister Colleen).

ACADEMY AWARDS 1996 OSCAR for BEST ACTRESS (Susan Sarandon).

IFF BERLIN 1996 SILVER BEAR for BEST ACTOR (Sean Penn).

*"I want the last face you see in this world to be the face of love, so you look at me when they do this thing."*

Never for a moment does this movie doubt the guilt of the condemned man, and the title makes it clear from the beginning that the execution will be carried out. Matthew Poncelet (Sean Penn), a vain, showy, shabby piece of white trash is to pay with his own messed-up life for the double murder of a pair of young lovers, symbol of America's hopes for a purer and better future.

Tim Robbins' second movie intentionally avoids the effects generally used in conventional prison thrillers to create suspense and win the audience's sympathy. There is no wrongly accused innocent saved at the last minute in a dramatic race against time, and no one pulls the condemned man's head out of the noose at the last moment. The movie does not set out to appeal against the death penalty, but rather to describe the grinding machinery of death row, with its strictly observed rituals and its wheels that turn with such agonising slowness.

Poncelet, the murderer in the film, has been waiting 6 years for his execution, while the national average is considerably more. He is not dragged to the gallows the way he would be in a Western or forced into the electric chair like in a classic gangster film, as modern-day Louisiana takes a far more clinical approach when it comes to deciding over the life and death of its citizens. Nevertheless, shortly before the injection machine begins to pump poison into Poncelet's veins, the table he is tied to is set in an upright position. The impression that a diseased animal is being released from its suffering and put to sleep is replaced by an image of the crucifixion. Here the deeply-rooted religious symbolism of American society is plain to see: through his crucifixion, God is with the sinner. This is however combined with a fundamentalist idea of revenge and retaliation, anchored in the Manichaean view of many American churches that only absolute good and absolute evil exist.

That conviction, and the cliché of America as a nation eternally wedded to violence are arguments that are often trotted out to make capital punishment seem acceptable even today in "God's own country". But the thinking is that even though evil must be rooted out mercilessly, the condemned

3  4

"As ... in lighting and setdesign, the film discards prison movie cliché: this jail is no shadowy gothic hell hole but institutionally dull, almost cosy in its way. *Sight and Sound*

1   It takes Sister Helen Prejean (Susan Sarandon) some time to win the trust of condemned murderer Matthew Poncelet (Sean Penn).

2   A courageous woman. Sister Prejean does not desert the murderer on his final journey.

3   Love for her fellow man also means overcoming her own repulsion at the barbarity of the execution.

4   Even in the face of death there are happy moments. Laughter reaches across where words fail.

5   Poncelet only accepts responsibility for the crime at the very end.

5

should not be deprived of spiritual comfort. Poncelet writes to Helen Prejean (Susan Sarandon), a Catholic nun who is also a social worker in a ghetto, and asks her to visit him in prison. Helen takes up his invitation and gets her first insight into the grim workings of the prison system, which both upsets her and inspires her decision to accompany the murderer on his way to death. The offensive, boasting, dishonest side of Poncelet breaks through again and again, and Sean Penn is magnificent in the way he constantly alienates the audience and thereby creates a wholly convincing criminal. By a huge act of will, Helen eventually succeeds in building up relationship of trust with Poncelet, a closeness the limits of which are subtly emphasised by the director's constant use of grids and dividing walls. Although there are no explicit hints of forgiveness or redemption, Helen does nonetheless develop the beginnings of an understanding for this totally alien man.

According to her partner Robbins, Susan's character was intended to be the eyes of the audience. As we accompany this uncertain, doubt-ridden handmaid of the Lord, we see many other perspectives on Poncelet's case, all presented in an unsentimental and non-judgemental way. We see the victim's embittered families crying out for retribution, the self-sacrificing, dedicated but incompetent legal aid lawyer, the contemptuous prison officials who fulfil their duties so unwillingly, and the sympathy of hypocritical local politicians who are hopelessly constrained by the limitations of the system – and all of these figures are treated with the necessary respect. Like all good movies, *Dead Man Walking* takes its audience seriously and demands that it come to its own conclusions. The viewers themselves must decide whether, given the terrible conditions of the prisons, it is more humane to lock someone up for life without any prospect of early release (the only alternative to the death penalty in the USA), or to execute him straight away. It is no secret that the overwhelming majority of Americans are in favour of the latter, and *Dead Man Walking* is clever enough to avoid launching a direct attack on that conviction.                                                                                          UB

# TOY STORY

1995 - USA - 81 MIN. - ANIMATION, COMEDY

DIRECTOR JOHN LASSETER (*1957)
SCREENPLAY JOSS WHEDON, ANDREW STANTON, JOEL COHEN, ALEC SOKOLOW DIRECTOR OF PHOTOGRAPHY JULIE M. MCDONALD, LOUIS RIVERA MUSIC RANDY NEWMAN PRODUCTION RALPH GUGGENHEIM, BONNIE ARNOLD for PIXAR ANIMATION STUDIOS (for WALT DISNEY PICTURES).

VOICES TOM HANKS (Woody), TIM ALLEN (Buzz Lightyear), DON RICKLES (Mr Potato Head), WALLACE SHAWN (Rex), JOHN RATZENBERGER (Hamm), JIM VARNEY (Slinky Dog), ANNIE POTTS (Bo Peep), JOHN MORRIS (Andy), LAURIE METCALF (Mrs Davis), R. LEE ERMEY (Sergeant).

## "You've got a friend in me."

Day breaks in Andy's playroom. After the boy has gone to school, it's time for his toys to stretch and scratch and sometimes even to fit themselves back together. Rex the neurotic dinosaur broadcasts his problems to the whole world, Mr Potato Head gives a running sarcastic commentary, Slinky Dog slopes through the room in his friendly and melancholic way and Woody, the cowboy doll, calmly watches over his herd. The toys live, they have feelings, and above all they have a fine sense of irony about their function, although the humans know nothing of all that.

One day the fine social balance that has developed in the playroom over the years is destroyed by the arrival of a newcomer. His name is Buzz Lightyear, his vocation is to save the universe, and he takes his mission seriously. Woody and the others recognise this childish fresh-out-of-the-pack-

aging syndrome right away and try to explain to Buzz that he is only a toy. To no avail. The situation is not improved by the fact that in no time at all Buzz is Andy's favourite toy, and he begins to neglect all his other old play partners. Woody is depressed and tries to win back his place in Andy's heart. If anything should upset Buzz Lightyear's electronics in the process, then so much the better.

Soon however a tricky situation comes about, and Woody, Buzz and all the other toys have to pull together to solve it.

Even if the story weren't the little masterpiece that it is, this movie would still have a place in cinema history, for it was the first film ever to be made using only computer animation. Everything from the smallest blade of grass to the plastic army was developed inside a computer, from the earliest

"To rephrase Wittgenstein, for all the characters in *Toy Story*, technology is the limit of their world." *Sight and Sound*

sketches to the three-dimensional finished object. Technical advances like that mean that some classic film jobs like camerawork can be simulated, although the eye of the cameraman, and above all his thinking are still vital to the project. *Toy Story* had its first contact with the outside world when the finished work was transferred from hard disc to 35mm film. When its sequel appeared four years later, alternative methods of distribution were already available: *Toy Story 2* was the first film in the world which was shown in selected cinemas via beam projection. *Toy Story* is a great movie independ-ently of its technical innovations. It demonstrates a belief in traditional cine-matic qualities which are often considered old-fashioned: the characters are well drawn and consistent, the plot is logical and beautifully constructed, and it's filled end to end with humour and suspense. The movie is also convinc-ing in the way it works on different levels, and has something to offer for every age group. It is an exciting adventure for children which passes on val-ues of friendship and trust. For adults it is an affectionate yet amazingly unsentimental homage to childhood and the difficulties of growing up.   OM

1    Woody sees to it that communal life is harmonious in Andy's playroom. The voice of Tom Hanks lends the wind-up cowboy a friendly, naïve soul.

2    Hamm, the piggybank, and Mr Potato Head, the funny-face doll, are compulsive card-players. One of many endearing pieces of fun in the world's first full-length animated feature film produced entirely using computer graphics.

3    Even a wind-up cowboy has feelings: Woody with Bo Peep, his beloved shepherdess doll.

4    Cosmic warrior Buzz Lightyear has an identity crisis. His role as Messiah to a race of three-eyed extra-terrestrials proves too much for him.

**PIXAR STUDIOS**    Pixar Studios originally belonged to George Lucas' "ILM – Industrial Light and Magic". Pixar was therefore responsible for the computer generated pictures in Richard Marquand's *Return of the Jedi* (1982), as well as for Nicholas Meyer's *Star Trek – The Wrath of Khan* (1982) and Barry Levinson's *Young Sherlock Holmes* (1985). In 1986 Pixar became an independent company under Steve Jobs, the founder of Apple. It began to concentrate on the development of the software necessary for the creation of movies that were totally computer-animated. After the production of various short films, Pixar finally succeeded in making *Toy Story*, which was the first movie in the world to have been produced entirely in a computer, under the direction of the creative head of the studio, John Lasseter.

# KIDS

1995 - USA - 91 MIN. - DRAMA

DIRECTOR LARRY CLARK (*1943)
SCREENPLAY LARRY CLARK, HARMONY KORINE DIRECTOR OF PHOTOGRAPHY ERIC ALAN EDWARDS MUSIC LOU BARLOW, JOHN DAVIS
PRODUCTION CARY WOODS for INDEPENDENT PICTURES, MIRAMAX.

STARRING CHLOË SEVIGNY (Jennie), LEO FITZPATRICK (Telly), JUSTIN PIERCE (Casper), YAKIRU PEGUERO (Darcy),
MICHELE LOCKWOOD (Kim), ROSARIO DAWSON (Ruby), BILLY VALDES (Stanly), BILLY WALDEMAN (Zack),
SARAH HENDERSON (Girl 1), SAJAN BHAGAT (Paul).

## "When you are young not much matters.
## When you find something you like, that's all you got."

New York: teenage boys sit together and talk loud and long about sex, especially Telly (Leo Fitzpatrick), who "specialises" in virgins. New York: girls sit together and talk – with only slightly more reserve – about sex. Both groups soon start to talk about AIDS, and the boys are determined not to let it spoil their fun. Two of the girls have just had an AIDS test, although Jennie (Chloë Sevigny) really only went to make it less embarrassing for Ruby (Rosario Dawson). But when they go to collect the results, Jennie turns out to be HIV positive. Telly is the only person she has ever slept with, and alone, she sets off to find him. He's on the streets with his friend Casper (Justin Pierce) buying grass with money that he has stolen from his mother. In the park they meet another couple of teenagers. Together they beat up a passer-by who they suspect is gay, and all the while they talk uninterruptedly about sex. Telly keeps talking about how he going to "crack a virgin" that evening, as

he did in that morning. This time the lucky girl is 13-year-old Darcy (Yakiru Peguero). He picks her up with his friends, and after dark they all they break into swimming pool. While the others start playing games in the water, Telly begins to tell Darcy tenderly of his love – just like he did with another girl in the opening sequence of the movie.

As she trails him around the city, Jennie keeps arriving just after Telly has left. She has to listen to a taxi driver telling her that she should just forget about the test result because when she laughs, she looks like a prom queen. In a disco where she hopes to find Telly a friend persuades her to pop a few pills of the latest "stuff". When she finally catches up with Telly she finds him ensconced in the parents' bedroom at a friend's party, in the midst of deflowering Darcy. Jennie has come too late. Horrified and half numbed by the drugs, she watches through the doorway as they have sex.

3

1   When Jennie (Chloë Sevigny) goes for an AIDS
    test to support her friend, she's the one who turns
    out to be HIV positive ...

2   ... while her friend Ruby (Rosario Dawson) had
    been worrying for nothing.

3   When looking for a suitable image, nothing beats
    dramatising your sexuality and showing it off.

## "I was trying to bring you into a reality that grownups just don't see. Think about what it's like to be a kid. How you're living for the moment. How you just want to have fun. How you're not thinking about tomorrow." *Larry Clarke, CNN*

4

5

4  The young boys emulate the older ones and experiment with their bodies and the topic of sex.

5  For they know not what they do: Telly (Leo Fitzpatrick) and Casper (Justin Pierce) aren't wicked or stupid, they just want to have fun.

6  For Telly this is just a kind of warm-up routine: he declares his love to any girl he likes, in order to be able to tell his mates about his sexual adventures afterwards.

**AMATEUR ACTORS**  It is much easier to work with non-professional actors in a movie than it is on the stage. Camera work and editing both exercise a selection process which means that neither the overall effect of a performance nor its single elements are important, and that unclear articulation or an imperfect physique are much less of a problem than they would be on the stage. On the other hand, film sometimes uses non-professionals precisely because of some distinguishing physical feature, but that is mostly the case for supporting roles. Amateurs are sometimes used – although rarely – for an alienation effect, as in the movies of Straub/Huillet. Their clumsy performances are a deliberate effect to remind us that we are watching an artificial product. Amateur actors often appear in children's films and youth movies. Capturing their spontaneity requires extremely careful filming and directing however, and they cannot be simply put in front of the cameras. Some directors specialise in this, like the French director Jacques Doillon, who after years of working with children has developed his own special technique to avoid cuteness, which has the effect of making the kids in his movies appear as fully rounded characters.

Eventually, she sinks down onto a couch in the last free corner in the living room which is full of drunken and doped up kids who have all fallen asleep. Only Casper – the friendly ghost – is still wandering around, sipping all the half-empty bottles. He tries to wake Jennie but gives up, removes her pants and penetrates her on the creaking leather sofa. The following morning, the sun shines down on the parks of New York. Casper opens his eyes and mutters: "Sweet Jesus, what happened?"

The kids of the title curse, smoke and have continual sex with each other (or at least talk about it) and yet the movie still manages to avoid shock effects and cheap thrills. Photographer Larry Clark gives us an impressive portrait of the kids in what was only his first movie. Despite what critics said when the movie first appeared, the kids are by no means clichéd monsters.

The simple images tell the story of a single day and the audience are forced observe the chaotic search for satisfaction without any moral yardstick. The mitigating factors which customarily appear in similar movies to explain the kids' extreme behaviour are intentionally omitted here, and neither the social milieu nor ethnic conflicts have an important role to play. Clark dissects his kids with a surgeon's scalpel. The film succeeds partly because Clark worked with young amateurs, and the result was an enormous variety of faces and gestures the like of which is rarely seen in standardised Hollywood movies. He also resisted the temptation to make his kids into pop stars with music, clothes and other outward signs of coolness. Nevertheless, Chloë Sevigny – who takes the role of Jenny – has since been much in demand as an actress and has appeared in other films like *Boys Don't Cry*.  MS

# CASINO

1995 - USA - 178 MIN. - GANGSTER FILM, DRAMA

DIRECTOR MARTIN SCORSESE (*1942)
SCREENPLAY NICHOLAS PILEGGI, MARTIN SCORSESE, based on the novel of the same name by NICHOLAS PILEGGI
MUSIC ADVISOR ROBBIE ROBERTSON DIRECTOR OF PHOTOGRAPHY ROBERT RICHARDSON PRODUCTION BARBARA DE FINA for SYALIS, LEGENDE, CAPPA (for UNIVERSAL).

STARRING ROBERT DE NIRO (Sam Rothstein), SHARON STONE (Ginger McKenna), JOE PESCI (Nicky Santoro), JAMES WOODS (Lester Diamonds), DON RICKLES (Billy Sherbert), ALAN KING (Andy Stone), KEVIN POLLAK (Phillip Green), L. Q. JONES (Pat Webb), DICK SMOTHERS (Senator), FRANK VINCENT (Frank Marino).

## "Anywhere else I would be arrested for what I'm doing. Here they're giving me awards."

Sam "Ace" Rothstein (Robert De Niro) is a genius book-maker. All addicted gamblers wait until Sam has laid his bets so that they can copy him. His perfectionism is legendary. If a jockey has problems with his wife or if a horse is ill, Sam is the first to know. That's why the Mafia choose him to manage Tangiers, their Las Vegas casino. Sam makes it his life's work and keeps the Mafia bosses happy by constantly increasing their profit margins. Nothing escapes his tireless eye.

The casino Scorsese shows us is a perfect system where everyone spies on everyone else. Everything goes perfectly until two newcomers suddenly upset the workings of Sam's life. To protect him adequately and presumably also to keep an eye on him, the Mafia send Nicky Santoro (Joe Pesci) to Vegas. Santoro is a psychopath who will do any dirty work necessary, a little man with big ambitions, who is obsessed with power and devoid of scruples. Nicky immediately begins to build up his own gangster mob, and in no time at all they have won control of petty crime in Las Vegas.

Sam sees Ginger McKenna (Sharon Stone) for the first time through the peep-hole in the casino's false ceiling. A prostitute who is as hardened as she is beautiful, she finds her clients among the ecstatic winners at the gambling tables. Sam falls in love with her. The only thing Ginger loves is her own self, but she is not adverse to Sam's money and power. To complicate matters, Lester, her former pimp, is still on the scene, and he still has a powerful hold on her. Scorsese retells a familiar tale of rise and fall, of powerful men who overreach themselves and end up losing everything, and he elevates his gangsters to the level of tragic heroes. Rothstein wants to rule the world by organising it perfectly and watching over it, and he ruthlessly uses everyone around him to his own immoral ends. But in the process, he unwittingly destroys his own happiness.

Nicky is intoxicated with Las Vegas, and he believes he can force his own rules on the city. He begins a brutal reign of terror at the bookmakers' and on the streets, only to fall victim of his own cycle of violence. Ginger, the third main figure, is unable to love and prefers to spend her life dependent on other people.

One of the great strengths of Scorsese's movies is they way they manage to present the Mafia and the underworld from constantly new and dif-

"I'm what's real out here. Not your country clubs and your TV show. I'm what's real: the dirt, the gutter, and the blood. That's what it's all about."

*Quotation from film: Nicky Santoro*

# "What interested me was the idea of excess, no limits. People become successful like in no other city."

*Martin Scorsese in: Sight and Sound*

1 Expressions that speak volumes: the paths of Sam "Ace" Rothstein (Robert De Niro) and Nicky Santoro (Joe Pesci) are not leading in the same direction.

2 A ruler and his empire: Robert De Niro as Sam Rothstein in an inferno of light.

3 Heavy guys throw dark shadows (Frank Vincent as Frank Marino, left): Nicky Santoro already senses that further humiliation awaits him.

4 The artificial smile of the professional: Ginger McKenna (Sharon Stone) at her place of work. This is where Sam Rothstein sees her for the first time. Ginger's glittering appearance comes to embody what he imagines happiness to be.

4

casual, almost comic way, like the men next door. *Casino* takes a radically different track, as though Scorsese had resurrected figures from Shakespearean tragedy. The film forces us to feel sympathy for these heroes, and as soon as we fall into that trap, we are forced stand by and watch their downfall. Sam's megalomania gets him into trouble with local politicians and suddenly life gets much more complicated; Nicky thinks he can run the racket to his own advantage without the Mafia noticing, and even Ginger's brilliant beauty starts to fade when she agrees to marry Sam Rothstein, who buys her love with jewellery, money and furs.

Casino is a searingly beautiful movie. It presents the audience with the characters' innermost desires and fears through its off-screen narration. It does far more than tell one story, but is a complex weave of tales relating how love cannot be bought, and how friendship can be easily betrayed Despite its tragic elements, the movie is witty in its depiction of the norma everyday life of the criminal fraternity. And Scorsese's special talent fo allowing comedy tip over unexpectedly into violence makes the movie a rea roller-coaster ride.

The story also reflects the rise and fall of Las Vegas itself. We see thi from Sam and Nicky's perspective, reflected in the everyday routine of the casino, and the endless struggle against cheats and con-men, the constan search for new ways to evade taxation, and ever more effective means o controlling employees. The movie's discursive structure is mirrored in Rober Richardson's camera work; he swings and zooms, looking curiously here and there. Scorsese's Vegas is a hell of sound and fury. The world, as ever, is his stage.

OM

---

**SAUL BASS**  We have the graphic designer and filmmaker Saul Bass to thank for the fact that uninspiring opening credit sequences have now become art works in their own right. His work with Otto Preminger, for who he made the credits, promotional material and above all posters and adverts from the mid-50s onwards, played a major part in his development. Bass cultivated a minimalist style, using a small number of colours and motifs to emphasize the main theme of a movie. Although Saul Bass had officially retired, Martin Scorsese managed to persuade him to work on his movies. From *Goodfellas* (1991) to *Casino* (1995) Saul made all the credits for Scorsese's movies with the help of his wife Elaine. Bass has also directed music videos and many prize-winning short films as well as the feature film *Phase 4* (1973).

---

5  They've made it. Sam and Ginger blithely adopt the status symbols of the wealthy and the beautiful, unaware that nothing can protect them from a precipitous fall.

6  A fatal ménage à trois: the husband and his wife, the ex-callgirl and her pimp. Lester Diamonds (James Woods) has a greater hold over Ginger than Sam ever will.

# "When you love someone, you've got to trust them. You've got to give them the keys to everything that's yours."

*Quotation from film: Sam Rothstein*

7   A dissolute icon of depravity: as Ginger McKenna Sharon Stone plays the most impressive role of her career.

8   A roll of the dice leads to deceptive success: Robert De Niro in his most complex Scorsese role to date.

9   Forbidden fruit: Nicky allows himself to be seduced by Ginger, in a relationship that will plunge him into oblivion.

8

# LEAVING LAS VEGAS

1995 - USA - 112 MIN. - DRAMA

DIRECTOR MIKE FIGGIS (*1948)
SCREENPLAY MIKE FIGGIS, based on the novel of the same name by JOHN O'BRIEN  DIRECTOR OF PHOTOGRAPHY DECLAN QUINN
MUSIC MIKE FIGGIS  PRODUCTION ANNIE STEWART, LILA CAZES for INITIAL PRODUCTIONS.

STARRING ELISABETH SHUE (Sera), NICOLAS CAGE (Ben), JULIAN SANDS (Yuri), RICHARD LEWIS (Peter), STEVEN WEBER (Marc Nussbaum), KIM ADAMS (Sheila), EMILY PROCTOR (Debbie), VALERIA GOLINO (Terri), LAURIE METCALF (Landlady), DAVID BRISBIN (Landlord).

ACADEMY AWARDS 1996 OSCAR for BEST ACTOR (Nicolas Cage).

## "I realised we didn't have much time, and I accepted him for what he was."

Ben (Nicolas Cage) is an alcoholic. He is so tired of life that he can't even bear it when he is completely drunk. When he loses his job, he takes it as a sign and decides to use his redundancy pay as a way of funding his alcohol consumption to the bitter end. As a failed scriptwriter, he feels that Las Vegas will be an appropriate setting for his intentions, as the bars in the city are open round the clock. On his way into town, he nearly runs over Sera (Elisabeth Shue), a young prostitute. She too is an addict, in her way: she is dependent on Yuri (Julian Sands), her Latvian pimp, who uses a knife on her whenever she disobeys. She has run away to Las Vegas in an attempt to regain control over her life, but Yuri has already tracked her down.

The next day, Ben and Sera meet again in a bar. Although Ben has been impotent for a long time, he takes her with him to his room. They get to know each other better. When Yuri finds out, he attacks Sera, as he has no patience with useless extras like emotional involvement. Luckily, it's for the last time:

a Mafia organisation from the former Soviet Union has a problem with Yuri and solves it by getting rid of him.

Sera likes Ben and decides to help him with his plan. She continues to earn on the streets and when she has time, she takes care of him.

One evening when Sera is at work, Ben goes to a casino, has an unexpected run of luck, and in a good mood hires a prostitute who happens to be free and takes her to Sera's apartment. When Sera returns home she finds them both there and, beside herself with jealousy and rage, she goes to the room of three college boys who rape her and beat her up. When she returns home completely distraught, Ben rings from a dosshouse. The end is near.

In the psychology of Ben and Sera's relationship there is no room for helper syndrome, so there is no need to fear sentimental last minute rescue scenes in the final act. Ben is serious, and that could have been a real dramatic problem: when the audience knows from the very beginning how the

movie will end, there is not much room left for suspense. Moreover, Yuri's forced exit from the scene removes the only unpredictable element from the constellation comparatively quickly. Mike Figgis uses this narrative stagnation to give his characters space to develop emotionally, and he gives his actors the chance to exercise their improvisation skills. This approach is emphasised by his much-discussed decision to film the movie on super 16, although in fact that was partly a budget decision. This method uses a compact, light camera and cheap, high sensitivity film. Although it had long been the material of choice for documentary filmmakers, it lost its place in the market when Digital Video appeared. As a material DV is even less expensive, and it quickly grabbed everyone's attention. It also inspired Figgis to make *Time Code* (2000), his most experimental film to date, a not entirely successful attempt at non-linear narration.

Technical aspects aside, *Leaving Las Vegas* is a movie truly remarkable for the honesty with which Figgis presents emotions it portrays. Occasionally he may be a little heavy on the Freud in the analysis of Ben and Sera – but it's their souls that remain his central concern.

OM

---

**ALCOHOLISM IN CINEMA**  Drugs have always been an important theme in feature films. Alcohol especially is a central motif, whether as a necessary attribute of hard men or as a source of inspiration for writers and artists. The consumption of alcohol with fatal consequences has also often been thematised, as for example in Billy Wilder's masterpiece *The Lost Weekend* (1945), Blake Edwards' *Days of Wine and Roses* (1962) or John Huston's *Under the Volcano* (1984). Lives drowned in alcohol and memory loss through drinking are leitmotifs of "Film Noir". Memorable performances of alcoholics include James Stewart seeing a six-foot rabbit in *Harvey* (1950), Dean Martin as a drunken assistant sheriff in Howard Hawks' Western *Rio Bravo* (1959) and Mickey Rourke playing the title role in Barbet Schroeder's Bukowski homage *Barfly* (1987). Seldom was alcoholism so erotic.

---

1   Las Vegas: city of lights but no dreams, the collection of curios that is the American dream.

2   The alcoholic Ben (Nicolas Cage) realises that there is still love even for the lost and fallen. Even if it manifests itself in the form of the prostitute Sera (Elisabeth Shue).

3   Sera at work: here she is part of the false veneer of happiness of Las Vegas.

4   Elisabeth Shue made a breakthrough as a serious actress with this portrayal of a woman on the brink of spiritual self-realisation.

5   Mike Figgis' favourite supporting actor Julian Sands as Sera's pimp Yuri.

6   Ben and Sera find common ground in the weightless world of a motel swimming pool.

3

"Are you some sort
of angel visiting me
in one of my drunk
fantasies?"

*Quotation from film: Ben*

# RUMBLE IN THE BRONX
## Hung Fan Kui

1995 - HONG KONG - 90 MIN. - ACTION FILM, COMEDY, MARTIAL ARTS FILM

DIRECTOR STANLEY TONG (*1960)
SCREENPLAY EDWARD TANG, FIBE MA DIRECTOR OF PHOTOGRAPHY JINGLE MA MUSIC J. PETER ROBINSON, JONATHAN WONG PRODUCTION RAYMOND CHOW, LEONHARD HO, BARBIE TUNG for GOLDEN HARVEST.

STARRING JACKIE CHAN (Ah Keung), ANITA MUI (Elaine), FRANÇOISE YIP (Nancy), BILL TUNG (Uncle Bill), MARC AKERSTREAM (Tony), GARVIN CROSS (Angelo), MORGAN LAM (Danny), KRIS LORD (White Tiger), AILEN SIT (Gang Member), CHAN MAN SING (Gang Member).

## "If you got the guts, drop the gun."

"Something's always happening here, that's New York for you." Keung (Jackie Chan) has just arrived from Hong Kong and he finds the American East Coast metropolis run-down and dangerous. At first his Uncle's words reassure him, but many adventures await him in the city and they're not all going to be fun,

Keung is a young man who has come over for the wedding of his Uncle Bill (Bill Tung), and on his very first night in America he has to defend the elegant white stretch limousine that Bill has borrowed for the occasion. Bill sells his supermarket in the Bronx and goes off on his honeymoon. Elaine (Anita Mui) buys the store, but still needs Bill's nephew's help and the very next day Keung discovers members of a biker gang raiding the place. He stops them and beats them up. After many chase scenes and fights between this gang, its leader Tony and Keung, the appearance of another gangster mob forces the rivals to pool their forces. Their new mutual enemies are unscrupulous

diamond thieves with automatic rifles who make Tony's boys look like harmless school kids. In the meantime, Keung also makes friends in New York; he meets little Danny (Morgan Lam) who is in a wheelchair and his sister Nancy (Françoise Yip), the girlfriend of gangster leader Tony.

In most Jackie Chan films the story is of secondary importance, but in *Rumble in the Bronx* he gets down to the essentials even faster than normal. The economy of the movie is remarkable. In the space of three minutes Keung is established in New York, he is set up as a loveable character and skilled fighter, and we have also met his uncle and the boy in the wheelchair. Moments later his troubles with the rocker gang begins, they get down to business and the carefully choreographed fighting begins. Whether Jackie Chan runs, jumps, climbs over high fences or water skis on trainers, whether he fights using refrigerators, shopping trolleys or chairs as shields and weapons – his element is still the material world and he moves effortlessly

2

# "I love action but I hate violence. For this reason, I think this choreographical solution is the best. In Asia I have become the children's idol and I do not want to set a bad example." Jackie Chan in: Abendzeitung

**JACKIE CHAN –
ASIA'S SUPERSTAR**

He does all his stunts himself and during the closing credits shows what went wrong in the process. Unique superstar Jackie Chan was born in 1954. He learned his amazing physical skills at a Peking opera school in Hong Kong, where he was sent at the age of 7. Since his debut in 1971 he has made movie after movie, since 1980 he has also directed films, and the combination of martial arts and comedy is an idea he originally developed himself. Chan's role models are the cinema's great comedians to whom he regularly pays homage, like Harold Lloyd, whose famous clock tower scene he refers to in *Project A* (1983) and Buster Keaton, from whose *Steamboat Bill, Jr.* (1928) he borrows a scene in *Project A, Part 2* (1987). *Rumble in the Bronx* brought the Asian superstar fame and fortune in the USA, as well as an MTV Lifetime Achievement Award. On that occasion Quentin Tarantino said: "If I could choose which actor to be, I would choose Jackie Chan."

1   Keung (Jackie Chan) doesn't use guns, the most he ever uses as a weapon is a ski.

2   Keung dispatches the unscrupulous diamond robbers as promptly…

3   … as the louts from Tony's gangster mob.

4   In 1996 *Rumble in the Bronx* was awarded Best Film at the Hong Kong Film Awards, and Jackie Chan and Stanley Tong Best Action Choreography.

5   In with the wrong crowd: Nancy (Françoise Yip), little Danny's sister.

3

hrough it. Speed, flexibility and elegance dominate his films, but the fights are never really brutal and Chan's boyish charm and slapstick humour take away their violent edge. That said, *Rumble in the Bronx* is a movie of unusual extravagance. It rejoices in destructive orgies, like the complete destruction of a supermarket while its owner sits on the lavatory. It allows itself the liberty of showing things which have precious little to do with the plot but look good, such as the truck loaded with balls which topples from a multi-storey car park. And it is full of breathtaking chase scenes, like the one where a hovercraft races through busy streets and over a golf course until the baddie is finally run over. He survives, if a little shaken.

As in all his films, Jackie Chan does the stunts himself. He broke his ankle jumping on to the moving hovercraft, but then hid the plaster with his trouser leg and carried on. *Rumble in the Bronx* was his breakthrough in America. The movie was made in Vancouver in English, as US audiences don't like dubbed films. The American distributor New Line Cinema shortened the original 105 minute version to 90 minutes by shedding scenes like a wedding duet and a moralising speech by Chan, and launched the film with a massive advertising campaign. It made $ 10,000,000 in its first week.

HJK

4

5

# MISSION: IMPOSSIBLE

1996 - USA - 110 MIN. - ACTION FILM, THRILLER

DIRECTOR BRIAN DE PALMA (*1940)
SCREENPLAY ROBERT TOWNE, DAVID KOEPP, based on characters from BRUCE GELLER'S TV series of the same name
DIRECTOR OF PHOTOGRAPHY STEPHEN H. BURUM MUSIC DANNY ELFMAN, LALO SCHIFRIN (theme tune) PRODUCTION TOM CRUISE, PAULA WAGNER for PARAMOUNT PICTURES.

STARRING TOM CRUISE (Ethan Hunt), JON VOIGHT (Jim Phelps), EMMANUELLE BÉART (Claire), KRISTIN SCOTT THOMAS (Sarah Davies), VANESSA REDGRAVE (Max), JEAN RENO (Krieger), VING RHAMES (Luther), HENRY CZERNY (Kittrigde), EMILIO ESTEVEZ (Electronics Expert), DALE DYE (Frank Barnes).

## "Dear boy, you are a sport."

Jim Phelps (Jon Voight) of the IMF (Impossible Mission Force) is supposed to be neutralising an enemy agent in Kiev. He succeeds thanks to the help of his wife Claire (Emmanuelle Béart) and his colleague Ethan Hunt (Tom Cruise),who specialises in disguise. He gets home to find the next assignment waiting for him – a traitor called Golitsyn must be found and stopped. Phelps sets a trap for him at the American embassy in Prague: during a reception he gives Golitsyn the opportunity to steal a list of names of double agents. Claire and Ethan also take part along with several other younger agents.

At the beginning it seems as if everything is going to plan and Golitsyn is soon unmasked, but gradually, successive members of the team are put out of action. At first we think only Ethan survives the trap that has been set for him, but later we realise that Claire has also survived. The failed trap means that Ethan becomes the CIA's prime suspect, and he is accused of being a double agent, especially as the actual aim of the operation was to unmask the traitors in their own ranks.

Ethan is able to escape but knows he will only be able to prove his innocence by finding the real culprit. He searches Jim Phelps' apartment and finds clues to a mysterious contact person called Max. Ethan meets up with Claire again who wants to join in his investigations and find out who murdered her husband. Max turns out to be an elderly lady who deals in top security information and is ready to pay a large sum of money for the real list of double agents' names. That list however only exists in the central CIA computer, and to get the data Ethan has to break in. He is helped by Luther (Ving Rhames), a technical genius and former CIA employee and Krieger (Jean Reno), an enigmatic killer.

The break-in and data theft are successful. Ethan, Claire, Luther and Krieger hide in London where Ethan sees his parents being arrested on the television news. To protect them, he leaves his hiding place and turns himself in to the CIA. Jim Phelps, who everyone thought was dead, unexpectedly reappears.

*Mission: Impossible* is basically typically 90s high-concept cinema, with Tom Cruise in some breathtaking action scenes. The opening scene is typical: Cruise blows up a restaurant that has massive aquariums built into its walls. He hangs on a thin line over a floor alarmed with a hypersensitive movement detector. Finally he clings to the roof of a high-speed train which is being followed by a helicopter into a tunnel.

But Brian de Palma's movie is also open to a second interpretation, and the breathless action sequences can also be seen as a meditation on the nature of images and the idea of deception as cinema's main inspiration. Spectators of *Mission: Impossible* are constantly forced to ask themselves what they are really watching, and wonder whether it is simply another trick. De Palma is brilliant at directing scenes where at first we believe what we see and then have to admit that we have been deceived. The central scene of the movie and its decisive moment is the meeting between Ethan Hunt and Jim Phelps – the only two figures who were taken from the TV series. Ethan and Jim discuss the things that have gone wrong, and we see individual moments again in flashback. At first the consequences and events seem clear, but the longer the discussion continues, the more the actual truth emerges: in fact, none of the images are to be trusted. They are all part of a cunningly conceived plot, which is uncovered step by step before our very eyes.                                                                    OM

---

**JEAN RENO**    Jean Reno made his cinema debut in 1978 in Raul Ruiz's *L'Hypothèse du tableau volé* (*The Hypothesis of The Stolen Painting*) after which he appeared in masterpieces such as Bertrand Blier's *Notre histoire* (*Our Rooms and Separate Rooms*, 1984) and Marco Ferreri's *I Love You* (1986). His big breakthrough came in 1987 with Luc Besson's successful movie *Le Grand Bleu* (*The Big Blue*, 1987). Reno's work with the director Jean-Marie Poiret was also very significant for his career. The three comedies *Operation Corned Beef* (1991), *Les Visiteurs* (*The Visitors*, 1993) and *Les Couloirs du temps: Les Visiteurs II* (*The Corridors of Time: The Visitors II*, 1998) made Reno a superstar in his native country. His role as a melancholy hired assassin in Luc Besson's *Léon/The Professional* (1994) made him known to a wider international audience.

3

4

# "*Mission: Impossible* makes of Brian de Palma the key analyst of the transformation of our society into a civilisation of image and technology."

*Cahiers du cinéma*

5

1  Tom Cruise is Ethan Hunt: a man of many masks, whose true character can't be read in his face.

2  One of the film's most striking images: Ethan Hunt gains access to the CIA's central computer.

3  Jean Reno plays mercenary agent Krieger.

4  Face to face: it doesn't take long for Hunt and Krieger to stop trusting each other.

5  Emmanuelle Béart plays Claire, wife of Hunt's boss Jim Phelps (Jon Voight).

6  The computer specialist Luther played by Ving Rhames proved to be a key figure in the film: he also plays a decisive role in John Woo's sequel.

6

# SHALL WE DANCE?

## Shall we Dansu?

1996 - JAPAN - 119 MIN. - COMEDY

DIRECTOR MASAYUKI SUO (*1956)

SCREENPLAY MASAYUKI SUO DIRECTOR OF PHOTOGRAPHY NAOKI KAYANO MUSIC YOSHIKAZU SUO PRODUCTION SHOJI MASUI, YASUYOSHI TOKUMA, YUJI OGATA for DAIEI, NIPPON TELEVISION NETWORK.

STARRING KOJI YAKUSHO (Shohei Sugiyama), TAMIYO KUSAKARI (Mai Kishikawa), NAOTO TAKENAKA (Tomio Aoki), ERIKO WATANABE (Toyoko Takahashi), AKIRA EMOTO (Toru Miwa), YU TOKUI (Tokichi Hattori), HIROMASA TAGUCHI (Masahiro Tanaka), REIKO KUSAMURA (Tamako Tamura), HIDEKO HARA (Masako Sugiyama), SHUCHIRO MORIYAMA (Ryo Kishikawa).

## *"Slow, slow, quick quick slow"*

Shohei Sugiyama (Koji Yakusho) leads the sober life of an average Japanese citizen. He is married with a daughter, owns his own home in the suburbs and has an office job in the city. But he still feels unfulfilled. One day on his way home in the train, he happens to see a woman standing at the window in the upper storey of a dance studio. The next day he sees her again. and soon he is waiting impatiently every day for the moment when his train will pass her building. One evening he can resist the temptation no longer and he gets out and goes to the studio. The beautiful stranger – whose name is Mai (Tamiyo Kusakari) – is a teacher there. Social dancing is not the done thing in Japan, but Shohei steels himself and puts his name down for a beginners' course. All he really wants is to get to know Mai. However, although his efforts in this direction fail, he begins to make real progress as a dancer after his first clumsy attempts. Gradually he is gripped by dance fever and his whole outlook on life begins to change, so much so that his wife becomes suspicious and engages a private detective to investigate the source of her husband's renewed vigour.

Back in 1937, Mark Sandrich directed *Shall We Dance?*, one of Hollywood's greatest musical successes. Fred Astaire and Ginger Rogers danced their way into the public's heart in the main roles, and for a few moments America could forget that its daily life was still overshadowed by the consequences of the Depression. Masayuki Suo's film of the same name was a smash hit in Japan in 1996 when economic recession hit the country. Decades of economic euphoria had come to an end, and more and more people began to question Japan's legendary work ethos and look instead for

ways of satisfying their individual needs. This social change is reflected in Suo's charming comedy. Unlike the Astaire film, Suo's movie does not use professional dancers to distract his audiences from their daily cares. Instead it shows how an ordinary family man in mid-life crisis discovers a love of dance that lifts him out of his depression. Shohei Sugiyama is a figure familiar primarily from European and American movies, but with whom many Japanese were able to identify.

The shape and narrative form of Suo's pictures are strongly influenced by the conventions of the Western. His references however are often ironic as he plays on the Americanisation of Japanese culture. Shohei is attracted by a woman in a window, a motif which has a long tradition in European and American film and has become something of a stale cliché. The mysterious beauty usually turns out to be a femme fatale, who threatens the man with sexual obsession and almost always with existential ruin, whereas in Suo's comedy, she turns out to be a comparatively harmless dancer who teaches the hero the simple lesson that there is pleasure in life outside work. Shohei's marriage still seems to be in danger, but only because he has to keep his dance course secret from his wife and work colleagues.

The drama and comedy of *Shall We Dance?* come above all from the heightened absurdity of daily routine at a time of national crisis. Despite his frequent ironic asides, Suo never fails to take his characters and their longing seriously – although their lives often seem banal, he gives them a heroic aspect. This opens the way for wonderful things at the movie's end.

JH

大関東アマチュアスポーツダンス大会

**FRED ASTAIRE**  Fred Astaire was born in 1899 in Omaha and died in 1987 in Los Angeles. He appeared on the stage as an actor, dancer and singer from his earliest youth. His film career began in 1933 during the most glamorous period of the Hollywood musical. Despite his skinny build and unusual looks Fred Astaire became one of Hollywood's most popular stars over the years that followed, with the help of his partner Ginger Rogers. He was famous above all for his extraordinary and incomparable dancing talent, which was a combination of precision, versatility and elegance. He was also very popular as a singer. Astaire made his last appearance as a singer and dancer in Francis Ford Coppola's *Finian's Rainbow* (1968) but continued acting to a ripe old age. His most famous musicals include *Top Hat* (1935), *Shall We Dance?* (1937), *Easter Parade* (1948) and *Daddy Long Legs* (1955).

1 And all your dreams will come true: Shohei and Mai (Koji Yakusho and Tamiyo Kusakari) find common ground in dancing.

2 The beautiful dance teacher shows the way.

3 Carried away by the music: at Mai's side Shohei really flies across the dance floor.

4 Beautiful and unattainable: the mysterious Mai arouses Shohei's passion.

5 Shohei is transformed from a run-of-the-mill pen-pusher into an elegant dancer.

6 Laborious first steps: at the beginners' course Shohei and his fellows are treading on unfamiliar ground.

6

"The movie has a great deal of zest and charm, and Yakusho gets so exactly that crest of melancholy that is a man's early 40s, until he decides to go for another kind of life, that the movie is infinitely touching." *The Washington Post*

7 Gripped by dance fever, Shohei adds unexpected élan to a normal day at the office.

8 The Japanese reveal their individual needs: spell-bound, Shohei watches the dance teacher's demonstration with his comrades-in-arms.

# WHEN WE WERE KINGS

&#8224;

1974/1996 - USA - 87 MIN. - DOCUMENTARY

DIRECTOR LEON GAST (*1936)
SCREENPLAY LEON GAST DIRECTOR OF PHOTOGRAPHY MARYSE ALBERTI, PAUL GOLDSMITH, KEVIN KEATIN, ALBERT MAYSLES, RODERICK YOUNG MUSIC WAYNE HENDERSON, TABU LEY PRODUCTION DAVID SONNENBERG, LEON GAST, TAYLOR HACKFORD, VIKRAM JAYANTI, KEITH ROBINSON for UFA NON FICTION.

STARRING MUHAMMAD ALI, GEORGE FOREMAN, DON KING, JAMES BROWN, B. B. KING, MIRIAM MAKEBA, MOBUTU SESE SEKO, SPIKE LEE, NORMAN MAILER, GEORGE PLIMPTON.

ACADEMY AWARDS 1997 OSCAR for BEST DOCUMENTARY.

## "Say it loud, I'm Black and proud."

Muhammad Ali was a rapper. His speech is poetic, melodic, full of images and rhymes. He insulted his opponents, humiliated them and predicted their downfall in the ring ("dissing" as this is known among rappers today). His charisma attracted people who went away inspired – that would be enough for any rap musician.

Documentary maker Leon Gast shows Ali as a rapper, he lets him do the talking and puts a drum beat under his words at the beginning of the movie; he also shows sport and the music of artists like James Brown and B. B. King as part of the Black Consciousness Movement. Gast documents the legendary fight between Ali and the then world champion George Foreman in Kinshasa, Zaire, today's Congo.

As a result of his refusal to fight in the Vietnam War, Ali received a five-year prison term in 1967 and lost the world champion title of the "World Boxing Association" (WBA). In 1970 his sentence was lifted and Ali set about trying to win back the title. The decisive fight between the 32-year-old and Foreman, who was six years younger, was a huge event, not just because Foreman had a unique record to defend (37 K. O. victories and no defeats since he turned professional) and Ali was considered an ageing sportsman in comparison. The circumstances were also spectacular: the boxing promoter Don King offered both Ali and Foreman five million dollars. He cast around for the total of ten million that he needed and finally received it from

Mobutu Sese Seko, military dictator of Zaire. The great fight, which quickly became known as "the rumble in the jungle", was supposed to take place on 25 September 1974 in the capital Kinshasa. The three days preceding the fight were reserved for a big music festival with James Brown, B. B. King, Miriam Makeba and The Spinners. The festival took place but the fight had to be postponed by six weeks as Foreman injured his eye during training and had to wait until it healed. In this six weeks, most of the documentary recordings that Gast filmed with Muhammad Ali were made.

Gast's Ali is a fascinating figure, and the director gives him plenty of opportunity to play up to the camera. What jumps out to the eye is Ali's tremendous musicality, which is made all the clearer by the way Gast sandwiches the Ali scenes between montages of the music festival. His speech, his movements and his fighting are filled with rhythm, and as Ali keeps repeating himself he's going to dance, dance, dance, so that Foreman won't even be able to find him in the ring. That was pure bluff, as the pictures of the fight prove. In interviews with the writer Norman Mailer and George Plimpton, who were there at the time, the situation before and during the fight is analysed over and over, and Ali's obvious fear of the giant Foreman is compared to his fighting strategy.

Gast finds wonderful rhythm for his images and the film is just as musical as its protagonist. Eyewitness statements, interviews from the time

> **"This film is more besides being a successful movie about Muhammad Ali – it is a film about Ali's skill at combining sport and politics and in so doing becoming the epitome of a people's hero."** *Frankfurter Allgemeine Zeitung*

2

3

**BOXING AT THE MOVIES**   Boxing has often been used as a film subject over the years, both in documentaries and feature films. At the beginning of cinema history, boxing was ideal for the static cameras used as it offered lots of movement in an enclosed space, and it is a subject that has remained popular with cinema audiences. It gives excellent scope for rags to riches stories about people who box their way to the top, like John Garfield as the Jewish boy in *Body and Soul* (1947) and Sylvester Stallone as the small fry hired fighter paid by gangsters in *Rocky* (1977). Rocky has remained the prototype of the boxer who loses in the ring but wins in life – he finds himself instead. Many biographies have made idols of the ring into film heroes, for example the American middle weight champion Jake La Motta played by Robert De Niro in *Raging Bull* 1980 and the IRA pugilist Danny Boy Flynn played by Daniel Day Lewis in *The Boxer* (1997). There is also another documentary film about Ali, a feature-length French documentary entitled *Muhammad Ali, The Greatest* (1964–1974).

1   Did he always believe he would win? In the ring, Ali seemed to have occasional doubts about himself.

2   Two icons of black culture: Muhammad Ali and soul star James Brown.

3   Ali won the Zairians' hearts with elaborate descriptions of his preparations, loud-mouthed threats against Foreman – and by kissing babies, just like a politician.

4   "Ali Bomaye!" – "Ali, kill him!" A thousand voices spur Muhammad Ali on.

5   Advance announcements that he would dance in the ring were a ruse – Ali let Foreman box himself into exhaustion.

archive material and music scenes are bound together in a harmonious whole – and the result is a gripping portrait of a genuine idol.

The film took decades to take on its finished form. Gast had already made several music movies (including *The Dead*, 1977, on The Grateful Dead) and originally was only supposed to document the music festival. When the fight was cancelled, he decided to stay on in Zaire and film. He used 100,000 metres of film, and needed nearly 15 years to get the money together to develop it all. The editing took another couple of years. His film-maker friend Taylor Hackford filmed the additional interviews with Mailer, Plimpton and the Black Cinema director Spike Lee, to complete Gast's material. Almost 22 years after the filming began, *When We Were Kings* was given its first showing at the Sundance film festival.    HJK

5

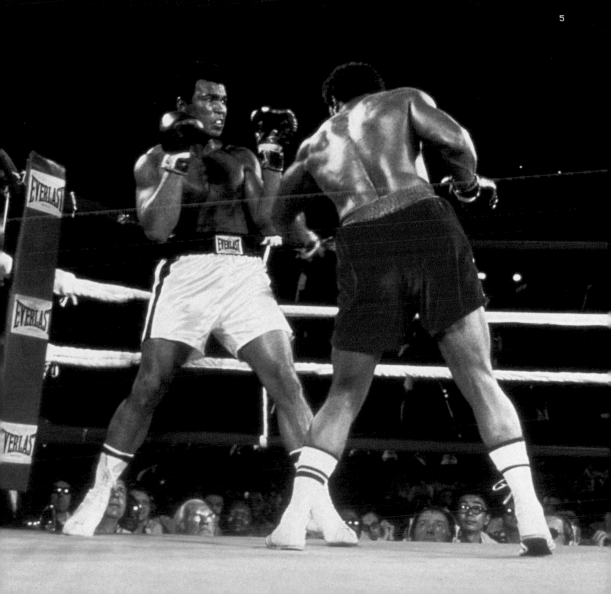

# FARGO

1996 - USA - 98 MIN. - CRIME FILM

DIRECTOR JOEL COEN (*1954)
SCREENPLAY JOEL COEN, ETHAN COEN  DIRECTOR OF PHOTOGRAPHY ROGER DEAKINS  MUSIC CARTER BURWELL  PRODUCTION ETHAN COEN
for WORKING TITLE FILMS.

STARRING FRANCES MCDORMAND (Marge Gunderson), STEVE BUSCEMI (Carl Showalter), PETER STORMARE (Gaear Grimsrud), WILLIAM H. MACY (Jerry Lundegaard), HARVE PRESNELL (Wade Gustafson), KRISTIN RUDRÜD (Jean Lundegaard), JOHN CARROLL LYNCH (Norm Gunderson), TONY DENMAN (Scotty Lundegaard), LARRY BRANDENBURG (Stan Grossman), BRUCE BOHNE (Lou).

IFF CANNES 1996 BEST DIRECTOR (Joel Coen).

ACADEMY AWARDS 1997 OSCARS for BEST ACTRESS (Frances McDormand) and BEST ORIGINAL SCREENPLAY (Joel Coen, Ethan Coen).

## "Jean and Scotty never have to worry about money."

Minnesota, 1987. Two tiny lights appear in the distance, vanish suddenly, and return somewhat larger. They are the headlights of a car in a hilly landscape. Winter, the movie seems to suggest, is the only possible season in Minnesota. The Coen brothers have a nasty story to tell. Car salesman Jerry Lundegaard (William H. Macy) is heavily in debt and has come up with a cunning plan to solve his problem: he's going to have his wife Jean (Kristin Rudrüd) kidnapped and demand a ransom from his father-in-law. Carl Showalter (Steve Buscemi) and Gaear Grimsrud (Peter Stormare) are to do the dirty work for him, and he'll pocket the one million dollars ransom money that he wants his rich father-in-law Wade Gustafson (Harve Presnell) to pay. He tells his accomplices that it's only a matter of 80,000 dollars, of which they'll get half for their pains. The two henchmen are total caricatures, Gaear in particular coming across as a complete fool. Their stupidity means that the abduction scene, where they snatch Jean from the shower, is a combination of the comic and the macabre, and cinema connoisseurs can hardly fail to recognise a parody of Hitchcock's *Psycho* (1960). Subsequently however the plan goes badly awry and the story becomes both brutal and grisly. When Carl and Gaear try to take Jean to the hiding place in one of Jerry's cars and are held up close to Brainerd by a police patrol, they kill a policeman and two tourists. Gaear seems devoid of any feeling, first killing Jean and then disposing of Carl.

Since it's one of her officers who has been murdered, the heavily pregnant police chief of Brainerd Marge Gunderson (Frances McDormand) decides to get personally involved in the hunt for the killers. Her husband Norm meanwhile paints nature pictures for a postage stamp picture competition. When Marge finds the remaining killer he is busy stuffing the corpse of his partner in crime through a woodchip shredder. He tries to run away and Marge shoots him dead. One of Norm's pictures is selected to go on a

postage stamp; the three cent stamp which is only needed for higher postage rates.

*Fargo* is a hard movie to categorise. It is grotesque and definitely absurd, but above all it is eerie. Cruelty and brutality become forces in their own right, and the story ends in an unexpected bloodbath because the protagonists have so little control over the situation. In *Fargo* everything moves a little more slowly. Not just because the world is deep in snow and each movement requires three times the usual effort, but also because the people of Minnesota, largely descendants of Scandinavian immigrants, are generally slower. Slow in the sense of speaking in a strange provincial drawl, and slow on the uptake. All of which has a role to play in this story about the real-

ity of crime and the ability of evil to assert itself. It is a movie which aims infallibly for the worst-case scenario with pessimistic Protestant determinism. The criminals are greedy, stupid and nervous, the police are powerless to do anything but trudge after them and pick up the pieces, counting the corpses and finally making a useless arrest criminals.

*Fargo* is the Coen brothers' coolest, most reserved movie to date, partly because it is so unspectacular optically. The colours are simple, almost monochrome, the music is practically minimalist and the dialogues are uncommunicative poetry intensified by the grinding singsong of the local dialect. The Coen brothers were born in Minnesota and *Fargo* is a grotesque and gruesome homage to their homeland.                                    OM

---

**WILLIAM H. MACY**  Character and ensemble actor par excellence and one of the most interesting faces of the 90s, Macy first became famous as part of David Mamet's team of actors. He is particularly convincing when he plays a small town characters whose livelihood is in danger. Above all, it was his brilliant interpretation of the desperate car salesman who becomes a criminal in *Fargo* that imprinted his face on audiences' memories. His convincing performance as the clinically precise family man who discovers the Nazi in himself (*Pleasantville*, 1998), is equally as striking as his role in *Magnolia* (1999) as a former quiz show child prodigy who feels unloved. Macy's brilliance shows above all in his capacity to give the most ridiculous figures their own dignity.

---

1  Dim petty criminals with a tendency to overreact: Steve Buscemi as Carl Showalter and Peter Stormare as Gaear Grimsrud.

2  Trudging along single-mindedly in pursuit of the criminals. Frances McDormand in the role of a lifetime as pregnant polices Officer Marge Gunderson.

3  A man with an enormous problem: William H. Macy as car salesman Jerry Lundegaard.

4

"***Fargo*** is undoubtedly our most traditional film. It's also the first time that we've used a news story."

*Ethan Coen in: Cahiers du cinéma*

4  After a meal like that the day can only turn out well: one of the many Minnesota-cum-Scandinavian idiosyncrasies that turn the film into a parody of a sentimental regional film.

5  A sticky end: stupidity and greed cause events to escalate.

5

# FROM DUSK TILL DAWN

1996 - USA - 108 MIN. - HORROR FILM, COMEDY

DIRECTOR ROBERT RODRIGUEZ (*1968)
SCREENPLAY QUENTIN TARANTINO, based on an idea by ROBERT KURTZMAN DIRECTOR OF PHOTOGRAPHY GUILLERMO NAVARRO
MUSIC GRAEME REVELL PRODUCTION GIANNI NUNNARI, MEIR TEPER for A BAND APART, MIRAMAX, LOS HOOLIGANS
PRODUCTIONS.

STARRING HARVEY KEITEL (Jacob Fuller), GEORGE CLOONEY (Seth Gecko), QUENTIN TARANTINO (Richard Gecko), JULIETTE
LEWIS (Kate Fuller), ERNEST LIU (Scott Fuller), SALMA HAYEK (Santanico Pandemonium), CHEECH MARIN (Border
Guard/ Chet Pussy/Carlos), DANNY TREJO (Razor Charlie), TOM SAVINI (Sex Machine), FRED WILLIAMSON (Frost).

## "All right, vampire killers – let's kill some fucking vampires!"

Mexico is so near and yet so far… The Gecko brothers are on the run, and Mexico is their only hope. The border is swarming with Texan policemen who close off every possible route into the promised land, but cool gangsters like the Geckos (George Clooney and Quentin Tarantino) shoot first and ask questions later: they currently have 16 dead men, a bank robbery and a bombed-out store on their conscience. Jacob (Harvey Keitel), a former priest, happens to cross their path, on holiday with his kids in a camper van. With his unwilling help the brothers smuggle themselves over the border by hiding inside the bodywork of the camper. The Geckos promise that they will set their hostages free as soon as they find Carlos, their Mexican contact man. They drink to their freedom with the family in an exotic, eccentric trucker bar called "Titty Twister". Too late, they realise that all five of them have landed in the pit of hell: the barman and the snake dancers suddenly turn into bloodthirsty vampires before their very eyes.

From Dusk Till Dawn is a double feature, a double whammy combining two completely different movies in one show. It begins like a gangster film and then completely out of the blue is transformed into a comic-like splatter film where blood hits the screen in bucketfuls and all kinds of limbs fly through the air. Whilst director Robert Rodriguez (Desperado, 1995) is allowed to spread gore to his heart's content in the fight scene in the "Titty Twister" bar, the first half of the movie is clearly the work of Quentin Tarantino. Screenwriter and main actor, Mr "Pulp Fiction" himself clearly had a strong influence on the look and the tone of the movie, from the gangsters' laid-back remarks ("Fight now, cry later") to insane dialogue like "Where are we going?" – "Mexico." – "What's in Mexico?" – "Mexicans."

Both Rodriguez and Tarantino love quotations and constantly refer to their cinematic models, so the characters eat "Kahuna Burger" and smoke the "Red Apple" cigarettes that we already know from Pulp Fiction (1994). "Precinct 13", written on a T-shirt, refers to John Carpenter's film Assault on Precinct 13 (1976), from which the directors also steal one dialogue word for word. They play this self-reflexive game so comprehensively that From Dusk Till Dawn is like a patchwork movie cobbled together from bits of other films.

It takes an especially bizarre twist when the figures begin to question their own roles. In a short break in the action, everyone who hasn't been

OPEN DUSK TILL DAWN

5

6

1   Wherever the Gecko brothers show up, there's sure to be blood. To prepare themselves for their roles as brothers, George Clooney and Quentin Tarantino spent whole nights wandering the clubs of Los Angeles.

2   The "Titty Twister", the wildest dive this side of the Rio Grande. What the Gecko brothers do not know is that the truckers' and bikers' bar is located right on top of an enormous vampires' grave.

3   Bar customer Sex Machine shows what's hiding in his trousers. Tom Savini is an expert in blood-thirsty films: he has written books on the art of make-up in horror movies, and even produced a few such films himself, as well as taking part now and then as an actor. He can be found, for instance, in *Martin* (1977) by George A. Romero.

**QUENTIN TARANTINO**   Tarantino was only just 31 years old when he was awarded the most important trophies in the movie business. He won the Golden Palm at Cannes for *Pulp Fiction* (1994) and an Oscar for the screenplay. The movie where killers shoot people as casually as they eat hamburgers caused a veritable outbreak of "Tarantinomania", and several directors tried to copy that special Tarantino touch. There was a sudden rash of gangsters dropping cool wisecracks against a backdrop of as much bloodshed as possible and a shameless parade of quotations from other films. Tarantino's enormous knowledge of films didn't come from any university, but from his job in a video shop in Los Angeles. To pass the time, he wrote film scripts. After the unexpected success of his first movie *Reservoir Dogs* (1991), a gangster story about a bungled bank robbery, the scripts he had in his bottom drawer suddenly became very desirable: Oliver Stone bought the rights to *Natural Born Killers* (1994) and Tony Scott filmed *True Romance* (1993). After *Pulp Fiction* Tarantino filmed an episode for the hotel film *Four Rooms* (1995) and made the comic-like horror comedy *From Dusk Till Dawn* (1996) together with Robert Rodriguez. Tarantino's last movie in the 90s was *Jackie Brown* (1997). This was a departure from the self-indulgent brutality of his early works and proved that he can also produce exciting narrative cinema without playing violent games.

chomped gets together to consider how to defend themselves against the monstrous vampires. Someone suggests crossing two sticks, as that was how Peter Cushing always defeated Dracula alias Christopher Lee. Jacob the ex-priest doesn't think much of this idea: "Has anybody here read a real book about vampires, or are we just remembering what some movie said?" What makes this scene so comical is that the film figures find themselves in a grotesque nightmare situation and yet they consider their options and come up with rational arguments. Jacob talks with contempt about "some movie" – and is himself part of one.

Unfortunately most critics didn't think this far, however. They weren't happy with *From Dusk Till Dawn* at all, and it was almost universally written off as too bloody and too self-satisfied. They only thing about the movie was George Clooney. The role of the gangster Seth, who has to deal not only with the vampires but also with his sex-obsessed younger brother Richard (Quentin Tarantino) liberated Clooney from the operating theatre of the TV series *Emergency Room* and smoothed his path to stardom on the silver screen.

NM

7

4   Santanico Pandemonium (Salma Hayek) bewitch-
    es the Titty Twister clientele with her erotic snake
    dance. To the horror of the Gecko brothers, she
    too turns into a bloodthirsty monster when the
    first drops of blood appear.

5   The vampires in the "Titty Twister" have little in
    common with Dracula-style bloodsuckers. Roberto
    Rodriguez based them on models from the mytho-
    logical culture of the Aztecs.

"Those who think that *From Dusk Till Dawn* is a fake horror movie, be
warned. Rodriguez gives the viewer *the real thing*: the high art of
tastelessness, pure unadulterated Punch and Judy." *epd Film*

6   George Clooney's screen career began with the
    role of Seth Gecko. Juliette Lewis plays Kate,
    daughter of Jacob the priest, who is taken
    hostage by the Geckos along with her brother and
    father.

7   The monsters in the "Titty Twister" come straight
    from the underworld. Tarantino originally wrote
    the screenplay for a special effects company, who
    give ample demonstration of their talents in the
    second half of the movie.

8   Seth pleads with the priest Jacob Fuller (Harvey
    Keitel) to find his faith again, since the preacher
    had turned his back on God after the agonising
    death of his wife. Now he is the final weapon in
    the battle against evil.

# TRAINSPOTTING

1996 - GREAT BRITAIN - 93 MIN. - DRAMA

DIRECTOR DANNY BOYLE (*1956)
SCREENPLAY JOHN HODGE, based on the novel of the same name by IRVINE WELSH  DIRECTOR OF PHOTOGRAPHY BRIAN TUFANO
MUSIC VARIOUS, including IGGY POP, LOU REED, LEFTFIELD, NEW ORDER, BRIAN ENO, BLUR, UNDERWORLD
PRODUCTION ANDREW MACDONALD for FIGMENT FILM.

STARRING EWAN MCGREGOR (Renton), EWEN BREMNER (Spud), JONNY LEE MILLER (Sick Boy), ROBERT CARLYLE (Begbie), PETER MULLAN (Swanney), KELLY MACDONALD (Diane), SUSAN VIDLER (Alison), KEVIN MCKIDD (Tommy), PAULINE LYNCH (Lizzy), IRVINE WELSH (Mikey).

## "And the reasons? There are no reasons, who needs reasons when you've got heroin."

Two youths run through the streets, the police hot on their heels. Off-screen, the voice of the protagonist debates the consequences of saying yes to "normal" life and concludes that heroin is a way of escaping from convention and banality. Danny Boyle's *Trainspotting* is one of the fastest-moving films of the 90s. To the sound of Iggy Pop's "Lust for Life", we see a rapid overview of the highlights of the lives of a group of youngsters. Mark Renton (Ewan McGregor), "Sick Boy" Simon (Jonny Lee Miller), "Spud" Daniel (Ewen Bremner) and Alison (Susan Vidler) – together with Dawn, the baby she has from one of the other three – all live together in a filthy, dilapidated apartment in a shabby neighbourhood of Edinburgh. The main thing they have in common is their drug addiction. The course of their daily lives revolves solely around the quickest possible way of getting a fix of drugs, preferably without ever having to take on gainful employment.

From time to time almost all of them try to kick the habit and begin a normal life. Their other interests are not so different from those of other young people: football, the pub, sex. "Sick Boy" is a snobby James Bond fan who holds forth about Ursula Andress and considers her to be the definitive Bond girl. Robert Carlyle gives an astonishing performance as the universally feared psychopath Begbie and Ewan McGregor appears in one of his best roles to date.

The movie may be gruesome, but above all, it is funny. At its best, *Trainspotting* is reminiscent of the British films of Swinging London, where social reality was dosed with a generous dollop of surrealism. Renton, for example, dives into the lavatory in search of his drugs and finds them at the bottom of the sea. Instead of moralising about the dangers of drug abuse we are shown pictures of the joys of drug taking – and the price that has to be paid.

The friends' situation escalates when Dawn's baby dies as a result of drug-induced neglect. Renton and Spud are caught shoplifting and Spud goes to prison. Renton is allowed out on parole, takes one of his many quar-

# "Mainly due to the ambivalence in McGregor's face, you get the feeling that Mark wouldn't say no to a bit of feeling. But he's numb – he can't say yes and he can't say no." *Sight and Sound*

anteed "last ever" shots and overdoses. At the hospital they just manage to save him, but his parents have had enough and they lock him up in his bedroom and force him to go cold turkey. Once he is clean he moves down to London and reinvents himself as an estate agent. But his past catches up with him when "Sick Boy" and Begbie turn up. To get away from his friends for good, Renton eventually has to betray them.

Irvine Welsh's novel *Trainspotting* came out in 1992 and quickly became a runaway cult success. The English edition quoted the self-confident comment "Deserves to sell more copies than the Bible; Rebel Inc.".

The novel was crying out to be made into a movie – and that cry was heard by a team with a sure instinct for works with cult status: Danny Boyle (director), John Hodge (screenplay), Andrew Macdonald (production) and Brian Tufano (director of photography), who had had a global success with their black comedy *Shallow Grave* (1994) and were able to go one better with *Trainspotting*. The movie became the cinema event of 1996, the first Britpop film with a promotion campaign using posters designed to look like concert publicity.

OM

1 An antihero for the 1990s: The only thing Renton (Ewan McGregor) cares about is where his next fix is coming from.

2 The working classes run amok: Begbie (Robert Carlyle) is the psychopath of the group. He embodies everything that goes wrong in all the pubs on the island every Friday and Saturday night.

3 Renton is swallowed up by the primeval sludge of his fears and dreams. This is one of the most frequently referred to scenes in the film, and became a commonplace among cinema images of the 1990s.

2

3

"(Sick Boy is) the chief trainspotter, with his encyclopedic riffs on the career and charisma of Sean Connery. Connery being Scotland's only super-star, what more apt than a Glasgow junkie high on movie junk to get off on earnest comparisons between Dr No and Thunderball. This is siege-warfare iconolatry." *Film Comment*

4

"The book is exciting, funny and dangerous in a way that a severe heroin addict's life isn't. The book has the vibrancy which connects with why people take drugs. It blazes away with this sense of experiment and risk." *Danny Boyle in: Sight and Sound*

**DANNY BOYLE**  Danny Boyle is head and director of a typical 1990s movie team. Alongside the director the team includes scriptwriter John Hodge and producer Andrew Macdonald. Their debut *Shallow Grave* (1994) was an immediate success. A thriller, it tells the story of the increasing paranoia that takes root in a group of young people who almost accidentally make money through an illegal drug deal. *Trainspotting* (1996) was without doubt their greatest success to date. *A Life Less Ordinary* (1998) was another elegant black comedy, but it didn't quite match their previous successes. Their movie of the best seller *The Beach* (2000) starring Leonardo DiCaprio, was also something of a disappointment.

**4** Renton at work: rarely has drug use been so casually portrayed as by Danny Boyle, who briefly became a superstar of European cinema thanks to this film.

**5** Air of defiance: Renton is not only sickened by consumer society, but also by the status of his native country as a supposed colony of England.

**6** Time for a change: Renton and his mates (Jonny Lee Miller, Kevin McKidd) take a trip to the country.

5

6

# MARS ATTACKS!

1996 - USA - 106 MIN. - SCIENCE FICTION, COMEDY

DIRECTOR TIM BURTON (*1958)

SCREENPLAY JONATHAN GEMS based on the TOPPS COMIC COLLECTOR'S CARDS "MARS ATTACKS!" DIRECTOR OF PHOTOGRAPHY PETER SUSCHITZKY MUSIC DANNY ELFMAN PRODUCTION TIM BURTON, LARRY FRANCO for WARNER BROS.

STARRING JACK NICHOLSON (President James Dale/Art Land), GLENN CLOSE (Marsha Dale), ANNETTE BENING (Barbara Land), PIERCE BROSNAN (Donald Kessler), DANNY DEVITO (Gambler), MARTIN SHORT (Jerry Ross), NATALIE PORTMAN (Taffy), ROD STEIGER (General Decker), SARAH JESSICA PARKER (Nathalie West), MICHAEL J. FOX (Jason Stone), LUKAS HAAS (Richie Norris), SYLVIA SIDNEY (Grandmother).

## "Nice Planet. We'll take it!"

A white dove of peace flies up into the air and is accidentally roasted by a stray shot from a laser gun. The Martians have landed! Unfortunately, things don't quite go the way earthlings had imagined. An enormous military contingent has travelled to the desert of Nevada, accompanied by hordes of media people, curious spectators, New Age disciples and alien fans. It's a warm welcome from the blue planet to the little green men, who must have come peace as they come from more highly-developed culture. But things don't quite work out as planned. The huge-brained creatures babble "dagg dagg dagg", open fire, and shoot wildly all around them. They take the reporter Nathalie (Sarah Jessica Parker) on board their space ship and subject her to useless medical experiments. They then leave a path of destruction in their wake as they rampage through the world – Big Ben is reduced to rubble, the faces of the presidents on Mount Rushmore are shot off and the sculptures on the Easter Islands tipped over.

For generations it was automatically assumed that beings from outer space would be belligerent warriors. At some point however, doubtless inspired by the television series *Star Trek – The Next Generation* and its message of tolerance, we moved away from such one-sided images, and started believing that aliens would have peaceful intentions. Director Tim Burton laughs openly in the face of such intergalactic political correctness. His aliens were moved to undertake the long journey from Mars by their most base instincts. For them the Earth is just one big galactic fairground shooting range, they fire at everything that moves and have a great time in the process. At the same time, they cunningly stress their peaceful intentions.

The people they meet are however not necessarily loveable and well meaning either. The powerless President James Dale (Jack Nicholson) is desperate for some kind of success in foreign affairs and wants to take up diplomatic relations with the Martians – even after their first attacks. Dodgy property speculator Art Land (Nicholson again) scents new – green! – clients for his casinos. A white trash family who live in a trailerpark only have one thought when the Martian invaders arrive: "They're not getting the TV!" Journalists want a sensation to sell, and the mad scientist Kessler (Pierce

1   "Lisa Marie as a seven-foot-tall, blankly gum-
    chewing bubble-coiffed, hip-swivelling, torpedo-
    breasted, alien-designed sex doll."
    *Sight and Sound*

2   With true British style and without the faintest
    idea of what he's talking about, Dr Kessler (Pierce
    Brosnan) explains all there is to know about the
    Martians.

3   "I'm not allowing that thing in my house." – The
    world is coming to an end, and the First Lady
    (Glenn Close, second from right) is worried about
    the carpet.

# "The Martians gabble like geese, and the President is a lame duck, yet they still fail to find a common language."

*Frankfurter Allgemeine Zeitung*

# "*Mars Attacks!* in particular arose from the certainty that it is itself an alien."

*Tim Burton in: Süddeutsche Zeitung*

**4** In keeping with the trash aesthetic of *Mars Attacks!* the Martians weapons look like toys. They're deadly all the same.

Brosnan) wants to show off his knowledge and skill although he hasn't a clue about the Martians or their motives. Ross (Martin Short), the President's spokesman is overcome by his animal instincts, and he allows a big-bosomed beauty into the White House (Lisa Marie, Vampira from *Ed Wood*) out of sheer lust, and thus opens the door for the invaders to the centre of American power.

Burton only permits a tiny number of earthlings to come out of it with any credit: soul legend Tom Jones plays himself, a cool and stylish singer who directly after the end of the Martian invasion is allowed to sing "It's Not

Unusual". Jim Brown plays the black boxer Byron Williams, who works in Las Vegas in a pharaoh costume. And last but not least, there is the deaf grandmother (Sylvia Sidney), who saves the world with appalling folk music, the yodel blues by Slim Whitman.

Once again, Burton gives us a loving adaptation of popular culture: *Mars Attacks!* is based on collector's cards from the chewing gum brand Topps. The original cards numbered 55 and went on the market in 1962 although they were withdrawn soon afterwards. Card titles such as "Crushed to Death" or "Destroying a Dog" make it easy to understand why.      HJK

5

> ## "Burton tells of a world that is no longer sure of itself and that therefore looks for meaning in the most stupid of things. However, 'daggdagg dag' simply means 'daggdagg dag'."
> *Süddeutsche Zeitung*

5  "Although *Mars Attacks!* often seems to parody *Independence Day*, it was actually longer in the production pipeline." *Sight and Sound*

6  The Martians not only use X-ray weapons, they can also see right through people's selfishness and delusions of grandeur (Danny DeVito).

6

7

**TIM BURTON: FILMMAKER AND FILM CONNOISSEUR**

The head of the journalist Nathalie, which has been transplanted onto the body of her own Chihuahua, and the free floating head of the scientist Kessler declare their undying love for each other – a moment which is pure Tim Burton. His films – from *Beetlejuice* (1988) to *Batman* (1989), from *Edward Scissorhands* (1990) and *Ed Wood* (1994) to *Sleepy Hollow* (1999) – are fairytales, fantasy stories which show his love of fantastic genres (science fiction, classic horror movies) and of the B-Movies of the 50s. This can be seen most clearly in his film biography of the trash filmmaker *Ed Wood*. Tim Burton worked for a short time as a cartoonist for Disney, and among his role models he includes the cartoonist Ray Harryhausen, who awakes fencing skeletons and mythological creatures to life in single image animation. This is known as Stop-Motion technique and was actually what Burton wanted to use for the little green men in *Mars Attacks!* However, the process was too lengthy and expensive and Burton decided on computer animation instead.

7  Highly advanced, particularly in the military
   domain: no terrestrial tank can withstand the
   Martians' "plastic weapons".

8  Voyeurs, hooligans, murderers – it was the
   Martians' baser instincts that brought them to
   Earth.

# ROMEO & JULIET

1996 - USA - 120 MIN. - LOVE FILM, LITERATURE ADAPTATION

DIRECTOR BAZ LUHRMANN (*1962)
SCREENPLAY CRAIG PEARCE, BAZ LUHRMANN, based on the drama of the same name by WILLIAM SHAKESPEARE
DIRECTOR OF PHOTOGRAPHY DONALD M. MACALPINE MUSIC NELLEE COOPER PRODUCTION GABRIELLA MARTINELLI, BAZ LUHRMANN
for MAZMARK PRODUCTIONS, 20TH CENTURY FOX.

STARRING LEONARDO DICAPRIO (Romeo), CLAIRE DANES (Julia), BRIAN DENNEHY (Ted Montague), JOHN LEGUIZAMO
(Tybalt), PETE POSTLETHWAITE (Father Laurence), PAUL SORVINO (Fulgencio Capulet), HAROLD PERRINEAU (Mercutio),
M. EMMET WALSH (Apothecary), CARLOS MARTÍN MANZO (Petruchio), CHRISTINA PICKLES (Caroline Montague).

IFF BERLIN 1997 SILVER BEAR for BEST ACTOR (Leonardo DiCaprio).

## "Did my heart love 'till now?
## For swear at sight, I never saw true beauty 'till this night."

"Two households, both alike in dignity (in fair Verona, where we lay our scene) from ancient grudge break to new mutiny, where civil blood makes civil hands unclean." The prologue of Shakespeare's *Romeo and Juliet* resounds from the television. Boys from the two rival gangs meet at a petrol station. One insult leads to another, guns are drawn and the petrol station goes up in smoke. The war between the Montague and Capulet families makes the whole city hold its breath and keeps the police on their toes. Romeo (Leonardo DiCaprio), old Montague's only son moons around in his unrequited love for Rosalinde and keeps out of the fighting. He lets his friend Mercutio (Harold Perrineau) persuade him to go to a fancy-dress party at the Capulet's where his beloved is also expected to appear. Instead however Romeo finds his true love: Juliet (Claire Danes), the daughter of his archenemy Capulet.

The works of William Shakespeare (1564–1616) have inspired movie adaptations since the beginning of cinema history, but it may well be the case that no other director has set an adaptation of a Shakespeare play so radically in his own times as the Australian Baz Luhrmann (*Strictly Ballroom*, 1991) did with *Romeo and Juliet*. The prologue is delivered by the most important news medium of the late 20th century: the television. "Fair Verona" is Verona Beach (although most of the film was made in Mexico City), a multicultural mega-city with a sunny beach, smog, skyscrapers, police helicopters and an enormous Jesus statue like the one in Rio de Janeiro. The offices of the Capulets' businesses are on one side of a wide street, those of the Montagues on the other. The rival families have been transformed into gangster dynasties. The Capulets are Hispanic Americans and the Montagues white Americans (as in *West Side Story*, another *Romeo and Juliet* adaptation). The Capulets wear black, the Montagues Hawaii shirts; one family drives cars with CAP numberplates, the other with MON. Their weapons are 9mm pistols made by the firm "Sword" (and can still therefore be referred to as "sword" in the script). The gangsters are like action movie heroes, their

1

2

rituals reminiscent of black gangster films like *New Jack City* (1990) or *Menace II Society* (1993). The fancy-dress ball at the Capulets' is a loud, trashy party featuring an appearance by a drag queen.

It's not just lovingly devised, creative details like those which transpose the play into the present (and that includes today's self-referential cinema and its world of quotations) but the production as a whole. Luhrmann permits himself a playfulness that goes far beyond the formal idiom of narrative cinema and does more than nod in the direction of the aesthetic of the video clip, with techniques like quick takes, high speed panning shots, slow motion and fast forward, extreme camera perspectives (shots from great heights,

shots through an aquarium or a wash basin), and a wide-ranging use of music and uneven acting styles (from serious to hammy overacting). The movie is a self-confident piece of pop culture and wallows in the superficial thrill of images that have become kitsch symbols in their own right: white doves, burning hearts, a priest with a tattoo of the Cross, and Juliet going to the fancy-dress party as an angel with Romeo as her knight. Amazingly, all of this combines to make a homogenous, seductively beautiful movie that miraculously maintains the magical rhythm of Shakespeare's language and verse.

HJK

3

4

"His works had to compete with bear fights and prostitutes. He was an entertainer, mixing comedy, song, violence and tragedy. Just like MTV today." *Baz Luhrmann in: Abendzeitung*

Three other Shakespeare films were made in 1997 as well as *Romeo & Juliet*, including Kenneth Branagh's 4-hour version of *Hamlet*. Cinema history is full of Shakespeare adaptations, and a scene from *King John* was seen on the silver screen as early as 1899. Branagh has made a considerable contribution to the number of adaptations. His *Henry V* started off a new Shakespeare boom in 1989 and in *Love's Labours Lost* (1999) he combined Shakespeare with more modern classics when he used the melodies of George Gershwin, Cole Porter and others. Alongside direct adaptations there are also films with looser links to the works of the bard, for example *West Side Story* (1960, based on *Romeo and Juliet*) and the science fiction classic *Forbidden Planet* (1956), which is a film version of *The Tempest*.

# "The language of Shakespeare, the acting of Quentin Tarantino." *Zoom*

5

# "All-consuming youth culture opens its greedy mouth and with great relish polishes off the classics hook, line and sinker." *Süddeutsche Zeitung*

1  Star-crossed lovers: a whole world separates Romeo (Leonardo DiCaprio) …

2  … and Juliet (Claire Danes) – but the lovers are unaware of this.

3  Grief at the death of his beloved – Baz Luhrmann sticks close to the Shakespeare original.

4  Objects "speak" in this film: Juliet floats into Romeo's life as if on wings; the fact that he is the "great enemy's only son" weighs him down like armour.

5  The priest is no longer wearing the Crucifix around his neck: Father Laurence (Pete Postlethwaite).

6  The quarrel between the Montagues and the Capulets – gangster warfare.

# THE ENGLISH PATIENT

1996 - USA - 162 MIN. - MELODRAMA, LITERATURE ADAPTATION

DIRECTOR ANTHONY MINGHELLA (*1954)
SCREENPLAY ANTHONY MINGHELLA, based on the novel of the same name by MICHAEL ONDAATJE DIRECTOR OF PHOTOGRAPHY JOHN SEALE MUSIC GABRIEL YARED PRODUCTION SAUL ZAENTZ, HARVEY WEINSTEIN, SCOTT GREENSTEIN, BOB WEINSTEIN for SAUL ZAENTZ PRODUCTIONS, MIRAMAX.

STARRING RALPH FIENNES (Graf Laszlo Almásy), KRISTIN SCOTT THOMAS (Katharine Clifton), JULIETTE BINOCHE (Hana), WILLEM DAFOE (Caravaggio), NAVEEN ANDREWS (Kip), COLIN FIRTH (Geoffrey Clifton), JULIAN WADHAM (Madox), JÜRGEN PROCHNOW (Major Müller), KEVIN WHATELY (Hardy), CLIVE MERRISON (Fenalon Barnes).

ACADEMY AWARDS 1997 OSCARS for BEST PICTURE, BEST DIRECTOR (Anthony Minghella), BEST SUPPORTING ACTRESS (Juliette Binoche), BEST CINEMATOGRAPHY (John Seale), BEST ART DIRECTION-SET DECORATION (Stuart Craig, Stepheny McMillan), BEST FILM EDITING (Walter Murch), BEST MUSIC, category DRAMA (Gabriel Yared), BEST SOUND (Chris Newman, Ivan Sharrock) and BEST COSTUMES (Ann Roth).

IFF BERLIN 1997 SILVER BEAR for BEST ACTRESS (Juliette Binoche).

## "The heart is an organ of fire."

The camera glides over an undulating yellow-brown surface. It looks like a desert, but in fact it's paper, and a brush starts to paint stylised human forms that swim about. We cut to a different yellow-brown surface that undulates more strongly – this time it is the desert. An aeroplane flies by, its shadows racing over the hillocks and valleys of the desert plain. Shots ring out, and we see that the biplane is being fired at from the ground. Dark flecks of flak dot the sky, getting ever closer, until suddenly they hit the plane. The aeroplane dives and bursts into flames.

*The English Patient* tells the story of the pilot and his great love – in an unhurried, old-fashioned way. The film unfolds gradually, slowly accumulating additional information and perspectives, and only at the end is the entire story revealed. The pilot is dubbed the "English patient" when he is delivered to an Allied hospital in Italy shortly before the end of the Second World War – he was in an English plane that was shot down by the Germans. He is deformed by hideous burns, and the flames have destroyed his face, his skin and his lungs. He doesn't have long to live, has lost his memory, and does not even seem to know his name or nationality. The only clue is the book he carries with him – Herodotus' *History*, a Greek tale from the 5th century BC with maps, photos and letters tucked in between the pages. He is too badly

injured to be transported any further and so Franco-Canadian nurse Hana (Juliette Binoche) stays behind with him in a half-ruined monastery in Tuscany. Here he spends his remaining days in peace, and gradually he recovers the memory of his great love.

The story begins in 1937. The "English patient" is Count Laszlo Almásy (Ralph Fiennes), a Hungarian aristocrat who has devoted himself to the study of the desert and joined a group of English cartographers in the Sahara. One day an English couple come to join them: Geoffrey and Katharine Clifton (Colin Firth, Kristin Scott Thomas). He is an enthusiastic pilot and she is a painter. To begin with, Katharine is dismissive and almost hostile towards the silent, introverted Laszlo. But after their car breaks down and they are forced to sit out a sandstorm together in the desert, their relationship changes. While exploring the interior of the Sahara, the group discovers a cave filled with unusual wall paintings of people swimming. The explorers are dispersed when war breaks out, but they meet again in Cairo. Love blossoms out of the friendship between Laszlo and Katharine, and they begin a passionate affair. Eventually, her husband realises, and reacts with an act of jealous rage: he flies into the desert with Katharine to find Laszlo and tries to kill all three of them in a plane crash.

As these memories and visions return to the "English patient", life continues around him. Hana treats him lovingly, not least because she believes that she is cursed. Everyone close to her – her lover, her friend, even a fellow nurse – have all died. She has no reason not to be fond of her patient as he is going to die anyway. She wants to make his last days bearable and give him an easy death. Their solitude is short-lived however, and they are soon joined in the ruined monastery by the devious Caravaggio (Willem Dafoe), a Canadian trader of Italian descent. He was also in North Africa when the war broke out, and in contrast to Hana, he asks critical questions when the English patient's memory begins to return. Caravaggio was tortured by the Germans in the Libyan town of Tobruk, where they cut off his thumbs. Two bomb disposal experts from the British Army also take up quarters in the monastery, the Sikh Kip (Naveen Andrews) and his colleague Hardy (Kevin Whately). A fragile love affair develops between Kip and Hana, although Hana will not let herself become too involved because she still believes that she is cursed. In the meantime Laszlo lives out his love for Katharine in his memories, and images return to him with ever greater power.

English director Anthony Minghella (*Mr. Wonderful*, 1993) films Michael Ondaatje's novel as a melodramatic epic, with grandiose images of desert adventure. The movie unfolds on two narrative planes that dove-tail elegantly and constantly mirror each other. The outbreak of war dovetails with its end, the burning yellow-brown of the desert is played off against the cool green of Tuscany, the great love between Katharine and Laszlo is set off against the fragile relationship between Hana and Kip, Katharine lies fatally wounded in a cave in the desert, and Laszlo faces death in the ruined monastery. The two narrative planes are not only separated by the war, but also seem to take place in entirely different eras. The cartographic exploration of the desert by the English is part of colonial history. Katharine is an aristocratic lady of the British Empire whereas practical, energetic Hana is a woman of the 20th century.

Ondaatje's 1992 novel, winner of the English Booker Prize, also works with flashbacks and dovetailing and spans the length of the Second World War. Minghella maintains the chronological framework but thins out the cast and the plot strands of what is an extensive novel. In the novel for instance

**THE RETURN OF THE MELODRAMA**

Love in a time of war. *The English Patient* tells the story of strong emotions in a tone of complete seriousness devoid of irony. This makes it part of the long cinema tradition of melodrama that began in the silent era. Its artistic highpoint came in the 50s with the movies of Douglas Sirk, and it reached a commercial peak with the tearjerker *Love Story* in 1969. Melodramas went out of fashion in the 80s and 90s, when emotions could only be shown mixed with irony, when they weren't being ridiculed altogether. Two films at the end of the 90s brought melodrama back into cinemas: *Titanic* (1997) and *The English Patient*. The latter was perhaps the most typical of the genre, as *Titanic* is a disaster movie as well as a love story and an adaptation of a historical event. *The English Patient* on the other hand is simply the simple story of a great love that can only be fulfilled in death.

"Of course David Lean's *Lawrence of Arabia* comes to mind. But the comprehensive way in which Minghella tells the story, leaving nothing in his film open to doubt, is something David Lean did not permit himself." *Frankfurter Allgemeine Zeitung*

1  Count Laszlo Almásy – he finds his great love in the desert.

2  "It is principally the actors, Ralph Fiennes as the dying, ironically broken Almásy…

3  … and Kristin Scott Thomas, who up until now had only appeared as a wallflower, who lift this film above the average." *Zoom*

the love story between Hana and Kip plays a much more important role. The movie never denies its literary origins, however, and literature and books feature throughout, and whatever happens, Laszlo also manages to save his copy of Herodotus – Hana reads it to him, and it eventually outlives him. Hana uses books to stop the gaps in the stairs, and the Sahara itself appears in the first scene as paper, on which the love story is written.

Production of the film was an adventure story in itself. Minghella had long cherished the idea of adapting the book for the screen. After eleven producers had refused it, *The English Patient* was eventually accepted by independent producer Saul Zaentz, winner of a total of 13 Oscars and maker of seven great films over the last twenty years, including *One Flew Over the Cuckoo's Nest* (1975) and *Amadeus* (1984). All seemed well at first but a funding crisis developed when 20th Century Fox pulled out of the project. Fox's casting preferences hadn't been taken into consideration: it wanted Hollywood stars whereas Zaentz and Minghella insisted on Ralph Fiennes, Kristin Scott Thomas and Juliette Binoche. Salvation finally arrived in the shape of Harvey Weinstein, head of Miramax. He contributed 26 of the movie's total budget of 32 million dollars and filming could go ahead. His courage was rewarded with nine Oscars.

HJK

# THE PEOPLE VS. LARRY FLYNT

996 - USA - 130 MIN. - DRAMA

DIRECTOR MILOS FORMAN (*1932)
SCREENPLAY SCOTT ALEXANDER, LARRY KARASZEWSKI DIRECTOR OF PHOTOGRAPHY PHILIPPE ROUSSELOT MUSIC THOMAS NEWMAN
PRODUCTION OLIVER STONE, JANET YANG, MICHAEL HAUSMAN for IXTLAN PRODUCTIONS, PHOENIX PICTURES.
STARRING WOODY HARRELSON (Larry Flynt), COURTNEY LOVE (Althea Leasure), EDWARD NORTON (Alan Isaacman), JAMES CROMWELL (Charles Keating), CRISPIN GLOVER (Arlo), JAMES CARVILLE (Simon Leis), BRETT HARRELSON (Jimmy Flynt), DONNA HANOVER (Ruth Carter-Stapleton), VINCENT SCHIAVELLI (Chester), LARRY FLYNT (Judge).
IFF BERLIN 1997 GOLDEN BEAR.

## "What is more obscene: Sex or War?"

Even as a child, Larry Flynt had a good nose for business. He distilled spirits with his brother and sold them to the local farmers. And when their father drank it all himself, Larry lost his temper and threw the jug at his head. Later he became a millionaire by selling sex magazines. And when someone got in his way, he broke china in the courtroom. *Entertainment Weekly* described *Hustler* editor Larry Flynt as a "pioneer of gynaecological photojournalism". Milos Forman is somewhat free with the truth in his account of the story, but Flynt himself worked on the movie as consultant and actually appears briefly as a judge in the first court case.

In 1972 Flynt (Woody Harrelson) was running strip-tease joints in Ohio with his brother Jimmy (Harrelson's brother Brett). To improve business he started publishing a magazine where the ladies can be "surveyed" in advance, and so *Hustler* was born. Circulation figures soared when he published naked pictures of Jackie Onassis, the first lady. Flynt became rich, married his girlfriend Althea (Courtney Love) and moved into a villa that had

exactly the same number of rooms as the mansion owned by *Playboy* editor Hugh Hefner. The first of a series of court cases then began where Flynt had to appear before the judge, and where time and again the core issues were the conflict between decency and freedom of speech. He lost his first case but won the appeal, and subsequently he began to style himself a guardian of the freedom of speech. He then formed an organisation for the freedom of the press at whose meetings he alternately showed pictures of naked women and of the destruction of war and concentration camps. Bizarrely, he found an ally in the evangelist Ruth Carter-Stapleton, sister of president Jimmy Carter (played by Donna Hanover, wife of squeaky-clean New York mayor Rudolph Giuliani).

In Forman's film, Flynt appears in court with an American flag wrapped round his hips. He throws oranges at a judge. He has a card on his desk that reads "Jesus H. Christ, Publisher". He has an epiphany in the shape of the American national symbol, the eagle, and he makes Santa Claus and the

1 Anyone can do it! – As the embodiment of the *American Dream* Flynt (Woody Harrelson) is a true patriot.

2 "Courtney Love lets all the raw, untamed, provocative impetus of her musical career and the echoes of her marriage to Kurt Cobain pour into her role as Flynt's lover Althea." *epd Film*

characters from the *Wizard of Oz* into sex figures. He likes to have sex six times a day but after an assassination attempt is stuck in a wheel chair and impotent. Doubtless it is hard to narrate the story of a figure so colourful figure with utter seriousness, but Forman finds a fine balance between irony, coarseness and a touch of mockery to describe his protagonist. Two things remain sacrosanct: Flynt's love for his wife, and his right to freedom of speech. The film makes no effort to turn Flynt into an aesthete, who makes pretty pictures of naked women (which would be far from the truth). Forman

presents him honestly as a pornographer, a tasteless horror, even a mean old devil – but he still supports his right to publish his magazines. Flynt is typical of Forman's film protagonists. Forman had previously given us figures like the rebel McMurphy, played by Jack Nicholson, who ends up in a psychiatric ward in *One Flew Over the Cuckoo's Nest* (1975), and the childishly sniggering Mozart who says obscenities backwards in *Amadeus* (1984). Flynt is a fool and rogue in that tradition, – a contrary spirit who questions the status quo with extraordinary nerve.

H.JK

**Larry Flynt, pornographer and lowest of the low, has achieved what he never dared to hope for – a place in American history."** *Frankfurter Allgemeine Zeitung*

**3** "Woody Harrelson's broad smile contains a hint of the "natural born killer" that he played for Oliver Stone." *epd Film*

**4** 25 years imprisonment! Charles Keating's (James Cromwell) first court action against Larry Flynt is successful.

# "What distinguishes Larry Flynt from Hugh Hefner is his almost messianic obsession with pursuing sex photography to the furthest limits permitted by law." *film-dienst*

**MILOS FORMAN**   Forman was born in 1932 in a small town near Prague and studied at the Prague Film Academy. In 1963 he made his debut with *Cerný Petr* (*Black Peter*), an autobiographical story about a teenager in a small Czech town, and he went on to become one of the foremost protagonists of the Czech Nouvelle Vague. He shot three films in his native land and then emigrated via France to America when the Soviets arrived in 1968. His big break in America was *One Flew Over the Cuckoo's Nest* (1975) which became the cult film of an entire generation and won five Oscars, including one for Forman as best director. His adaptation of the musical *Hair* was less successful, as his version of the hippie idyll simply arrived too late (1977). Nine years later, he won a second Oscar for best director with *Amadeus*. The movie of the theatre play of the same name by Peter Shaffer was filmed in Prague, and that gave Milos Forman his first opportunity to return to his native country.

5   His own lawyer (Edward Norton), a private jet: Flynt is almost a normal entrepreneur.

6   Flynt appears in court wearing battle dress like a freedom fighter.

7   Scantily clad girls empty out bags of dollar bills: this is how Larry Flynt pays his cash fine.

# L. A. CONFIDENTIAL

♛♛

1997 - USA - 138 MIN. - POLICE FILM, DRAMA, NEO FILM NOIR

DIRECTOR CURTIS HANSON (*1945)
SCREENPLAY CURTIS HANSON, BRIAN HELGELAND based on the novel *L. A. CONFIDENTIAL* by JAMES ELLROY
DIRECTOR OF PHOTOGRAPHY DANTE SPINOTTI MUSIC JERRY GOLDSMITH PRODUCTION CURTIS HANSON, ARNON MILCHAN,
MICHAEL G. NATHANSON for REGENCY ENTERPRISES.

STARRING RUSSELL CROWE (Bud White), KEVIN SPACEY (Jack Vincennes), GUY PEARCE (Ed Exley), KIM BASINGER (Lynn
Bracken), DANNY DEVITO (Sid Hudgeons), JAMES CROMWELL (Dudley Smith), DAVID STRATHAIRN (Pierce Patchett),
RON RIFKIN (D. A. Ellis Loew), MATT MCCOY (Brett Chase), PAUL GUILFOYLE (Mickey Cohen).

ACADEMY AWARDS 1998 OSCARS for BEST SUPPORTING ACTRESS (Kim Basinger), AND BEST ADAPTED SCREENPLAY (Curtis
Hanson, Brian Helgeland).

## "Why did you become a cop? – I don't remember."

Sun, swimming pools, beautiful people: "Life is good in L.A., it's a paradise …" That Los Angeles only exists in commercials. In *L. A. Confidential* – set in the early 50s – the city looks quite different, and is a morass of crime and corruption. Three policemen try to combat this with varying dedication and varying motives. Ambitious young police academy graduate Ed Exley (Guy Pearce) is a champion of law and order, and his testimony against his colleagues in an internal police trial catapults him straight to the top of the station house hierarchy. Bud White (Russell Crowe) is a hardened cynic who is prepared to extract confessions with force, but cannot stand violence against women and Jack Vincennes (Kevin Spacey) is nothing more than a corrupt phoney who uses his police job to get in with the entertainment

industry. He is advisor to the television series "Badge Of Honor" and sets up stories for Sid Hudgeons (Danny DeVito), slimy reporter on the gossip magazine "Hush-Hush".

Exley's first case is a spectacular bloodbath in the Nite Owl bar. Five lie dead in the bathroom, killed with a shotgun. Three back youths seen near the scene of the crime are swiftly arrested, and with his brilliant interrogation technique, Exley gets them to admit to having kidnapped and raped a Mexican girl. While White frees the victim and shoots her captor, the three blacks escape from police custody. Exley hunts them down and shoots them dead. He is hailed as a hero and awarded a medal, and it would seem that that is the end of the case. But it doesn't seem to quite add up, and Exley,

3

4

1   He may have deserved it much more for this film, but Russell Crowe didn't win an Oscar until 2001 for *Gladiator*.

2   Bud White (Russell Crowe) doesn't waste any time with the kidnapper of the Mexican girl.

3   Kim Basinger's Oscar for the part of Lynn Bracken brought her long-overdue universal acclaim.

4   A Christmas angel: Lynn out on business until late in the evening with her employer.

5   A few moments of melancholy apart, Bud White doesn't let the corruptness of the world get to him.

6   Brief moments of happiness: is there a future for Bud and Lynn's love?

White and Vincennes continue their investigations until they discover a conspiracy which reaches up into the highest echelons of police and city administration, involving drugs, blackmail, and a ring of porn traders.

*L.A. Confidential* is a reference to the first and perhaps most brazen American gossip magazine "Confidential" (1952–1957), and Hudgeons, the reporter played by Danny DeVito (who is also the off-screen narrator) is an alter ego of Robert Harrison, its infamous editor. Hudgeons gets his kicks from filth and sensationalism, and typifies the moral decadence that seems to have infected the entire city. The police make deals with criminals, the cops who uncover the conspiracy are far from blameless and even the naive greenhorn Exley looses his innocence in the course of the film.

Director Curtis Hanson conjures up the brooding atmosphere of the film noir crime movies of the 40s and 50s, but *L.A. Confidential* is far more than a throwback of a simple nostalgia trip. Cameraman Dante Spinotti shoots clear images free from any patina of age and avoids typical genre references like long shadows. The crime and the corruption seem even more devastating when told in pictures of a sunny, crisp Los Angeles winter. The plot is complex and difficult to follow on first viewing, but Hanson does not emphasise this so much as individual scenes which condense the city's amorality into striking images, like Vincennes saying he can no longer remember why he became a cop. Above all, the director focuses on his brilliant ensemble. Australians Russell Crowe and Guy Pearce, who were virtually unknown before the movie was made, make a great team with the amazing Kevin Spacey. Kim Basinger is a worthy Oscar winner as prostitute and Veronica Lake look-alike Lynn.

HJK

5

6

# "When I gave Kevin Spacey the script, I said I think of two words: Dean Martin."

*Curtis Hanson in: Sight and Sound*

7

**JAMES ELLROY: L.A.'S INDEFATIGABLE CHRONICLER**

His own life sounds like a crime story. James Ellroy was born in Los Angeles in 1948. When he was ten, his mother fell victim to a sex killer, a crime he works through in his 1996 novel *My Dark Places*. The shock threw Ellroy completely off the rails: drugs, petty crime and 50 arrests followed, and he came to writing relatively late. His first novel *Brown's Requiem* was published in 1981 and made into a movie with the same name in 1998. He then wrote a novel trilogy on the figure of the policeman Lloyd Hopkins. The first of this series *Blood on the Moon* (1984) was filmed in 1988 as *Cop* starring James Woods in the title role. Ellroy's masterpiece is the L. A. tetralogy, novels on historical crimes from the period 1947 to 1960. *L. A. Confidential* is the extensive third volume of the series; it took Hanson and co-author Brian Helgeland a whole year and seven different versions to adapt it as a screenplay.

7  Tabloid reporter Sid Hudgeons (Danny DeVito) loves digging up other people's dirt.

8  Officer Vincennes (right) likes to take Hudgeons and a photographer along to his arrests.

9  Vincennes (Kevin Spacey) makes sure that first and foremost he's looking after number one.

10  Officer Ed Exley (Guy Pearce) earns praise from the press and from his boss Dudley Smith (James Cromwell, right).

8

**DIRECTOR** PAUL THOMAS ANDERSON (*1970)

**SCREENPLAY** PAUL THOMAS ANDERSON **DIRECTOR OF PHOTOGRAPHY** ROBERT ELSWIT **MUSIC** MICHAEL PENN **PRODUCTION** JOHN LYONS, LLOYD LEVIN, PAUL THOMAS ANDERSON, JOANNE SELLAR for GHOULARDI (for NEW LINE CINEMA).

**STARRING** MARK WAHLBERG (Eddie Adams/Dirk Diggler), JULIANNE MOORE (Amber Waves), BURT REYNOLDS (Jack Horner), DON CHEADLE (Buck Swope), PHILIP SEYMOUR HOFFMAN (Scotty), JOHN C. REILLY (Reed Rotchild), HEATHER GRAHAM (Rollergirl), WILLIAM H. MACY (Little Bill), NICOLE PARKER (Becky Barnett), ALFRED MOLINA (Rahad Jackson).

# *"Everyone's blessed with one special thing."*

His fans waited in vain: for years, Abel Ferrara (*Driller Killer*, 1979; *Bad Lieutenant*, 1992), iconoclast and untiring rebel of the US movie scene, invited the wildest speculations by declaring that he was going to make a film about the life of pornstar legend John C. Holmes. In the end Paul Thomas Anderson got there before him. His effervescent, epic portrayal of the rise and fall of a pornstar and his clique in San Fernando Valley, California is however only loosely based on the biography of the world's most famous male pornstar. Anderson was only 27 when *Boogie Nights* was made, but he succeeded in producing what is perhaps the definitive movie about the American sex film industry of the 70s and 80s, despite – or perhaps because – of conscious omissions. In *Boogie Nights* we see nothing of its Mafia structure or the organised exploitation of women that is endemic in the business. Instead, Anderson depicts a tender, sympathetic, almost romanticised portrait of a surrogate family. In *Hard Eight* (1996), the melodrama that marked his debut as a director, Anderson's solitary gambling figures sought comfort by bonding together as a replacement family, and *Magnolia* (1999), his Berlin Festival winner, also underlines the strength and uniqueness of family ties.

*Boogie Nights* was not just a breakthrough for its young director, but also for its main actor. Previously known as a model for Calvin Klein under-

wear and as white bad boy rapper Marky Mark, Mark Wahlberg had already found a measure of success in small supporting roles, but here he conclusively proved his potential as a character actor. His character Eddie Adams is the focal point of the movie: a boy from the 'burbs who works as a bouncer in a disco, convinced that he was born both for and with greater things. His impressive penis length of 32 centimetres gets him noticed by porno producer Jack Horner, who takes him under his fatherly wing. Burt Reynolds, who made a great comeback with this role, plays Horner with wonderful coolness; he is a man with a vision. He wants to make porn films that are so entertaining and gripping that people will stay in the cinema even after they have been sexually satisfied to find out what happens next. He works on this with his new superstar Eddie under the name Dirk Diggler, with his porn muse Amber (Julianne Moore) and with the many other crew members who hang around his fashionable villa. The porn star Dirk Diggler quickly learns to take for granted all the luxurious idols of the 'American way of life' which as high school drop-out Eddie he could only worship on posters in his room: fast cars, hot dates, cool clothes, endless pool parties, cocktails and coke brought to him on a tray. But in the early 80s the idyll races to a crash as the classic porn movie is replaced by videos made quickly and cheaply with

3

1  Sex sells: porn film director Jack Horner (Burt Reynolds) gambles with the secret fantasies of his viewers.

2  Group portrait with porn star: his colleagues come to be a substitute family for high school drop-out and runaway Eddie Adams (Mark Wahlberg).

3  In the porn industry people have seen just about everything. But Eddie's natural talent surprises even the oldest hands.

anonymous amateurs lolling about in front of the cameras. The big stars' careers are over and the porn cinemas close. Dirk's drug consumption spirals out of control, and he is even involved in an armed robbery on a millionaire – this is one of the episodes taken from the true story of John Holmes.

*Boogie Nights* is a hedonistic film. It revels in the sounds of the 70s and the well-proportioned California bodies. It is provocative and politically incor-

rect, but as a movie it exploits neither its actors nor its theme for cheap thrills. Dirk Diggler's greatest asset is only seen once in the final shot. This seriousness made the tragicomic melodrama a hit even in prudish America. In its wake, the cable channel HBO produced *Rated X* (2000) a mainstream film on the brothers Jim and Artie Mitchell, who began a porn revolution in the 70s with the classic movies *Behind the Green Door* (1972) and *Inside Marilyn Chambers* (1975).

AK

# "It kind of got me down, watching six hours of solid fucking. You really don't have any desire to go home and kiss your girlfriend."

*Paul Thomas Anderson in: Sight and Sound*

4  A star is born! With his multifaceted and sensitive portrayal ex-rapper Mark Wahlberg finally achieved his transformation into actor.

5  Horner's girlfriend Amber (Julianne Moore) leads a double life. Fascinated and tempted by luxury, drugs and sex, she is fighting a losing battle for custody of her child …

4

5

6

6   With its disco soundtrack and garish costumes, *Boogie Nights* celebrates the hedonistic lifestyle of the 1970s.

7   Heather Graham as Rollergirl, an artificial figure she created herself. We don't find out her real name, which she disowns as she does her past, until the end of the film.

"Razor-sharp dialogue, interlocking destinies splendidly contrived, and a blend of humour and melancholy: this film might have turned out uniform grey. In fact, it's wonderful. You emerge with the conviction that a glimpse of paradise, a moment of grace has been vouchsafed." *Le nouvel observateur*

**PHILIP SEYMOUR HOFFMAN**

Although he claims to have become a professional actor only to impress a girl, Philip Seymour Hoffman, born in 1967 in Fairport, New York, seldom gets the leading roles. With his massive build, dull complexion and unmanageable red-blond hair, he doesn't fit into the part of typical film beau at all – which is probably what gets him the perhaps more exciting roles such as the drag queen in *Flawless* (1999) cursed with a homophobic neighbour played by Robert De Niro or the snob Freddy in the movie of Patricia Highsmith's novel *The Talented Mr. Ripley* (1999). Not that Hoffman's characters are devoid of romantic impulses: it's hard to think of any movie moment in recent years as touching as the scene in *Boogie Nights* when, in a badly-fitting tank top, he asks Mark Wahlberg if he can kiss him on the mouth. The magazine *Talk* hit the nail on the head when it claimed that Hoffman is "a new sort of Hollywood handsome: real." Hoffman has played leading roles in all of Anderson's movies. The director first noticed him in *Scent of a Woman* (1992) and in the Broadway play *True West* where he appeared with his friend John C. Reilly, another actor who often works with Anderson.

# GOOD WILL HUNTING

♟♟

1997 - USA -> 126 MIN. - DRAMA

DIRECTOR GUS VAN SANT (*1952)
SCREENPLAY MATT DAMON, BEN AFFLECK DIRECTOR OF PHOTOGRAPHY JEAN-YVES ESCOFFIER MUSIC DANNY ELFMAN, JEFFREY KIMBALL
PRODUCTION LAWRENCE BENDER, KEVIN SMITH, SCOTT MOSIER for BE GENTLEMEN, A BAND APART (for MIRAMAX).

STARRING ROBIN WILLIAMS (Sean Maguire), MATT DAMON (Will Hunting), BEN AFFLECK (Chuckie), MINNIE DRIVER (Skylar),
STELLAN SKARSGÅRD (Gerald Lambeau), COLE HAUSER (Billy), CASEY AFFLECK (Morgan), JOHN MIGHTON (Tom),
RACHEL MAJOROWSKI (Krystyn), COLLEEN MCCAULEY (Cathy).

ACADEMY AWARDS 1998 OSCARS for BEST ORIGINAL SCREENPLAY (Matt Damon, Ben Affleck) and BEST SUPPORTING ACTOR
(Robin Williams).

## "Real loss is only possible when you love something more than you love yourself."

Matt Damon and Ben Affleck love throwing red herrings to journalists when asked in interviews for the secret of their successful collaboration: "we're lovers" is the invariable reply. The two boyhood friends, who grew up just a few houses away from each other, have every reason to joke about things. *Good Will Hunting* was received enthusiastically by critics and fans alike. Robin Williams was by far the movie's biggest star, but it was still basically their movie, despite the controlling hand of cult director Gus Van Sant (*Drugstore Cowboy, My Own Private Idaho*) and the fact that cinema tycoons Bob and Harvey Weinstein saved the movie by buying the rights for their company Miramax. The two young shooting stars do more than play main parts, they also wrote the screenplay – and it took Bob and Harvey Weinstein to recognise the potential of this atmospherically intense drama about a rebellious but emotionally isolated genius.

Matt Damon, who himself studied at Harvard and left the elite university shortly before graduating, plays Will Hunting, a cleaner at MIT. The cleaning job is one of his probation orders, for Will can't keep out of trouble.

Whenever the opportunity for a fight or a quick buck presents itself, he's there. He spends almost as much time in the young offenders' centre as he does in his run-down apartment in the centre of Boston.

But Will is a many-sided character. When Professor Lambeau (Stellan Skarsgård) discovers the answer to a difficult maths problem on the board and none of his students will own up to having solved it, he sets out to find the mysterious mathematical genius – and finds him of all places in the boy who cleans the institute's floors. Lambeau saves Will from another stay in prison by taking him under his wing and making sure he goes to the therapy sessions the court has decreed with an old friend from his student days, psychologist Sean Maguire (Robin Williams). While Will and Lambeau work together in euphoric harmony on complicated mathematical equations, Maguire has his work cut breaking through Will's emotional defences. Williams plays the widowed Maguire without pathos, and shows him to be an affectionate yet saddened man with the smallest of gestures. Befriending his stubborn patient is a lengthy process, but Maguire quickly realises that

behind Will's rebellious and angry façade an unhappy and vulnerable boy is hiding ...

As so often in Hollywood, success didn't arrive over night, not just in the movie but in real life as well. Damon and Affleck wrote the screenplay years previously on a scriptwriting course and several Hollywood studios had even shown an interest in it. Damon and Affleck's condition however was that they should both star in the movie, and as they were completely unknown at the time, none of the studios accepted. That changed instantly with Damon's great success in the main role of Francis Ford Coppola's film of the Grisham novel *The Rainmaker* (1997).

Miramax finally bought the rights to *Good Will Hunting* after its authors took the advice of their experienced colleagues Rob Reiner, Terrence Malick and William Goldman, cutting the suspense element and adding love interest to the plot. In the revised version, Will, the social outsider, falls in love with Skylar (Minnie Driver) a British medical student who is the daughter of a respectable family. The emotional conflict which dominates Will's life is intensified by the love Skylar offers him and which he finds almost impossible to accept. Maguire gives him the courage to let his cynical, smart alec mask fall and face his feelings – even if this means that the world will have to do without the next Albert Einstein ...          AK

4

5

# "A heart-warming, credible piece of cinema full of human impressions and sparkling wordplay." *Neue Zürcher Zeitung*

**MATT DAMON**     Hollywood's latest golden boy was born in Cambridge, Massachusetts in 1970. His breakthrough was the starring role in Francis Ford Coppola's adaptation of John Grisham's legal bestseller *The Rainmaker* (1997), where he played a young, inexperienced but indomitable lawyer who fights against a dishonest multimillion dollar insurance company and its star defence lawyers. Everything he has done since has been a success. With his boyish charm and understated good looks he seems predestined to play the sensitive heroes of American film. He received enthusiastic reviews for the title role in Steven Spielberg's *Saving Private Ryan* (1998) and fascinated critics with the contrast between his innocent boyish face and cynical indifference as the cold-blooded murderer in the film of Patricia Highsmith's novel *The Talented Mr. Ripley* (1999). Together with his boyhood friend Ben Affleck, Damon has also written successful screenplays, and the script for *Good Will Hunting* won a Golden Globe and an Oscar. They went on to found a production company together aimed at giving young hopefuls like themselves a chance.

1   Hollywood clown Robin Williams is brilliant in his role as psychologist Sean Maguire, acting with an earnestness that is not merely by chance reminiscent of Peter Weir's *Dead Poets' Society* (1988).

2   Knowledge as power? All the knowledge he has picked up from books has given Will (Matt Damon) a feeling of superiority – but hasn't brought him happiness.

3   Medical student Skylar (Minnie Driver) embodies the complete opposite of social underdog Will, who doesn't dare to love her.

4   Professor Lambeau (Stellan Skarsgård) discovered Will's genius. But how honourable are his motives?

5   Shortly before a brawl: Will is still sitting peacefully with his mates (Ben Affleck, right) watching a baseball game.

# MEN IN BLACK

1997 - USA - 98 MIN. - SCIENCE FICTION, COMEDY

DIRECTOR BARRY SONNENFELD (*1953)
SCREENPLAY ED SOLOMON, based on a MALIBU comic by LOWELL CUNNINGHAM DIRECTOR OF PHOTOGRAPHY DON PETERMAN
MUSIC DANNY ELFMAN PRODUCTION WALTER F. PARKES, LAURIE MACDONALD for AMBLIN ENTERTAINMENT, COLUMBIA
PICTURES.

STARRING TOMMY LEE JONES (K), WILL SMITH (J), LINDA FIORENTINO (Laurel), VINCENT D'ONOFRIO (Edgar), RIP TORN
(Zed), TONY SHALHOUB (Jeebs), SIOBHAN FALLON (Beatrice), MIKE NUSSBAUM (Gentle Rosenberg), JON GRIES (Van
Driver), SERGIO CALDERÓN (José).

ACADEMY AWARDS 1998 OSCAR for BEST MAKE-UP (David LeRoy Anderson, Rick Baker).

## "There are approximately 1500 aliens in Manhattan."

Sylvester Stallone is an alien. Elvis isn't dead, he's just gone home. And every word you read in the *National Enquirer* is true. – If you've ever had the feeling that you have to deal with aliens in your terrestrial life, this movie is the confirmation you've long been waiting for: "Sometimes there are up to 1500 aliens on earth, most of them here in Manhattan." Two things are necessary to ensure that humans and aliens can coexist peacefully: cover-up jobs and ceaseless vigilance. The "Men in Black" are responsible for both of these, black-clad agents from the department six, the immigration board. They do everything to stop the humans from realising that they are not alone on their blue planet, and make sure that the guests from outer space don't step out of line. At an interstellar airport the MiB supervise the arrival of creatures from far-off planets. They inspect their luggage and grant them entry permits to limited areas of New York and the world. If they try to travel in other parts, the agents fetch them back or shoot them dead. Alien civil rights are fairly low down on the agenda.

We see an example of this on the Mexican border. Police hold up a dilapidated truck full of illegal immigrants from the neighbouring Latin American country. State officials muscle in on their local colleagues; "Man in Black" K (Tommy Lee Jones) and a colleague take over and release all the refugees except one – he comes from further afield than Mexico. Under his poncho he is hiding a slimy body and tentacles, and the blue ooze in his veins sprays out all over one of the sheriffs when K summarily blows the creature up with a "De-atomiser". With a gadget know as a "Neuralyzer" which looks like a pen with a light instead of a nib, the agent then wipes all trace of the incident from the sheriff's memory.

In New York another policeman is chasing someone right through Manhattan, without realising of course that he is an alien. Cop James Darrel Edwards (Will Smith) stays hot on the criminal's heels even when he runs up the wall of the Guggenheim museum like a fly. James stops him on the roof, but the runaway avoids capture by throwing himself to his death. This attracts K's attention to James. And since the cheeky cop often clashes with the authorities, he's a good candidate to be K's new partner. Edwards passes an absurd test in which he is the only competitor and is taken on. The ends of his fingers are cauterised to stop him leaving any fingerprints. He is

"Mind you, the best thing is the two stars Will Smith and Tommy Lee Jones, whose humour is so bone-dry that they can deliver lines and keep their cool, where others would let the lines die on their lips." *Süddeutsche Zeitung*

fitted up with the black uniform and given dark glasses and a new name. Henceforth he is J, reduced like his colleagues to a single letter of the alphabet. Anonymity is their name, silence their language.

J and K's very first assignment is big. An alien bug has landed secretly on earth, a dangerous species that would never have been given an entry permit in the first place. The bug has killed Farmer Edgar (Vincent D'Onofrio), sucked out his entrails and put on his skin. He manages – more or less – to pass himself off as a human and is looking for the Galaxis, a valuable jewel worn by the son of the Aquilians' ruler who is living unobtrusively on earth

disguised as a jeweller. K and J's assignment becomes really difficult when the Aquilians decide they want the jewel back. If they don't get it, they're going to destroy the world. The time limit is a stellar week – a mere sixty earth minutes!

*Men in Black* is an almighty parody. Goggle-eyed, slimy aliens like the monsters in 50s movies, secret government organisations reminiscent of the television series *The Man From U.N.C.L.E.,* (1964–1968) and the uncanny modern mystery series *The X Files* (1993–), the *Blues Brothers*' black gear (1980) and *Casablanca*'s escape scenario (1942) – it's all there. Director

1  They have to make sure they keep their shades on, otherwise the neutraliser would wipe the memories of the "Men in Black" as well.

2  Edwards (Will Smith, left) wins through in the aptitude test, against candidates who follow the regulations.

3  "Here come the Men in Black" – the song performed by Will Smith in the film also became a hit.

4  Perfectly disguised among humankind: son of the ruler of the Aquilians.

5  Dry humour and futuristic mega-weapons were the secret of *Men in Black*'s success.

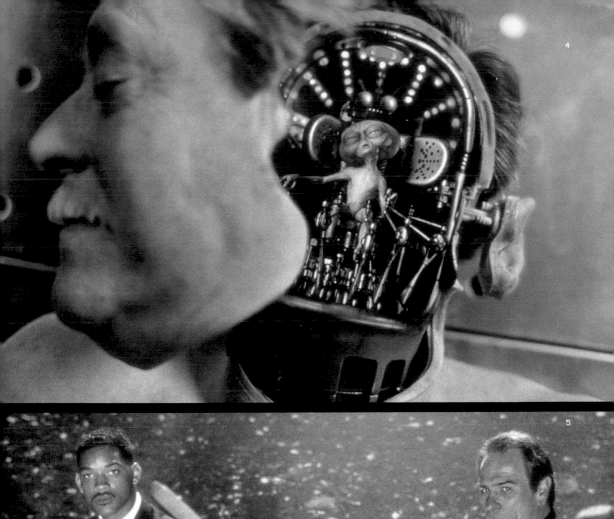

6 Useful aliens: at "M.I.B." headquarters they dish out coffee along with cheeky comments.

7 Disguised as a Mexican: an extraterrestrial immigrant tries to get into the USA, but he can't fool K.

8 Aliens bring some strange luggage with them on their trip to Earth.

Barry Sonnenfeld creates a funny, exciting mix from these quotations, and then goes a step further and adds historical dates and real events: the steel remains of the 1964 world exhibition in Queens are nothing less than the remnants of a space ship. The New York powercuts of 1977 were caused by … aliens. Microwaves, zips and silicon implants were all invented somewhere in another galaxy, and confiscated from alien tourists when they arrived on earth. Elvis lives. We learn that we are surrounded by aliens – not only Sylvester Stallone and the Republican politician Newt Gingrich, but singer Dionne Warwick too are all aliens. Sonnenfeld and his scriptwriter Ed Solomon take the game with facts and outrageous UFO fantasies to the extreme when the headlines of a gossip magazine read: "Aliens stole my husband's skin!" – scandal sheets are an important source of information for the MiB.

Men in Black is also a buddy movie. Rapper Will Smith – best known as an actor for the television series The Fresh Prince of Bel-Air (1990–96) – is seen here in his first main role as an energetic, go-getting action character. Tommy Lee Jones is the wise old-timer experienced in the alien business, and the two of them make an irresistible team. With stoicism and laconic

humour, they go about their daily alien work; their immaculate black suits are spattered with one burst of slime after another. K is eaten alive by an alien and J helps deliver an alien baby. Although it often conjures up the charm of old B features, Men in Black is actually a huge modern production with a 100 million dollar budget and effects by George Lucas' Industrial Light and Magic company. Rick Baker (Gremlins), perhaps Hollywood's most brilliant monster creator, made the aliens. His creativity was allowed free rein: one bug-eyed alien in human form grows a new head every time it is shot off; a quartet of curious beings – naked pipsqueaks on two legs – live by the coffee machine in the MiB headquarters and make sarcastic wisecracks; a tiny creature with enormous eyes operates a huge machine from a control tower – the machine is a human body and the control tower is its head. Baker won a well-deserved Oscar for the make-up effects.

The efforts were well rewarded, as the production was by far the most successful movie of 1997. It had millions of viewers in Europe and was a box-office smash in the USA where it earned over 250 million dollars. In the same year a television series started with the alien hunters as cartoon figures. A sequel to the movie Men in Black is planned for 2002.     HJK

"In the best sci-fi movie tradition, *Men in Black* gets straight to the point in the very first scene." *epd Film*

**BARRY SONNENFELD** With the comic adaptations *Addams Family* (1991) and *Men in Black*, the Hollywood novel *Get Shorty* (1995) and the television series *Wild Wild West* (1998) Barry Sonnenfeld has made a name for himself as specialist in pop culture. He studied politics and then film and began his career as a cameraman, first of all for documentary films. He made his first feature film *Blood Simple* (1983) for his former classmates, the Coen brothers. He worked with them two more times, on *Raising Arizona* (1987) and *Miller's Crossing* (1990). The first *Addams Family* film was Sonnenfeld's debut as a director. He was asked to direct *Forrest Gump* and refused; Robert Zemeckis took over and the film won six Oscars. Sonnenfeld's disappointment didn't last long. He filmed the Elmore Leonard Adaptation *Get Shorty* which was a huge hit, and it became Sonnenfeld's ticket to the upper echelons of Hollywood.

# FACE/OFF

1997 - USA - 138 MIN. - ACTION FILM

DIRECTOR JOHN WOO (*1946)
SCREENPLAY MIKE WERB, MICHAEL COLLEARY DIRECTOR OF PHOTOGRAPHY OLIVER WOOD MUSIC JOHN POWELL PRODUCTION DAVID PERMUT, BARRIE M. OSBORNE, TERENCE CHANG, CHRISTOPHER GODSICK for DOUGLAS-REUTHER PRODUCTION, WCG ENTERTAINMENT.

STARRING JOHN TRAVOLTA (Sean Archer), NICOLAS CAGE (Castor Troy), JOAN ALLEN (Eve Archer), ALESSANDRO NIVOLA (Pollux Troy), GINA GERSHON (Sasha Hassler), DOMINIQUE SWAIN (Jamie Archer), NICK CASSAVETES (Dietrich Hassler), HARVE PRESNELL (Victor Lazarro), COLM FEORE (Dr Malcolm Walsh), CCH POUNDER (Dr Hollis Miller).

## "In order to catch him, he must become him."

Sepia pictures, images in someone's memory. A father rides with his son on a carousel horse. A shot rings out. The father is wounded and the son is killed. Six years later L. A. cop Sean Archer (John Travolta) still hasn't caught up with Castor Troy (Nicolas Cage), the psychopathic sharp shooter who killed his son. He gets another chance at a private airfield. Castor and his brother Pollux (Alessandro Nivolla) are about to take off, and Archer tries to stop them.

A shoot-out ensues where Pollux is arrested and Castor is injured and falls into a coma. But Archer still hasn't shaken off Castor Troy's evil legacy. His brother is carrying a disc that contains information on a gigantic bomb attack in Los Angeles, but the whereabouts of the bomb is a mystery. Pollux insists that he will only speak to his brother. To find out the truth about the bomb, a team of scientists from a secret project make Archer an unbelievable offer.

The parallel between hunter and hunted is a well-worn theme: the cop has to empathise with the criminal in order to predict his next move. Many movies have used this device, perhaps none so systematically as *Heat* (1995), where cop Al Pacino and gangster Robert De Niro meet for a tête-à-tête. *Face/Off*'s director John Woo takes the motif to new heights when he turns the cop into the gangster. With the help of the latest medical technology, Archer is given the face, stature and voice of the gangster Troy. He already knows more than enough about Troy's story, deeds and accomplices as he has been chasing him for years. To get the information out of him, Archer is admitted to the high security prison where Pollux is being kept. The mission remains a secret, and not even Archer's boss or his wife know anything about it. At any time, with the help of the same techniques, he can be given back his own body. But suddenly that escape route is suddenly blocked. Troy wakes out of his coma and appears in the prison – as Archer.

4

1 A shock: police officer Archer (John Travolta) wearing the face of the villain he has been pursuing like a man possessed for the last six years.

2 "Ridiculous chin", says Castor (Nicolas Cage) when Archer's face is fixed onto his.

3 The parallel between the hunter and the hunted is a well-known film motif, but nobody has ever taken it as far as John Woo.

4 It's not easy for Archer: locked up in the body of Castor in a high-tech jail.

5 The moment of truth: Archer (as Castor) runs his arch-enemy to ground.

6 Sean and Eve Archer (Joan Allen) have lost their son. Their grief lends a dark mood to the whole film.

---

**JOHN TRAVOLTA**  John Travolta's career began in 1975 with the role of Vinnie Barbarino in the popular television series *Welcome Back, Kotter*. His enormous success in the dance movies *Saturday Night Fever* (1977) and *Grease* (1978) was based on his clichéd roles as attractive lady's man, and as a result Travolta practically disappeared from the screen in the 1980s. He wasn't able to return to Hollywood's premiere league until Quentin Tarantino cast him as the off-beat killer Vincent Vega in *Pulp Fiction* (1994). Since then, Travolta has established himself as a versatile character actor who is just as at home in comedy roles as in action films (for example, *Operation: Broken Arrow*, 1995) or in existential dramas such as *Mad City* (1996). Travolta has become one of Hollywood's biggest earners in the 1990s: following *Pulp Fiction*, which made him 140,000 dollars, his fee per movie has risen to 20,000,000 dollars.

---

He has had the cop's face put on and shot the scientists and the people who witnessed the "swap". Archer manages to escape from the prison and has to make his way as an outlaw while Troy lives in his comfortable home with his wife and daughter.

Two movies gave new life to the Hollywood Action Film genre in the 90s: *Speed* (1994) and *Face/Off. Speed* is a fast-paced, light-footed celebration of pure movement, whereas *Face/Off* – despite its virtuoso action scenes – has dark, elegiac undertones and a much more complex plot. Archer is a tragic figure from the outset, first losing his son and then his life. The idea of changing bodies might seem far-fetched, but it offers the director plenty of opportunities to play with the hunter/hunted motif. John Woo

goes through all of them one by one. Troy in Archer's body becomes a more subtle kind of gangster: he defuses his own bomb, becomes a hero and decides he wants to run the whole police department. Archer in Troy's body holds Troy's son in his arms as he used to hold his own. And Archer's wife Eve is delighted with the reawakened passion of her husband, who seems like a new man.

The doppelgänger motif reaches a visual highpoint in the scene where Archer and Troy stand on two sides of a mirror and aim their pistols at their own reflections, each of them wearing the face of their archenemy. The visual stylisation typical of Woo is everywhere in the movie – like the white doves in a church, or the slow motion billowing overcoat.          HJK

5

6

"Woo is such an action wizard that he can make planes or speed boats kick box, but his surprising strength this time is more on a human level." *New York Times*

# TITANIC

1997 - USA -194 MIN. - MELODRAMA, DISASTER FILM

DIRECTOR JAMES CAMERON (*1954)
SCREENPLAY JAMES CAMERON DIRECTOR OF PHOTOGRAPHY RUSSELL CARPENTER MUSIC JAMES HORNER PRODUCTION JAMES CAMERON, JON LANDAU for 20TH CENTURY FOX, LIGHTSTORM ENTERTAINMENT, PARAMOUNT PICTURES.

STARRING LEONARDO DICAPRIO (Jack Dawson), KATE WINSLET (Rose DeWitt Bukater), BILLY ZANE (Cal Hockley), KATHY BATES (Molly Brown), GLORIA STUART (Rose as an old woman), BILL PAXTON (Brock Lovett), BERNARD HILL (Captain Smith), DAVID WARNER (Spicer Lovejoy), VICTOR GARBER (Thomas Andrews), JONATHAN HYDE (Bruce Ismay).

ACADEMY AWARDS 1998 OSCARS for BEST PICTURE, BEST DIRECTOR (James Cameron), BEST CINEMATOGRAPHY (Russell Carpenter), BEST FILM EDITING (Conrad Buff, James Cameron, Richard A. Harris), BEST MUSIC, category DRAMA (James Horner), BEST SONG ("My Heart Will Go On"; Melody: James Horner, Text: Will Jennings, Performed by Céline Dion), BEST ART DIRECTION – SET DECORATION (Peter Lamont, Michael Ford), BEST COSTUMES (Deborah Lynn Scott), BEST VISUAL EFFECTS (Robert Legato, Mark Lasoff, Thomas L. Fisher, Michael Kanfer), BEST SOUND (Gary Rydstrom, Tom Johnson, Gary Summers, Mark Ulano), BEST SOUND EFFECTS EDITING (Tom Bellfort, Christopher Boyes).

## "So this is the ship they say is unsinkable."

The sinking of the passenger ship Titanic is usually interpreted as a warning of the catastrophic end of the modern belief in progress, which was confirmed in the trenches of World War One only a few years later. The numerous film versions of the event demonstrate the fascination that the luxury liner's fate has always held. The movies themselves have had an influence on the Titanic myth, which in turn has become an integral part of our cultural memory. The story never varies: technology clashes with nature, human inventiveness with destructive natural power, arrogant presumption with impassive creation. Film versions were made almost immediately after the accident, like the long-forgotten *Saved From the Titanic* (by Etienne Arnaud, 1912) and Pier Angelo Mazzolotti's *Titanic* (1915).

Subsequently many vast and expensive films were made in which private unhappiness and technical disaster developed side by side only to fuse together in an infernal catastrophe at the end. Jean Negulesco's film version of the event was awarded an Oscar for best original screenplay in 1953. Cameron's *Titanic* cost 200 million dollars and was awarded a total of eleven Oscars – the time any film had matched the previously unbeatable *Ben Hur* (1959).

Cameron's interpretation of the Titanic myth is more proof of his talent for telling melodramatic love stories. The proletarian prince almost accidentally rescues the world-weary princess while "polite society" postures and poses to conceal its spiritual and moral decay. The megalomania that inspired the construction of a gigantic luxury liner like the Titanic is part of that modern decadence.

The film's recipe for success could be summed up as strong emotion reflected by huge disaster. And it works. The penniless painter Jack Dawson

2

3

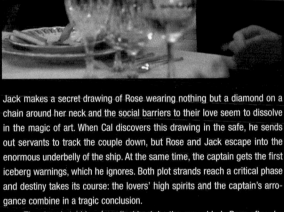

# "The scene where a lifeboat is carefully edging its way between frozen corpses floating in the water as it searches for survivors is as horrific as it is unforgettable."

*Frankfurter Allgemeine Zeitung*

meets beautiful, of noble birth but unhappy Rose DeWitt Bukater. She tries to kill herself, he saves her and they fall in love. A passionate romance develops between this young man from the lower decks and the upper class lady from the top echelons of society. The love story becomes a social drama where class differences become apparent not just in location and decor but also in everyday life. Upstairs there is distinguished, arrogant small talk about money accompanied by pleasant string music, downstairs there is wild dancing to fast and furious Irish folk music. The class barrier becomes extremely real. Rose's fiancé Cal Hockley (Billy Zane) wants to put an end to the subversive relationship and eventually manages to have Jack forbidden from coming up to the top deck, but this is not enough to drive the two apart

Jack makes a secret drawing of Rose wearing nothing but a diamond on a chain around her neck and the social barriers to their love seem to dissolve in the magic of art. When Cal discovers this drawing in the safe, he sends out servants to track the couple down, but Rose and Jack escape into the enormous underbelly of the ship. At the same time, the captain gets the first iceberg warnings, which he ignores. Both plot strands reach a critical phase and destiny takes its course: the lovers' high spirits and the captain's arrogance combine in a tragic conclusion.

The story is told in a long flashback by the now elderly Rose after she has seen on television that a diving team has found Jack's drawing in a safe lying on the bottom of the sea. The movie takes great care to adopt a light

---

**LEONARDO DICAPRIO**  DiCaprio was born in Hollywood in 1974 and stood in front of the camera for the first time when he was only five years old. The boyish star began his career with publicity spots and television series before getting his first big movie breakthrough with *This Boy's Life* (1993) alongside Robert De Niro and Ellen Barkin. He was nominated for an Oscar for his performance as the mentally retarded Arnie Grape in *What's Eating Gilbert Grape* (1993). Similarly difficult roles followed, for example as drug-addict and sports scholarship holder in *The Basketball Diaries* (1993) or as the homosexual poet Rimbaud in *Total Eclipse* (1995). DiCaprio also shone in his role as a youthful Romeo in Baz Luhrmann's contemporary adaptation of *Romeo & Juliet*. After *Titanic* (1997), the most successful box office hit of all time, DiCaprio played the lead role in the dark adventure film *The Beach* (1999).

---

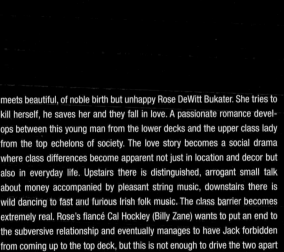

1   Impending disaster reflected in the lovers' eyes (Leonardo DiCaprio as Jack and Kate Winslet as Rose).

2   Tenderness in a time of decadence.

3   Humanity's presumptuousness embodied as a machine on her journey into the abyss.

4   The betrayed fiancé (Billy Zane) loses his appetite.

"The outside shots of the stern breaking up, the tidal waves inside, the drama around and in the lifeboats rank among the best special effects Hollywood has ever produced." *Frankfurter Allgemeine Zeitung*

5   An arrogant society falls from a great height.       · 6   Classical grandeur in a watery grave. Any hope of
                                                              being saved is ebbing away.

touch with just a hint of melancholy when passing from this fairytale beginning to an atmospheric portrayal of the early years of the 20th century.

This was the first Titanic movie to use pictures of the actual wreck after
it had been located and explored, giving an added note of authenticity.
*Titanic* fuses the two time dimensions of its tale in many poetic pictures: like
Kubrick's famous "match cut" in *2001: A Space Odyssey* (1968) where a
bone is thrown into the air and the editing turns it into a space ship, past and
present are combined with blend-ins and morphing effects. All of which of
course is enhanced by the movie's impressively atmospheric soundtrack.

When the inevitable finally happens and the Titanic sinks after colliding
with the iceberg, Jack drowns in the icy water. But their love survives. When
Rose, now an old woman, returns to her lover's watery grave for the last time
at the end of the film, she throws the blue diamond that she saved from the
wreck into the sea as a symbol of her eternal love. The ship may not have
been unsinkable, but the myth of the Titanic is. Watching the movie is like
looking at an old photograph. We can only discover its secrets by looking at
it many times from different angles, like a sparkling diamond that always has
new facets to be discovered.                                              BR

3

1 She has the potential to play the blonde bomb-shell, but Helen Hunt generally feels more at home in the role of the homely girl-next-door. Here she plays waitress and single mum Carol Connelly.

2 Misanthrope Melvin Udall, grimly fighting his way through the jungle of the metropolis: a showpiece role for Hollywood veteran Jack Nicholson.

3 With his hatred of dogs, Udall proves a worthy fol-lower of W. C. Fields, who once declared: "Anyone who hates small dogs and children can't be all bad."

## "The cascades of words and succinct punch-lines of this film make you realise the amount of impoverished dialogue that contemporary comedy usually fobs you off with."

*Abendzeitung*

4

5    6

4  Enemies can become friends – in spite of the age
   difference there is a real spark between Carol and
   Melvin.

5  Greg Kinnear as Simon, the gay painter who is
   beaten up by a gang and forced to rely on his
   horrible neighbour for help.

6  When health is a matter of money: Carol's son
   Spencer (Jesse James) can only get the best
   medical care with Udall's financial support.

**HELEN HUNT**  From the age of six, Oscar award winner Helen Hunt only ever wanted to be an actress. The daughter of director Gordon Hunt was born in California in 1963, and already at the age of nine had her first role in a television film (*Pioneer Woman*). In 1986, she came to the attention of a broader public playing the daughter of Kathleen Turner and Nicolas Cage in *Peggy Sue Got Married*. In the successful sitcom *Mad About You*, Hunt was not only brilliant as the newly wed wife, but also acted as producer, and occasionally took on the direction. Her first international breakthrough came with Jan de Bont's disaster film *Twister* (1996). Since then "the hardest working girl in show biz" (according to fellow actor Eric Stoltz) has celebrated one hit film after another, playing alongside the likes of Kevin Spacey (*Pay it Forward*), Mel Gibson (*What Women Want*, 2000), and Tom Hanks (*Castaway*, 2000).

DIRECTOR TOM TYKWER (*1965)
SCREENPLAY TOM TYKWER DIRECTOR OF PHOTOGRAPHY FRANK GRIEBE MUSIC TOM TYKWER, JOHNNY KLIMEK, REINHOLD HEIL
PRODUCTION STEFAN ARNDT for X FILME CREATIVE POOL, ARTE, WDR.

STARRING FRANKA POTENTE (Lola), MORITZ BLEIBTREU (Manni), HERBERT KNAUP (Lola's father), ARMIN ROHDE (Mr Schuster), JOACHIM KRÓL (Norbert von Au – Bum), HEINO FERCH (Ronnie), NINA PETRI (Jutta Hansen), SUZANNE VON BORSODY (Mrs Jäger), LARS RUDOLPH (Kassierer Kruse), SEBASTIAN SCHIPPER (Mike).

# "Ball's round. Game lasts 90 minutes. I can follow that much. All the rest is just theory."

Tom Tykwer's first films caused a stir – his elegiac debut *Deadly Maria* (*Die tödliche Maria*, 1993) and the prize-winning *Wintersleepers* (*Winterschläfer*, 1997), although naturally the interest came more from critics and impassioned art house fans than it did from the general public. *Run Lola Run* came as a surprise in every respect. Its content is as complex as his previous film, the mournful, difficult melodrama *Wintersleepers*, but formally it is exactly the opposite with its hip, contemporary look. It combines classic means of expression such as split screen, slow motion, time lapse and animated sequences with a modern pop video aesthetic resulting in some impressive visual fireworks. Those visuals are complimented by Franka Potente and Moritz Bleibtreu, its fresh, cool, attractive young stars, but above all by its speed. *Run Lola Run* is a throwback to the childish enthusiasm inspired by the earliest cinema pictures, the simplest of all film images: a person in motion.

It's high-speed cinema. Tykwer's movie is literally a running film, and spectators are carried along with it through the streets of Berlin, where Lola (Franka Potente) races panting over the asphalt and cobblestones, over bridges, building sites and squares, puffing and gasping but determined,

driven on by the pumping techno soundtrack. The movie was also a welcome surprise where the image of German films abroad was concerned. Humour is difficult to translate, and while domestic German cinema had turned out some excellent relationship comedies like *Maybe ... Maybe Not* (1994) in the 90s, they had never really made it abroad. *Lola* on the other hand ran not only all over German cinema screens but was also invited to international festivals such as Venice and Sundance.

Hers is a race against time, for love: Lola has 20 minutes to find 100,000 marks. That's the amount of money that her boyfriend Manni (Moritz Bleibtreu) has lost in the subway – money which actually belonged to the gangster boss Ronnie (Heino Ferch), and if Manni doesn't deliver the sum on the dot of 12, he's a dead man – "it's as simple as that". And so Lola runs through Berlin, first to her father, who is a bank director, then to meet Manni, who is threatening to rob a supermarket.

*Run Lola Run* is physical, dynamic, speed-dominated action cinema. With her fire-red shock of hair, Lola runs like the Pippi Longstocking of the ecstasy generation. "I make the world how I like it ..." she seems to say, and Lola's streets are empty and wide. Anyone who knows Berlin soon realises

3

1  After *Knockin' on Heaven's Door* Moritz Bleibtreu's role as Manni in *Run Lola Run* finally made him a star.

2  79 minutes of speed, 79 minutes of life in the fast lane: Franka Potente as Lola.

3  The film slackens its pace for a few moments during conversations about love.

4  German heart-throb Heino Ferch, barely recognisable as shaven-headed gang leader Ronnie.

5  Lola's costume, a city brat outfit representing something near permanence in the metropolitan jungle with boots, combat trousers and vest quickly found a place in the Berlin Film Museum.

**DIGITAL PICTURES**  With the development of the computer, a completely new realm of possibilities opened up for Special Effects experts. Pictures scanned into the computer can be changed at will – whether it is to delete a price label left on a coffee cup by mistake, or to integrate actors with pictures of historical personalities as in Robert Zemeckis' *Forrest Gump* (1994) or to save an army of extras by copying digital pictures as in Wolfgang Petersen's *In the Line of Fire* (1993) and Ridley Scott's *Gladiator* (2000). CGI (Computer Generated Images) open up an entire new dimension of trick techniques. Pictures can now be created completely in the computer without needing initial photographs or drawings, and can then be combined with live action pictures. This is how the dinosaurs were created for Steven Spielberg's *Jurassic Park* (1993).

that the routes she runs have nothing to do with the real geography of the city. But that's not just an error, for *Run Lola Run* is also a philosophical film, an illustration of chaos theory, a hypothetical game of "what if …". Lola sets off three times to save Manni, in three lots of twenty minutes. Her way across town is different every time, according to how she reacts to the dog that snarls at her in the stairwell of her apartment building. Does she jump over it? Is she momentarily frightened? Or does the child with the dog stick a leg out and trip her up? Every second won or lost in leaving the house changes her own fate and that of many others. The first time Lola bursts into her father's office to discover him embracing his lover, the second time he has

just discovered that she is pregnant, and a third time it becomes clear that the child is not his. One time Lola dies, another time Manni dies and there is one happy ending. This game with destiny, with possibilities, options and their effects on time and space is also played on an emotional level in the few quiet moments of the movie. Manni and Lola lie in bed together and talk like Valentine's Day cards, asking "Well, do you love me or not?". Spectators immediately identify with the dialogues – Manni wants to find out whether Lola would still love him if he were dead, or if she met someone else or if she didn't even know that he existed.

AK

AK

> "This image of the running woman contains everything: despair, emotion, dynamism – all the reasons why you actually wanted to make films ..."
>
> *Tom Tykwer in: Süddeutsche Zeitung*

4

"In an age where the mass media of television and film are exploiting their very own simulation strategies and how these relate to 'reality' with wavering quality, we were crying out for a satire on these media." *epd Film*

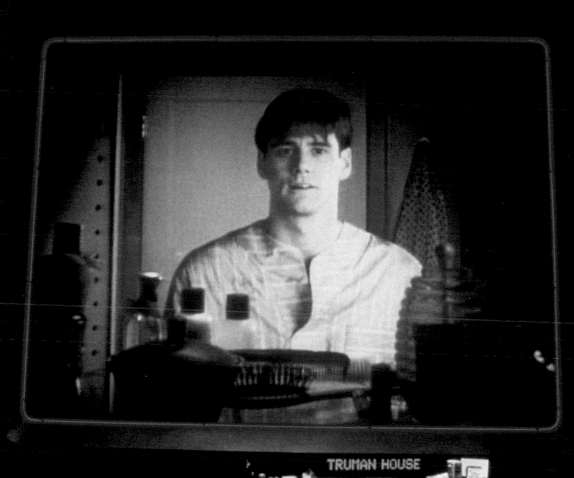

**4** A god of artifice: director Christof (Ed Harris) as creator and supreme father of the world.

**5** Television-style TLC.

**6** The view in the mirror: who is watching whom?

He is the main character in a perfect illusion that is shattered by one of its own elementary principles, repetition. The same actor is hired to play the homeless man as played by his father in his fake yet traumatic childhood memories. Additional goofs mount up: spotlights repeatedly fall from the sky, it only rains where Truman happens to be, stage directions are broadcast on the radio by mistake and passers-by and cars move at implausibly regular intervals along the same trajectories. The movie cleverly combines ironic humour and important truths. The pictures of Truman's life are framed by iris patterns that constantly remind us of the secret observers, the voyeuristic gaze of the hidden camera which registers Truman's every move with no less than 5000 lenses.

Luckily, however, there is a limit to this entertaining yet deeply disturbing scenario. When Truman tries to escape from his home on Seahaven Island in a sailing dinghy, he crashes into the painted horizon on the scenery wall and both audiences breathe a sigh of relief. Life as a cliché in a cliché comes to a – happy – end here in the literal sense of the word.  BR

"As a visual spectacle, *The Thin Red Line* meets the expec-tations raised by *Badlands* and *Days of Heaven*. There's no question that Malick's ability to lend depth and texture to his images is without rival in Hollywood at the moment."

*Sight and Sound*

"As a visual spectacle, *The Thin Red Line* meets the expectations raised by *Badlands* and *Days of Heaven*. There's no question that Malick's ability to lend depth and texture to his images is without rival in Hollywood at the moment."

*Sight and Sound*

# War and Creation

The main part of the movie shows how the American soldiers try to conquer a hill occupied by the Japanese. The soldiers lose themselves in the waving grass of the hill: bent double, the scouts sneak forward through waist-high vegetation, half-crawling, half-running. The other soldiers watch anxiously and tensely. Shots ring out like whip-cracks in the silence. The fallen soldiers disappear into the hill like stones dropped in a pond; the hill remains as still and seemingly untouched as before. When the weapons fall silent for a moment, nothing can be heard but the soft rustling of the wind as it blows through the blades of grass, forming a constant acoustic accompaniment to the attack. Then all hell breaks loose in a maelstrom of rockets, machine guns, grenades, shots, explosions and shouts. In the midst of this commotion, a soldier trips over a snake in the grass. For a split second the battle fades into the background and nature penetrates our consciousness with all her power. Again and again the movie turns away from the immediate threat

in moments of danger or tension and shows colourful exotic birds, gnarled logs or the tropical tree tops with the sun shining brightly through them.

Malick contrasts the majesty of nature with the corruption of war and its culture of destruction. These diversions are not self-indulgently picturesque or irrelevant animal images, they serve to sharpen our eyes for the contrast between nature and culture and therefore also for war. There are unforgettable images, the like of which is rarely seen in other war movies, like a dying bird hit by a bullet, writhing in agony, or a native striding past a jungle patrol, who shows no sign of having seen the soldiers. Another soldier stares fascinated at a bizarrely-shaped leaf in the midst of the battle while his comrades die around him.

Unlike Steven Spielberg's *Saving Private Ryan* (1998), which was made at more or less the same time, the viewer is never told exactly why or for what the soldiers are fighting. The actors go through the movie seemingly without an aim or motivation. They retreat into the background for half an hour or so or leave the picture completely, then unexpectedly reappear. This makes them a symbol of the expendability of soldiers in war. It is therefore

1 Battle plans during a temporary lull: First Sergeant Welsh (Sean Penn), Colonel Tall (Nick Nolte) and Captain Staros (Elias Koteas).

2 Mail from home: Bell (Ben Chaplin) misses his wife, who eventually leaves him for an Air Force Captain.

3 Captain Staros, of Greek origin, refuses to send his men into a battle they have no hope of winning, bringing great trouble upon himself.

4 Staring the high casualty rate in eye. The natural surroundings so prominent in the film remain unmoved by the war.

5 An innocent paradise? Two blueprints for civilisation collide on a Pacific island (Jim Caviezel, right).

5

**TERRENCE MALICK**    When Terrence Malick finished *Days of Heaven* in 1978, two years had passed since the end of filming. Through endless fights with the producers and Richard Gere, the movie's leading actor, the stubborn and self-willed Malick stuck to his vision. *Days* was a jealousy drama among harvesters in Texas set during World War One, and it followed his debut movie *Badlands* (1973) in which a young criminal couple flees through the deserted landscapes of Dakota and Montana. Terrence Malick, the son of an oil magnate from the south of the US, studied at Harvard and worked as a journalist for the *New Yorker* and other papers. After his first two movies, Malick moved to Paris in the 80s and 90s and made his living as an uncredited scriptwriter, before returning to the Hollywood limelight after an absence of 20 years.

# "Death appears in the endless sea of green like an episode in Nature's never-ending drama." *Die Zeit*

6  Facing death: Keck (Woody Harrelson) has accidentally pulled the pin from a hand grenade.

7  Commander Tall wants to capture the hill at any price.

8  Keck and Welsh still find something to laugh about.

all the more surprising that famous stars agreed to be treated this way; however, as with Woody Allen or Stanley Kubrick, working with Malick is a distinction for which many actors are prepared to waive their usual conditions.

John Travolta appears at the beginning of the movie for three brief minutes as a brigadier general who does little other than cast meaningful glances out to sea, and George Clooney appears in an even shorter scene at the end of the movie in a pastiche of the patriarchal "family man" who talks down to his soldiers as though they were children. Scenes filmed with Lukas Haas and Bill Pullman were later cut and the role planned for Gary Oldman never materialised.

At the end of the movie the survivors return on a battleship and we see new recruits arrive on the island. The movie may be over, but the war goes on.

Malick once again confirmed his place as a leading outsider in Hollywood with *The Thin Red Line*. By mixing chaotic images of war with sublime pictures of the natural world, he shows the ambivalence of human nature. The movie claims the right to ask questions which go beyond visible reality. Who are we, if we are capable of such utter madness, while still being able to appreciate and experience the beauties of nature?

MH

# THE BIG LEBOWSKI

1998 - USA - 113 MIN. - COMEDY

DIRECTOR JOEL COEN (*1954)
SCREENPLAY JOEL COEN, ETHAN COEN DIRECTOR OF PHOTOGRAPHY ROGER DEAKINS MUSIC CARTER BURWELL, T-BONE BURNETT
PRODUCTION ETHAN COEN for WORKING TITLE PRODUCTIONS.

STARRING JEFF BRIDGES (Jeffrey "The Dude" Lebowski), JOHN GOODMAN (Walter Sobchak), JULIANNE MOORE
(Maude Lebowski), STEVE BUSCEMI (Donny), DAVID HUDDLESTON (The Big Lebowski), PETER STORMARE (Nihilist no.1),
FLEA (Nihilist no. 2), TORSTEN VOGES (Nihilist no. 3), PHILIP SEYMOUR HOFFMAN (Brandt), JOHN TURTURRO (Jesus
Quintana), SAM ELLIOTT (The Stranger), BEN GAZZARA (Jackie Treehorn).

## "Quite possibly the laziest man in Los Angeles County ... which would place him high in the runnin' for laziest worldwide."

Woe betide anyone who calls him Mr Lebowski. "I'm the Dude", he insists, "so that's what you call me. That, or Duder. His Dudeness. Or El Duderino." A hairy old hippy whose nourishment consists entirely of White Russian cocktails, likes to smoke his joints in the bathtub and listens to whale calls at great length.

It's 1991. The Gulf War rages at the other end of the world, but the Dude (Jeff Bridges) is still floating in the serene intoxication of the psychedelic 70s. The centre of his life is the bowling alley where he meets his friends Walter (John Goodman) and Donny (Steve Buscemi) to prepare for the next tournament, although even there his main aim is to move as little as possible. However, these leisurely days come to an abrupt halt when some debt collectors confuse the Dude with a millionaire of the same name from Pasadena and pee on his beautiful Persian carpet as a warning. The Big Lebowski is Joel and Ethan Coen's third movie about kidnapping, following Raising Arizona (1987) and Fargo (1996); their weakness for this particular plot mechanism is because "everything can go so very wrong". Accordingly,

the Dude's life runs completely out of control when Bunny, the wife of the other Lebowski, is kidnapped. After the Dude and his bad-tempered friend, Vietnam veteran Walter, have messed up handing over the money, they suddenly find themselves involved in an absolutely impenetrable tangle of interests and are threatened by a legendary porn producer, the police and a trio of German nihilists.

Unmistakably a Coen movie, this hash-fuelled comedy is filled with quotations, hints and post-modern mannerisms. The Big Lebowski begins like a parody of the standard Western and develops into a gloriously laconic and ironic homage to the classics of hard-boiled literature. It may be a disinterested day dreamer who lopes through Los Angeles instead of a cool, hardened private detective, but the plot is just as confused as Raymond Chandler's The Big Sleep where even Philip Marlowe's creator couldn't say for sure who shot the chauffeur. At the end of The Big Lebowski nobody knows exactly what's going on, nor how the events hang together – least of all the Dude himself. The Coens are only superficially interested in estab-

lishing the logical reconstruction of a crime, they are much more interested in indulging their weakness for bizarre characters, crazy situations and sophisticated bluffs. Aspects of the movie are even reminiscent of the great musicals of the 30s, and one of its highlights is a flashy musical sequence that seems to have been choreographed by Busby Berkeley on acid. Under pressure from all sides, the happy hash dreams of the Dude give way to fearful fantasies where he ends up in a porn film being made by one of his enemies. With its characteristic top shots, the long legs of the glamour girls and its symmetrical choreography, his dream production (called "Gutterballs") looks like a down-market version of a famous Warner Bros musical from the 30s. But fear creeps into the glittering arrangement of paste jewels and feathers, Saddam Hussein grins slyly in front of a shelf of bowling shoes and the German nihilists in flaming red catsuits brandish enormous scissors and threaten to remove Lebowski's "Johnson". Apparently, according to the Coen brothers, the figure of the Dude is based on an uncle of theirs – although who knows if they're to be trusted!

AK

# "The Coens have an incredible sense for the crazy spirit of the contemporary age. They can't fall short of their surreal standard, and *The Big Lebowski* casts a glimmer of nightmare comedy on life." *Neue Zürcher Zeitung*

1   "The Dude" Lebowski (Jeff Bridges): one man and his drink. A White Russian is a mixture of vodka, kahlua and cream.

2   "You said it, man. Nobody fucks with the Jesús!" – The most uptight challenger of the threesome is Jesús Quintana (John Turturro), a macho Latino dressed head to toe in purple.

3   "Losers like the Dude like hanging out at bowling alleys best. Bowling is a comfortable sport where you don't have to worry about keeping fit. We were also attracted by the design with the retro fifties and sixties feel to it." *Joel Coen*

4

5

4   When Jesús makes fun of him yet again, Walter (John Goodman) flips and pulls a gun on him. The Dude tries to calm him down, *"This is not Nam. This is bowling."*

5   Julianne Moore as the devious Maude Lebowski.

6   After his exaggerated role as the *kinda funny looking* kidnapper in *Fargo* (1996), Coen regular Steve Buscemi played Lebowski's withdrawn, almost melancholy buddy Donny.

6

# BUENA VISTA SOCIAL CLUB

1998/1999 - GERMANY/USA/FRANCE/CUBA - 105 MIN. - MUSIC FILM, DOCUMENTARY

DIRECTOR WIM WENDERS (*1945)
SCREENPLAY WIM WENDERS DIRECTOR OF PHOTOGRAPHY ROBBY MÜLLER, JÖRG WIDMER, LISA RINZLER MUSIC RY COODER, BUENA VISTA SOCIAL CLUB PRODUCTION ULRICH FELSBERG, DEEPAK NAYAR for ROAD MOVIES, KINTOP PICTURES, ARTE, ICAIC.

STARRING IBRAHIM FERRER, RUBÉN GONZÁLES, ELIADES OCHOA, OMARA PORTUONDO, COMPAY SEGUNDO, PIO LEYVA, MANUEL "PUNTILLITA" LICEA, ORLANDO "CACHAÍTO" LÓPEZ, RY COODER, JOACHIM COODER.

## "It's good not to have to pass the hat round anymore, but you don't forget."

Right at the beginning of the movie, we see pictures of Castro in front of the Lincoln Memorial in Washington. "David and Goliath" is the photographer's dry comment. It would be wrong however to expect *Buena Vista Social Club*, the film version of the album recorded by Ry Cooder with legendary Cuban Son musicians, to be a political movie. If the musicians portrayed are not at all concerned with material possessions, that is not because of their socialist convictions, but rather because there is only one meaning to their lives: music.

The movie came about through a series of coincidences. Producer Nick Gold and guitarist Ry Cooder had planned to record an album with African and Cuban musicians in the mid-90s, but when they arrived in Havana for the recording they found that the Africans were stuck in Paris. Since they were already in Cuba, they looked round for alternatives and got hold of numerous old Son legends. Cooder named the demo tape of this session after the legendary "Buena Vista" dance club of the 40s and 50s, and gave it to his old friend Wim Wenders. Cooder had previously written the music for two Wenders movies, *Paris, Texas* (1984) and *The End of Violence* (1997). Before the actual boom took off, Wenders accompanied Cooder to Cuba on a trip to record Ibrahim Ferrer's solo album and also filmed the only concerts the Buena Vista Social Club performed together, in the Carré Theatre in Amsterdam and New York's Carnegie Hall.

The Buena Vista Social Club ensemble did not exist before its one and only album and after these concerts, it will in all probability cease to exist. The musicians of the all-star project of popular Cuban music of past decades already knew each other well, but it was the first time they had played together in this combination. Most of them already had successful solo careers. We get to know and love many of them in the movie: the die-hard philanderer Compay Segundo, who at 90 has fathered five children and, as

3

1 Ry Cooder and his son Joachim (in the back-ground) got the Buena Vista Social Club musicians together and set the ball rolling for one of the most astounding success stories in all Cuban music.

2 A line-up of old men: the Buena Vista Social Club takes the audience's applause.

3 Guitarist Eliades Ochoa accompanies Omara Portuondo singing "Dos Gardenias para ti", her duet with Ibrahim Ferrer.

4 A triumphal reception in the heart of the USA: standing ovations from the New York audience in Carnegie Hall.

5 Director Wim Wenders described the dilapidated charm of Havanna as a "submerged city of the future".

**CONCERT MOVIES** The US film maker D.A. Pennebaker is a veteran of music documentary films, having begun with the movie *Don't Look Back* about Bob Dylan's 1965 England tour. Two years later, he filmed a predecessor of the legendary Woodstock concert, *Monterey Pop*, for posterity. The years that fol-lowed saw what are perhaps still the best-know "rockumentaries" ever: *Woodstock* (1969, Michael Wadleigh), which branded the event onto the collective memory and *Gimme Shelter* (1971, David & Albert Maysles) about a Rolling Stones concert where Hell's Angels acting as stewards kill a black man right in front of the stage. Various other film auteurs have also tried their hand at the genre, for example Jean-Luc Godard in *One Plus One* (1968), also about the Rolling Stones, and Martin Scorsese's *The Band* (1978), while projects such as *U2 – Rattle and Hum* (1988) or *In Bed with Madonna* (1991) show the music industry's increasing commercialisation.

he says with a grin, is currently working on the sixth; the gifted pianist Rubén Gonzáles who for ten years did not even possess a piano and claimed he could no longer play, the amazing Ibrahim Ferrer, who had promised himself never to sing again, and the *grande dame* Omara Portuondo. Almost completely forgotten, most of the one-time music stars of Son and Bolero of the 40s, 50s and 60s were eking out a miserable existence in Havana.

Many little things remain unforgettable – Ferrer surreptitiously wiping tears of emotion from Portuondo's eyes during their concert duet; Portuondo striding through the streets of Havana, shot by Wenders in nostalgic pastel tones and filmed with all the charm of decay. She waves to some women who join in her song. The Cubans give a triumphant concert at the Carnegie Hall, stronghold of US music, and then wander through New York wondering at many things that we have long taken for granted. Gonzáles accompanies children's gymnastics and exercises in an old dance hall, and gradually draws them around his piano in a clumsy dance.

House walls display slogans like "The revolution will last for ever", but the musicians seem to have little interest in that. The audience in New York presents them with a Cuban flag at the end of their concert and they gather around it. However, even in the anti-Cuban United States, this doesn't resemble a political gesture so much as a symbol of belated recognition for these captivating performers and their beautiful music.

MH

"I came to Havana, because I wanted to let these musicians speak for themselves, since their music speaks so powerfully for itself."

*Wim Wenders in: Sight and Sound*

# THERE'S SOMETHING ABOUT MARY

1998 - USA - 119 MIN. - COMEDY

**DIRECTOR** PETER FARRELLY (*1957), BOBBY FARRELLY (*1958)
**SCREENPLAY** ED DECTER, JOHN J. STRAUSS, PETER FARRELLY, BOBBY FARRELLY **DIRECTOR OF PHOTOGRAPHY** MARK IRWIN
**MUSIC** JONATHAN RICHMAN **PRODUCTION** FRANK BEDDOR, MICHAEL STEINBERG, CHARLES B. WESSLER, BRADLEY
THOMAS for 20TH CENTURY FOX.

**STARRING** CAMERON DIAZ (Mary Jensen Matthews), MATT DILLON (Pat Healy), BEN STILLER (Ted Stroehman), LEE EVANS
(Tucker), CHRIS ELLIOTT (Dom Woganowski), LIN SHAYE (Magda), JEFFREY TAMBOR (Sully), MARKIE POST (Mary's
mother), KEITH DAVID (Mary's father), W. EARL BROWN (Warren Jensen).

## "Husband ... negative. Children and a Labrador ... negative. Tight little package ... affirmative."

How about this for a nightmare experience: you pick up your dream girl for the school prom, first you get beaten up by her little brother and then you get a body part so sensitive caught in your zip in her family bathroom that half of the town arrives to witness the rescue attempts by the police and the fire brigade. Perhaps this hasn't actually happened to many people, but generations have dreaded of this or similar disasters on their first date.

The Farrelly brothers have a passion for everyday visions of horror. They take the underside of the everyday life of moderately intelligent small town inhabitants with an average number of complexes, and then take them to extremes. They don't really care much whether their assortment of coarse, dirty jokes and grotesquely embarrassing situations is bearable for less hardened viewers or not.

*Dumb & Dumber* (1994) sounded the depths of absolute stupidity and *King Pin* (1996) dared to investigate the seedy world of American professional bowling, a world of sweaty feet and damp hotel beds. In *There's Something About Mary* the Farrellys decided to try their hand at a love story. With inevitable results: painful fishing accidents, spunk as hair gel, burning ears, gross jokes about gynaecology and the disabled — let's face it, not

everyone will share the Farrellys' view of romance. But in the end, and this is what *Something About Mary* brings home with a vengeance, they do make us aware that the confused, impoverished and disadvantaged of this world have a love life too.

Ever since the memorable bathroom fiasco, Ted (Ben Stiller) hasn't been able to get Mary (Cameron Diaz) out of his head. Years later, his monstrous braces and bowl cut have gone, but he still has a despairing conviction that a woman like Mary could never be interested in a loser like him. Dom (Chris Elliott), his best friend, is full of useful advice, and he sends Ted off to see shady private detective Pat Healy (Matt Dillon), who sets off to find Mary and promptly falls in love with her himself.

When Ted discovers that Mary is by no means the wheelchair-bound enormously overweight woman with four children that Healy describes to put him off the scent, he screws up his courage and goes to Miami to the scene of the action to try and conquer Mary's heart. He soon comes to the unwelcome realization that her hordes of admirers are larger than he thought. Before the key issue of whether he gets the girl or not is resolved, the heavy hand of fate deals Ted some mighty blows, to the delight of sadistic viewers

1

2

"Peter and Bobby Farrelly are Hollywood's 'bad boys' of the moment: two cunning confidence tricksters who have found their place in mainstream cinema with a mixture of catchy material and provocative disregard for taboos."

*film-dienst*

3

4

5

1 A hair-style to the taste of the Farrelly brothers: Mary (Cameron Diaz) tries out a very unusual hair gel made from purely natural ingredients.

2 Asking for trouble: the loathsome Pat Healy (Matt Dillon) thinks he knows how to win women over and see off any annoying competition.

3 With a winning smile Ted (Ben Stiller) demonstrates his stylish but passion-killing dental adornment.

4 A little kiss for mummikins: fans of the Farrellys have to have a strong stomach.

5 Terrier in plaster: the battle over Mary leaves its mark on people and animals alike.

6 Who could resist this smile? To win the beautiful Mary as their girl, her admirers will stoop to any nastiness.

CAMERON DIAZ    Born in San Diego, California in 1972 as the daughter of a Cuban and a German American, Cameron Diaz left home at the age of 16 to travel the world. She spent the following five years in Japan, Australia, Mexico, Morocco and Paris. When she returned to the USA she worked as a model until she was given her first role in *The Mask* (1994) with Jim Carrey. Her natural, open way of acting instantly made her famous. Subsequent important movies are *Head Above Water* (1996) and *My Best Friend's Wedding* (1997).

There is no kind of silly joke or disgusting substance that the transparent plot is not prepared to feature, and it is mostly saved from banality by the unscrupulous womanisers Matt Dillon and the English stand-up comedian Lee Evans. That tricky task was carried out with great panache by Jim Carrey and Jeff Daniels in *Dumb & Dumber* and Woody Harrelson and Randy Quaid in *King Pin*. Part of the Farrellys' success is that high quality actors are always more than ready to work with them, even Cameron Diaz, who is as breathtakingly beautiful as ever. The music for the movie was composed by independent cinema icon Jonathan Richman. One rule seems to do for the production team and audience alike where the Farrelly brothers' movies are concerned: put aside your political correctness, good taste and common sense, and you will have loads of fun.                    SH

6

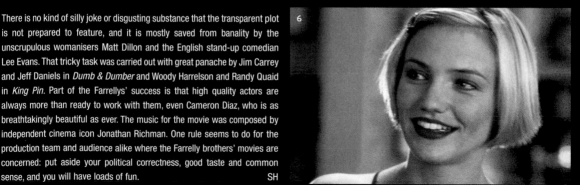

# SHAKESPEARE IN LOVE

1998 - USA - 123 MIN. - LOVE FILM, COSTUME FILM

DIRECTOR JOHN MADDEN (*1949)
SCREENPLAY MARC NORMAN, TOM STOPPARD DIRECTOR OF PHOTOGRAPHY RICHARD GREATEX MUSIC STEPHEN WARBECK PRODUCTION DAVIT PARFIT, DONNA GIGLIOTTI, HARVEY WEINSTEIN, EDWARD ZWICK, MARC NORMAN for BEDFORD FALLS PRODUCTIONS.

STARRING JOSEPH FIENNES (William Shakespeare), GWYNETH PALTROW (Viola de Lesseps), GEOFFREY RUSH (Philip Henslowe), JUDI DENCH (Queen Elizabeth), SIMON CALLOW (Tilney), BEN AFFLECK (Ned Alleyn), COLIN FIRTH (Lord Wessex), JOE ROBERTS (John Webster), TOM WILKINSON (Hugh Fennyman), RUPERT EVERETT (Christopher Marlowe).

ACADEMY AWARDS 1999 OSCARS for BEST PICTURE, BEST ACTRESS (Gwyneth Paltrow), BEST SUPPORTING ACTRESS (Judi Dench), BEST ART DIRECTION-SET DECORATION (Martin Childs, Jill Quertier), BEST ORIGINAL SCREENPLAY (Marc Norman, Tom Stoppard), BEST COSTUMES (Sandy Powell), BEST MUSIC, category COMEDY (Stephen Warbeck).

IFF BERLIN 1999 SILVER BEAR for BEST SCREENPLAY (Marc Norman, Tom Stoppard).

## "I know something of a woman in a man's profession."

Viola (Gwyneth Paltrow) loves William (Joseph Fiennes), and William loves Viola. This becomes clear relatively quickly and seems to be a good thing, but it's also where all the problems begin. For William's surname is Shakespeare, and being a writer in Elizabethan England is not a particularly respectable profession. Viola on the other hand is a member of the respectable de Lesseps family and is promised in marriage to the aristocrat Lord Wessex (Colin Firth), who may be in dire financial straits but can at least offer her a title. We understand immediately that there is going to be a conflict of interests as far as matters of the heart are concerned: but what we don't suspect are the questions of money and art.

Unfortunately, theatre owner Philip Henslowe (Geoffrey Rush) is also in dire financial straits. He is desperate for Shakespeare to finish the play he has promised Henslowe's Rose Theatre, *Romeo and Ethel – The Pirate's Daughter*, but Shakespeare is suffering from writer's block. He only overcomes it when he meets Viola, who turns up disguised as a boy – women

were not allowed to act in Shakespeare's day – to audition for the main part of Romeo. However, Lord Wessex soon gets wind of the unbecoming plans of his future wife and decides to get rid of the inconvenient and disreputable writer.

These events are mirrored in the plot of the play that Shakespeare writes during the rehearsals in the theatre. The movie's two levels are closely connected and intelligently dovetailed but never become incomprehensible, and their interaction is the driving force of the film. Art neither imitates life nor life art – the two feed off each other instead.

Against a well-researched backdrop of Elizabethan theatrical life, the plot speculates about Shakespeare's private life, which in fact remains a mystery to experts even today. The screenplay skilfully combines elements from his plays with historical fact and pure fantasy. But there's nothing dry or dusty about it, it's not only about English theatre in the 16th century but is also a radical modernisation of Shakespeare. Its authors were inspired by the

1 Writer's block, Renaissance-style: when Shakespeare (Joseph Fiennes) isn't in love, he can't write a single line.

2 All the world's a stage and we are merely players: a stage battle becomes a real skirmish.

3 Shakespeare's enigmatic object of desire: Lady Viola (Gwyneth Paltrow).

4 "Shall I compare thee to a summer's day…"

5 Always on his guard against creditors: Henslowe (Geoffrey Rush), the notorious bankrupt theatre director.

6 Gwyneth Paltrow disguised as Thomas Kent on the way to her first Oscar.

"We had 25 million dollars, not that much for a project of this size. The set was hugely expensive. We had to build not only two theatres, but also a whole district of the city from a brothel to Shakespeare's digs, behind Shepperton Studios in London." *John Madden in: Abendzeitung*

dea that if Shakespeare lived today he would be a screenplay writer and a Hollywood star, so they fill the film with comic anachronisms and quotes from other movies: Shakespeare goes to confess on the psychoanalyst's couch, Philip Henslowe is introduced in the opening sequences as a businessman with cash flow problems, and with a sharp "Follow that boat!" Shakespeare directly quotes innumerable crime movies.

Rather than allowing the movie to be dominated by opulent costumes and imagery, director John Madden gathered a first-class ensemble whose talent shines in every scene. Judi Dench may only appear in a few scenes as Queen Elizabeth, but she is all the more impressive for that. Joseph Fiennes is convincing as the bard and Gwyneth Paltrow as his muse, particularly in her breeches role. The rest of the ensemble, from Geoffrey Rush and Ben Affleck to a brief but memorable appearance from Rupert Everett as Christopher Marlowe, lend great naturalness and texture to the wonderful recreation of 1590s London.

*Shakespeare in Love* is intelligent and well-made entertainment cinema. It was rewarded with a shower of Oscars, not least because Hollywood was flattered to see the US film industry portrayed as the legitimate heir to Shakespeare's theatre.

MH

**7** A queen with a natural wit: Judi Dench as Queen Elizabeth, with scowling villain Lord Wessex (Colin Firth).

**8** Their world is the Globe Theatre, as the ill-fated love of William and Viola can only exist on stage.

**GWYNETH PALTROW**

Some found her enchanting, others insufferable: when Gwyneth Paltrow accepted an Oscar for her performance as Viola in *Shakespeare in Love*, her voice was choked with tears. Born in Los Angeles in 1972, she quickly became famous for her roles in costume movies and literature adaptations. She earned early recognition in the historical biographies *Jefferson in Paris* (1995) and *Mrs Parker and her Vicious Circle* (1994). She played the title role in the film version of Jane Austen's *Emma* (1996) which brought her to the attention of a wider public even before she won an Oscar as Shakespeare's muse. Her penchant for literary material is also apparent in the 1997 version of Charles Dickens' *Great Expectations* and in the Patricia Highsmith adaptation *The Talented Mr Ripley* (1999).

"The heterogenous mixture, a rich and satisfying pudding, works really well, (...) and changes from one mood to another with hardly any effort."

*Sight and Sound*

8

# SAVING PRIVATE RYAN

1998 - USA - 170 MIN. - WAR FILM

DIRECTOR STEVEN SPIELBERG (*1947)
SCREENPLAY ROBERT RODAT DIRECTOR OF PHOTOGRAPHY JANUSZ KAMINSKI MUSIC JOHN WILLIAMS PRODUCTION STEVEN SPIELBERG, IAN BRUCE, MARK GORDON, GARY LEVINSOHN for AMBLIN ENTERTAINMENT, DREAMWORKS SKG, MUTUAL FILM COMPANY (for PARAMOUNT).

STARRING TOM HANKS (Captain Miller), TOM SIZEMORE (Sergeant Horvath), EDWARD BURNS (Private Reiben), BARRY PEPPER (Private Jackson), ADAM GOLDBERG (Private Mellish), VIN DIESEL (Private Caparzo), GIOVANNI RIBISI (Wade), JEREMY DAVIES (Corporal Upham), MATT DAMON (Private Ryan), TED DANSON (Captain Hamill).

ACADEMY AWARDS 1999 OSCARS for BEST DIRECTOR (Steven Spielberg), BEST CINEMATOGRAPHY (Janusz Kaminski), BEST FILM EDITING (Michael Kahn), BEST SOUND (Gary Rydstrom, Gary Summers, Andy Nelson, Ronald Judkins), BEST SOUND EFFECTS EDITING (Gary Rydstrom, Richard Hymns).

## "What's the use in risking the life of the eight of us to save one guy?"

With an abrupt, muffled crack, a bullet pierces a steel helmet. Boats landing on the beach are met by salvos of machine gun fire, soldiers run into a hail of bullets. Death and blood are everywhere. One soldier is hurled into the air, his thigh is blown off, another searches for his left hand. Steven Spielberg shows D Day, the landing of the allied forces on the French Atlantic coast 6 June 1944, like something out of a horror movie that grabs the viewer with physical force. It lasts 25 almost unbearable minutes, before we cut to America, where military bureaucracy is dealing with the administration of the dead. Secretaries sit at desks and compose telegrams of condolence like a production line. Here people type, while in Europe they die. From afar the invasion is a strategic necessity, while on the beaches of Normandy, as one critic wrote, the participants experience it as a meaningless "chaos of noise, filth, blood, vomit and death". Immediately after this shocking opening, Spielberg establishes the contrast between military tactics and their practicalities, which result in nothing but undignified death.

A decision by the military leadership then introduces the actual theme of the film. During the Normandy landing three sons of the Ryan family in Iowa have died, while a fourth, James Ryan (Matt Damon), has been parachuted into France behind the German lines. To save mother Ryan from losing him as well, he must be sent home. The task of finding Ryan is given to Captain Miller (Tom Hanks), an experienced and reliable soldier, but a man badly affected by the burdens of the war as we see from his trembling hands. Together with a small group of soldiers – Mellish, a sniper (Adam Goldberg), Wade, a first aider (Giovanni Ribisi), and Upham, an interpreter who has no experience of war (Jeremy Davies) – he sets off to find Ryan. He finds him, and he and his troops take part in a battle over a strategically important bridge. Only one of them survives, the solider who we see in the framework of the movie, set in our times.

War movies are fraught with problems. Should the horrors be presented realistically or metaphorically? Should a director show the action on the battlefield or should he describe its consequences for the survivors? Spielberg chose a realistic mode for the opening and final sequences of this movie. They mirror each other, although the final sequence is not quite as ferocious. He filmed the opening sequence with 3000 extras in 30 days on the Irish coast, and the intensity that resulted may not be unique in modern cinema, but is certainly a rare thing. The camera mingles with the soldiers,

1  He hardly talks about his life back home, and his
men are not supposed to see his shaking hands.
Captain Miller (Tom Hanks) doesn't doubt the

sense of the war, but he does doubt whether he can
survive it.

2  Miller and Sergeant Horvath (Tom Sizemore, left)
have to lead their men straight towards the
German positions.

blood and filth spurt onto the lens, and the sound cuts out when we see underwater pictures of sinking corpses. The viewer is directly involved in the events and there is no option to retreat into the position of an observer.

The middle part of the movie has a more distanced narrative perspective. During his search for Ryan, Miller is busy with the arithmetic of death. He has lost 94 men, he reckons, but has saved ten or twenty times as many. A gruesome sum, but one way for the soldiers to make their daily work of death more bearable. However, another calculation seems to contradict this

logic: risking the life of eight soldiers and Miller to save one life, that of Ryan. Is that morally justifiable? Aren't they just as human as he is? Is he worth more than they are?

The movie doesn't have an answer to that question, but it does raise the issue and the characters repeatedly turn it over in their minds. And the resulting tension shows us the grisly absurdity of war perhaps more effectively than any of the realistic action scenes can.

HJK

> "I asked myself throughout, is this a mission of mercy or a mission of murder? But I can't answer the question. I don't think anyone can."
>
> *Steven Spielberg in: Time Magazine*

3  The American military cemetery where the film begins.

4  "Since the end of World War II and the virtual death of the western, the combat film has disintegrated into a showcase for swagger, cynicism, obscenely overblown violence and hollow, self-serving victories. Now, with stunning efficacy, Spielberg turns back the clock." *New York Times*

**TOM HANKS**

The *New York Times* claimed that Hanks had never put his everyman qualities to better effect than in *Saving Private Ryan*. Born in 1956, Hanks is the James Stewart of the 90s, the boy next door. Hardly any other American actor invites such a high level of audience identification, whether he plays a burned out ex-baseball player who trains a women's team, as in *A League Of Their Own* (1992) or a widowed single father in *Sleepless in Seattle* (1993). He won the hearts of many with his portrayal of AIDS suffer and lawyer in *Philadelphia* (1993) and became a prototypical American in the title role of *Forrest Gump* (1994) which takes us through three decades of American history. He played another historical role in *Apollo 13* (1995), appearing as the astronaut Jim Lovell. After Spencer Tracy in 1937 and 1938, Hanks was the first person to receive an Oscar for best actor two years running: in 1994 for *Philadelphia*, and in 1995 for *Forrest Gump*. 1996 saw his debut as a director with *That Thing You Do*, a nostalgic musical comedy.

5   Master of death: sniper Jackson (Barry Pepper) on     6   An allusion to the German film *Die Brücke* (*The*
    the lookout.                                              *Bridge*, 1959): after they have found Ryan, Miller
                                                              and his men have to defend a bridge.

"It has its place in cinema history, due to the first 25 minutes.
The picture it gives of this war is already as mythically transfig-
ured as the violent event in its entirety, just as *Gone with the
Wind* showed the numbers of wounded in the ruins of Atlanta."

*Süddeutsche Zeitung*

# THE MATRIX

1999 - USA - 136 MIN. - SCIENCE FICTION

DIRECTOR ANDY WACHOWSKI (*1967), LARRY WACHOWSKI (*1965)
SCREENPLAY ANDY WACHOWSKI, LARRY WACHOWSKI DIRECTOR OF PHOTOGRAPHY BILL POPE MUSIC DON DAVIS PRODUCTION JOEL SILVER, DAN CRACHIOLO for SILVER PRODUCTIONS.

STARRING KEANU REEVES (Neo), LAURENCE FISHBURNE (Morpheus), CARRIE ANNE MOSS (Trinity), HUGO WEAVING (Agent Smith), GLORIA FOSTER (Oracle), JOE PANTOLIANO (Cypher), MARCUS CHONG (Tank), JULIAN ARAHANGA (Apoc), MATT DORAN (Mouse), BELINDA MCCLORY (Switch).

ACADEMY AWARDS 2000 OSCARS for BEST FILM EDITING (Zach Staenberg), BEST SOUND EFFECTS EDITING (Dane A. Davis), BEST VISUAL EFFECTS (Steve Courtley, John Gaeta, Janek Sirrs, Jon Thum), BEST SOUND (David E. Campbell, David Lee, John T. Reitz, Gregg Rudloff).

## "The Matrix is the world that has been pulled over your eyes to blind you from the truth."

A Cinderella story in a technological Wonderland: Thomas Anderson (Keanu Reeves) spends his days in a tiny office at a computer firm, doing his best to avoid working. At night, using the pseudonym "Neo", he hacks his way through the international data network. His boss's threats to kick him out are as much a part of the daily routine as dealing in illegal diskettes, which he keeps hidden inside a book titled *Simulacra and Simulation* – an early reference to the central theme of the film, which is the rift between reality and perception. Somewhere out in cyberspace Morpheus (Laurence Fishburne) is waiting for him, believing him to be the Saviour, but Neo has not yet heard his call.

That call is a call to revolution, and for liberation from the machines. Morpheus is the leader of a rebellion whose sole aim is to free mankind from its undeserved bondage. In *The Matrix*, the human race has been enslaved by the artificial intelligence of its electronic apparatus, which derives its energy from human cells. People are lined up in endless rows, like units in a power station, and while their bodies are trapped in this giant battery, their minds roam free in a computer-generated parallel universe. This prison that gives the illusion of freedom is the matrix of the title, and it has all the appearance of reality.

The movie initially inspired controversy on account of its cross-cultural plundering, but critics were united in the opinion that *The Matrix* would set stylistic trends. Techno discos, crumbling Victorian houses, abandoned subway stations, and wastelands of social housing – images of global turbo-capitalism alternating with pictures of post-industrial decay present a portrait of the post-modern world. *The Matrix* marks the spot where late capitalism tips over into the new economy, where the oversized production grounds of mono-industry make way for the revolutionary cells of the new market. In that new economy questions like the limits of our knowledge become increasingly pressing, and it is questions like those that are raised by *The Matrix*, with giddy twists and disorienting turns. Our world is revealed to be a façade and the real world looks more like the hippest and coolest music videos of the nineties. The monopoly on the interpretation of reality no longer belongs to the person who has the strongest arguments or the best evidence, it belongs instead to the person who's most good-looking. Style is

"Our main aim in *The Matrix* was to shoot an intellectual action movie. We like action movies, guns and Kung Fu, so we'd had enough of watching mass-produced action movies that didn't have any kind of intellectual content. We were determined to put as many ideas as possible into the film." *Larry Wachowski in: American Cinematographer*

1  Trinity (Carrie Anne Moss) and the other rebels can only escape the illusory world of the Matrix using telephone lines.

2  Neo (Keanu Reeves) is the chosen one, who will inform the world about all the computer-generated scenery, that at least is the claim made by…

3  … Morpheus (Laurence Fishburne), leader of the rebels in the fight against the Agents.

reality and truth says the film, its greenish tint an imitation of the screen colour of early computer monitors.

In Ovid's *Metamorphoses*, Morpheus is the son of Sleep, and the god of dreams. "Neo" is the Greek prefix for "new". Trinity (Carrie Ann Moss), the third protagonist, completes this pop-culture three-in-one as the Holy Spirit. In practically every scene and dialogue, *The Matrix* delights in pointing out parallels between ancient mythology and modern pop culture, piling up quotations from other films on top of references to philosophical disputes before pulling them apart in the scenes that follow. Accusing this movie of not being serious is like expecting pop music to follow the rules of mathematical logic. The scene with the Oracle is especially brilliant: the Oracle is an old woman who bakes cookies and spouts platitudes, but her prophecies turn out to be true in the end. *The Matrix* makes ingenious use of anything that can serve as a stone in its mosaic: the world is a mine of these stones for our imagination.

MH

"On the visual front, it's been such a success that most sub-sequent action films include a passing genuflection to *The Matrix*. Which probably defines the genius of the Wachowski brothers: by sheer ingenuity in making new from old, they've become a point of reference." *Télérama*

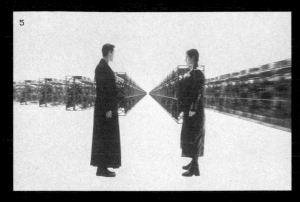

5

6

4  In skin-tight black leather, angel of death Trinity fights an Agent.

5  Computer batteries generate the illusion of the world that we live in.

6  Next summer's fashion: *The Matrix* not only set standards in the domain of special effects, but even created a "look" which was taken up by films and music videos.

7  The rebel base is located on a neo-noir version of the legendary Nautilus submarine, which cruises through the interior of the Matrix.

7

# "The Wachowskis clearly designed *The Matrix* as a comic-book, before it became a screen-play, and many decisions taken 'because it's cooler' disregard the discipline that you would expect of a literary film."

*Sight and Sound*

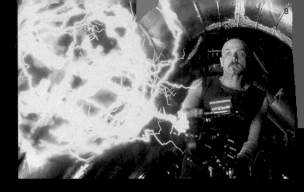

**ANIMATION TECHNOLOGY** The Wachowski Brothers are great fans of Anime (Japanese comics and animated films) and of action films from Hong Kong, both of which left their mark on the special effects in *The Matrix*, elevating it above run-of-the-mill Hollywood films where effects are confined to rapid cutting and a small number of explosions. The brothers managed to persuade Hong Kong kung-fu film veteran Yuen Woo-Ping to design the elaborate choreography, before Yuen went on to give a further demonstration of his talents in Ang Lee's *Crouching Tiger, Hidden Dragon* (2000). Specialist John Gaeta was brought in for the computer-animation. Rather than fast editing and simulation, dozens of cameras were placed in a circle around Keanu Reeves and the film was shot simultaneously by all of them in extreme slow motion. This meant that the actor could then be frozen in one position and a camera shot simulated all the way around him.

8   Burn, baby, burn: mutiny on the rebels' ship.

9   Mind triumphing over matter: Neo and Smith (Hugo Weaving) defy the laws of gravity with perfect balance.

1O   Morpheus and Agent Smith both await sequels, which have already been shot and are scheduled to reach cinemas in 2002

# ALL ABOUT MY MOTHER

## Todo sobre mi madre

999 - SPAIN / FRANCE - 101 MIN. - MELODRAMA

DIRECTOR PEDRO ALMODÓVAR (*1951)

SCREENPLAY PEDRO ALMODÓVAR DIRECTOR OF PHOTOGRAPHY AFFONSO BEATO MUSIC ALBERTO IGLESIAS PRODUCTION AGUSTIN ALMODÓVAR, CLAUDE BERRI for EL DESEO, RENN PRODUCTIONS, FRANCE 2 CINÉMA.

STARRING CECILIA ROTH (Manuela), ELOY AZORÍN (Estéban), MARISA PAREDES (Huma Rojo), PENÉLOPE CRUZ (Sister Rosa), ANTONIA SAN JUAN (Agrado), CANDELA PEÑA (Nina), ROSA MARÍA SARDÀ (Rosa's mother), FERNANDO FERNÁN GÓMEZ (Rosa's father), TONI CANTÓ (Lola), CARLOS LOZANO (Mario).

IFF CANNES 1999 SILVER PALM for BEST DIRECTOR (Pedro Almodóvar).

ACADEMY AWARDS 2000 OSCAR for BEST FOREIGN LANGUAGE FILM.

## "The only genuine thing about me is my feelings."

The loss of a child is the worst thing that can happen to a mother. Manuela (Cecilia Roth) never mentioned the child's father, even when asked, but now that she is completely on her own she continues her son's search for his other parent. Bowed by suffering and yet filled with strength she is driven back deep into her own past, and she travels from Madrid to Barcelona, from her present existence back to an earlier one. The people she meets on this journey to the end of the night generally only appear on our screens as the bad crowd in television crime series, as pathetic informers or more likely as corpses. Here, transsexuals and junkie prostitutes, pregnant nuns and touchy divas are not only the main characters, but with all their failings and weaknesses, they also win our sympathy.

In her search for comfort, Manuela eventually finds the father of her dead son Estéban (Eloy Azorín), and he has now become a dark angel of death, a terminally ill transsexual who earns his living as a prostitute. Eighteen years ago when they were a couple he was also called Estéban, but now (s)he calls herself Lola (Toni Cantó). Although (s)he was once attractive, those days are long gone: Estéban the First no longer exists and Lola is not long for this world either. Nevertheless, at the end of the movie a third Estéban is born, giving us a utopian hope against all the odds.

The audience shares Manuela's perspective and the Spanish director guides us skilfully through the glittering microcosm of Barcelona's transsex-

ual scene. Almodóvar however has no intention of giving us a documentary; he does not claim to portray objective reality in an authentic manner, and neither is it his intention to teach us a lesson in pity. Instead he takes all the expressive means at the disposal of a melodrama to their extreme: tears, blood, blows, violence, fucking, birth, love, hate, life and death. The plot may sound unlikely, but nothing seems artificial or false and that is the true miracle of this movie, an effect due in no small part to its fantastic actresses.

They all play actresses in the movie as well: Manuela does role plays with hospital employees to teach them how to deal with the families of deceased patients, and when Nina (Candela Peña), partner of the theatre diva Huma (Marisa Paredes) can't go on stage because she's too doped up, Manuela takes her place. The faithful companion Agrado (Antonia San Juan) is perhaps the greatest actress in the true sense of the word; her body has been operated on innumerable times until it is nothing but artificial illusion. One of the best scenes is where she has to announce the cancellation of a play but manages to whip up the disappointed audience into storms of enthusiasm with an autobiographic monologue. This movie about mothers is also dedicated to all actresses who have ever played actresses.

At their best Almodóvar's men are senile like the father (Fernando Fernán Gómez) of AIDS sufferer Rosa (Penélope Cruz), but for the most part men are conspicuous by their absence. However, even in his short appear-

1 Women in the mirror: Marisa Paredes (with lip-pencil) and Cecilia Roth.

2 Three women, three different stories: Manuela (Cecilia Roth, left), whose son died, and Rosa (Penélope Cruz, right), whose son provides a glim-

mer of hope at the end of the film, on either side of Rosa's mother (Rosa María Sardà).

3 The actress Huma Rojo (Marisa Paredes), larger than life, looks through the railings at her fan Estéban (Eloy Azorín), who is soon to die.

4 Penélope Cruz, *shooting star* of Spanish cinema, finds herself on the road to Hollywood.

5 It's the "End of the line for desire" not only for the dreams of Almodóvar's heroines, but also as a play in the film.

ances the double father Estéban/Lola – who is in theory the villain of the piece – is given a dignity which no other character acquires in the course of the whole movie. Almodóvar respects every single human emotion, however bizarre his characters might appear. "The only genuine thing about me is my feelings," says Agrado, the faithful transsexual girlfriend in *All About My Mother*. This also applies to Almodóvar's movie, where feelings always remain genuine despite the visual artistry. And that's more than can be said of most films. MH

## " *All About My Mother* is all about art, women, people, life, and death, and must be one of the most intense films I've ever made."
*Pedro Almodóvar in: Cahiers du cinéma*

**PEDRO ALMODÓVAR**  In the 1980s Almodóvar was hailed as an icon of Spain's gay subculture and was a welcome guest at international festivals. His biting satire ensured that midnight showings of his films were invariably sold out and eventually he became a great figure of European art cinema. In the 90s he was awarded all of cinema's most important prizes and came to be considered one of the most important contemporary filmmakers. He started off being provocative for the sake of it, but gradually he has given his figures depth and complexity whilst still taking a critical look at conventional bourgeois family life and sexual morals. Nowadays Almodóvar is seen as part of the great tragicomic tradition alongside directors such as Fassbinder or Buñuel.

# EYES WIDE SHUT

1999 - USA - 159 MIN. - DRAMA, LITERATURE ADAPTATION

**DIRECTOR** STANLEY KUBRICK (*1928, † 1999)
**SCREENPLAY** STANLEY KUBRICK, FREDERIC RAPHAEL, based on Arthur Schnitzler's *Dream Story* (*Traumnovelle*)
**DIRECTOR OF PHOTOGRAPHY** LARRY SMITH **MUSIC** JOCELYN POOK, GYÖRGY LIGETI, DMITRI SHOSTAKOVICH, CHRIS ISAAK
**PRODUCTION** STANLEY KUBRICK, JAN HARLAN for POLE STAR, HOBBY FILMS (for WARNER BROS.).

**STARRING** TOM CRUISE (Dr William Harford), NICOLE KIDMAN (Alice Harford), MADISON EGINTON (Helena Harford), JACKIE SAWIRIS (Roz), SYDNEY POLLACK (Viktor Ziegler), SKY DUMONT (Sandor Szavost), MARIE RICHARDSON (Marion), TODD FIELD (Nick Nightingale), RADE SERBEDZIJA (Milich), LEELEE SOBIESKI (Milich's daughter).

## "May I ask why a beautiful woman who could have any man in this room wants to be married?"

Traditionally, Hollywood is only interested in marriage insofar as the customary kiss at the end of the movie provides the obligatory happy ending and hints at a future wedding, whose preparation has filled the preceding two hours. The marriage takes place during and after the credits and Hollywood remains in a state of infantile bachelordom. In mainstream films, married couples seldom appear in prominent roles; in Stanley Kubrick's *Eyes Wide Shut* by contrast, sexuality, faithfulness and desire inside marriage are the main themes.

*Eyes Wide Shut* is admittedly not a Hollywood film in any conventional sense. It was made in England, but as Tom Cruise and Nicole Kidman played the main roles, the film qualified automatically for the premiere multiplex league. They play what they were real life, at least at the time the movie was made: a married couple. Bill Harford is a doctor, his wife Alice paints. Unambiguous advances are made to both of them – separately – at a party they go to together. Although they reject them, the possibility of unfaithfulness sparks off a crisis in their marriage.

Driven by his wife's confessions of her sexual fantasies about another man, Bill sets off aimlessly into the night and into the abyss of his subcon-

scious. His wanderings are punctuated by black and white images of Alice's imagined night of passion with a naval officer – or are we seeing her memories? Bill's sexual odyssey spins him around in a whirl of desirable women who for one reason or another are all forbidden: the daughter of a patient who has just died, a prostitute, the underage daughter of the owner of a costume shop and the masked, naked beauty he met at an orgy that he should not have attended.

The model for *Eyes Wide Shut* is Arthur Schnitzler's *Dream Story*, which is set in Vienna at the turn of the 19th century. The movie is set in contemporary New York. It isn't a literature adaptation in the conventional sense, but an experiment that follows Schnitzler's model for long stretches and then deviates at important points. There was much critical debate about whether enough of the bourgeois ideal of marriage has survived the last hundred years to make Schnitzler's Freudian investigation of married morals still relevant today. Kubrick's opponents accused him of having an antiquated concept of society and morality, whereas others considered his movie a successful modernisation, particularly as today's sexual behaviour is still relatively conservative in spite of the sexual revolution.

2

1   In spite of the length of time taken to shoot *Eyes Wide Shut* Nicole Kidman and Tom Cruise were prepared to accept pay cheques way below their usual income.

2   The portrayal of marital sexuality is a rarity in Hollywood.

3   The Harfords' marital crisis forces William, a successful doctor working on the Upper East Side, to take a long painful look inside himself.

4   Nicole Kidman was highly regarded as an actress well before her marriage to Cruise.

**STANLEY KUBRICK**   Many English have moved to America and live and work in Hollywood, but there are very few American filmmakers who have settled in England. Stanley Kubrick was an exception. Following his experiences of the Hollywood system (*Spartacus*, 1959/1960) this doctor's son from New York moved to England. His largely independent productions in England showed his mastery of various genres and won him complete freedom and control over all the aspects of his movies, for example *Dr Strangelove* (1964), *2001: A Space Odyssey* (1968) and *A Clockwork Orange* (1971). Kubrick became a living legend, and withdrew from the public eye whilst continuing to make films at longer and longer intervals: *Barry Lyndon* (1975), *The Shining* (1980), *Full Metal Jacket* (1987) and his legacy *Eyes Wide Shut*.

Many legends surround the story of the movie's production: instead of the nine months originally planned, Kubrick filmed in complete secrecy for 19 months in a studio near London. Stars such as Harvey Keitel and Jennifer Jason Leigh were swapped around and edited out, during or even after the filming. In the orgy scene, which is a cross between a Venetian carnival and a Baroque inquisition in Moorish halls, digital figures and objects were added in the US to obscure the audience's view of the proceedings to prevent the movie from ending up on the porn shelves in video shops. When Kubrick, control freak and grand master of PR, died a week after the film was finished, it was even claimed that his death was his ultimate, best-ever public-

Even if Bill defends monogamy with rational arguments in his discussions with Alice, his behaviour betrays his forbidden desires. At what point does secret sexual desire break the vow of married faithfulness and where do reality and dreams converge? Paradoxically, the marriage partner is both beloved subject and desired object: Alice's self-confidence and freely admitted desire is as much a witness to the insufficiency of language as Bill's weak attempts to justify his behaviour. Both are attracted to outsiders, but in the final instance, they remain faithful to each other.

MH

"If a scene basically consists of acting, and the feelings of the actors show ninety percent of what you want to say, then you have to do everything you can so that the actors achieve this result." *Stanley Kubrick in: Positif*

3

4

5  William Harford roams through Manhattan by
   night, a driven man – and "lucky", as the newspa-
   per proclaims, he certainly is not.

6  Not long after *Eyes Wide Shut* was completed the
   press announced the separation of Cruise and
   Kidman after more than ten years – half an eterni-
   ty for Hollywood.

7  For a long while Cruise, born in New York state in
   1962, was considered to be a good-looking boy
   with no acting talent – but roles in *Eyes Wide Shut*
   and *Magnolia* (1999) won many critics over to his
   side.

8  Director Sydney Pollack played the part of roué
   Viktor Ziegler for his colleague and friend Kubrick.

"There are many questions left unanswered in *Eyes Wide Shut*. However, these are questions that viewers themselves can answer. Everything is there."

*Kubrick's brother-in-law Jan Harlan in:*
*Stanley Kubrick. The Director as Architect*

# AMERICAN BEAUTY

1999 - USA - 121 MIN. - DRAMA

DIRECTOR SAM MENDES (*1965)

SCREENPLAY ALAN BALL DIRECTOR OF PHOTOGRAPHY CONRAD L. HALL MUSIC THOMAS NEWMAN PRODUCTION BRUCE COHEN, DAN JINKS for DREAMWORKS SKG, JINKS/COHEN COMPANY.

STARRING KEVIN SPACEY (Lester Burnham), ANNETTE BENING (Carolyn Burnham), THORA BIRCH (Jane Burnham), WES BENTLEY (Ricky Fitts), MENA SUVARI (Angela Hayes), PETER GALLAGHER (Buddy Kane), CHRIS COOPER (Colonel Frank Fitts), ALLISON JANNEY (Barbara Fitts), SCOTT BAKULA (Jim Olmeyer), SAM ROBARDS (Jim "JB" Berkley).

ACADEMY AWARDS 2000 OSCARS for BEST PICTURE, BEST ACTOR (Kevin Spacey), BEST CINEMATOGRAPHY (Conrad L. Hall), BEST DIRECTOR (Sam Mendes), and BEST ORIGINAL SCREENPLAY (Alan Ball).

## "You have no idea what I'm talking about, I'm sure. But don't worry, you will someday."

In one year's time Lester Burnham (Kevin Spacey) will be dead: that much we learn right at the beginning of the movie. And he already knows this himself, for he's the one who tells his own story. A dead man speaks to us from off screen, and the strangest thing about it is his amused detachment. With a sweeping movement making the off-screen narration seem like a message of salvation, the camera moves down on the world from above and closes in on the dismal suburban street where Lester lives. We are introduced to the situation in which he finds himself: his marriage to Carolyn (Annette Bening) is over, and she considers him a failure, while his daughter Jane (Thora Birch) hates him for not being a role model. The only highpoint of Lester's sad daily routine is masturbating under the shower in the morning while his wife gathers roses in the garden to decorate the dinner table where they conduct their daily fights.

Family happiness, or whatever passed for it, only ever existed in the photos that Lester often looks at to remind himself of his past, and of the interest in life which he once had but which is now buried under the pressure of conformity. It is only when he falls in love with Angela (Mena Suvari), his daughter's Lolita-like friend, that he rediscovers his zest for life. This second spring changes Lester, but his wife Carolyn meanwhile is doing worse and worse as a property dealer. He reassesses his position and discovers old and forgotten strengths. She by contrast becomes inextricably entwined in the fatal cycle of routine and self-sacrifice. As Lester puts it, trying to live as though their life were a commercial nearly destroys them both. Outward

conformity and prosperity results in inner impoverishment. The business mantras that Carolyn repeats over and over to herself to bolster her self-confidence sound increasingly ridiculous under the circumstances.

At this point, it becomes abundantly clear what we are intended to understand by "American Beauty". The title is not a reference to the seductive child-woman who helps Lester break out of the family prison – that would be too superficial. The subject of *American Beauty* is the question of the beauty of life itself. Mendes' movie is about whether or not it is possible to live a fulfilling life in a society where superficiality has become the norm. To put it in more philosophical terms, *American Beauty* uses the expressive means of drama and satire to go through all the possibilities for leading an honest life in a dishonest environment. Sadly this turns out to be impossible, or at least Lester's attempt ends in death.

It's a gem of a movie, thanks to Sam Mendes' careful use of film techniques. He never exposes his characters to ridicule and he protects them from cheap laughs by giving them time to develop. He also gives depth to their relationships and arranges them in dramatic constellations. Mendes' experience as a theatre director shows in a number of carefully staged scenes whose strict form is well suited to the Burnham's oppressive and limited family life. Many scenes put us in mind of plays by Samuel Beckett, like the backyard sequence where Rick teaches Lester not to give in to circumstance. The symmetrical arrangements of characters around the table or the television are further reminders of family dramas on the stage.

1   A seductively beautiful image.

2   Hollywood's new bright young things: saucy
    Angela (Mena Suvari) …

3   … and sensitive Jane (Thora Birch).

4   Carolyn Burnham (Annette Bening) on the brink
    of madness.

5   Liberation from the familial cage brings happiness
    to Lester Burnham (Kevin Spacey).

## "At first the film judges its characters harshly; then it goes to every effort to make them win back their rights." *Frankfurter Allgemeine Zeitung*

In an important subplot, Lester's daughter Jane falls in love with Rick, the boy next door, who is never seen without his video camera and films constantly, to "remind himself", as he says. He documents the world and discovers its beauty in grainy video pictures of dead animals and people. It is his father, the fascist ex-marine Colonel Frank Fitts – brilliantly acted by Chris Cooper – who in a moment of emotional turmoil shoots Lester Burnham and thereby fulfils the prophecy made at the beginning of the film. The hopeless struggle between internal and external beauty comes to a bloody end, but the issue remains open. The movie points to a vague possibility for reconciling these two opposites, but at the end this seems to have been an illusion. Despite our right to the "pursuit of happiness", material and spiritual wealth seem to be mutually exclusive, and the good life remains a promise of happiness which is yet to be fulfilled. With irony and humour, *American Beauty* shows that modern American society's mental state is by no means as rosy as the initiators of the Declaration of Independence would have hoped.

BR

---

**KEVIN SPACEY**   What would the cinema of the 90s have been without Kevin Spacey? Born in 1959, this friendly looking actor with his ordinary face portrayed some of the most complex and disturbing characters of the decade with impressive depth. Nobody demonstrated so clearly the difference between being and appearance, between a deceptive façade and the brutal reality behind it as drastically as Kevin Spacey playing John Doe, "The Man Without Qualities" in *Se7en* (1995), or the sinister Keyser Soze who pulls the strings in *The Usual Suspects* (1995). Spacey is an enigmatic minimalist who needs only a few striking gestures, and with cool irony can play great emotional cinema as he shows in the role of Lester Burnham in *American Beauty*. When he dies at the turning point of a story – as he does in *L.A. Confidential* – it's a great loss, both for us and for the movie.

"When I made *American Beauty*, I wanted the film's vision to offer every spectator a very intimate experience. I hope it's a universal work, which helps one understand life that little bit better." *Sam Mendes in: Le Figaro*

6 Grotesque victim of his own ideology: sinister neighbour Colonel Fitts (Chris Cooper) shortly before his surprise coming out.

7 Scenes from a marriage in ruins.

8 Wes Bentley is very convincing as Ricky Fitts, the introverted young man from next door.

9 Jane is fascinated by Ricky's puzzling hobby.

10 Life's true beauty can only be appreciated in a video image.

# THE BLAIR WITCH PROJECT

1999 - USA - 87 MIN. - HORROR FILM

DIRECTOR DANIEL MYRICK (*1964), EDUARDO SANCHEZ (*1969)
SCREENPLAY DANIEL MYRICK, EDUARDO SANCHEZ DIRECTOR OF PHOTOGRAPHY NEAL FREDERICKS MUSIC TONY CORA PRODUCTION GREGG
HALE, ROBIN COWIE, MICHAEL MONELLO for HAXAN FILMS, ARTISAN ENTERTAINMENT.

STARRING HEATHER DONAHUE (Heather), MICHAEL WILLIAMS (Michael), JOSHUA LEONARD (Joshua), BOB GRIFFIN (Angler),
JIM KING (Interview partner), SANDRA SANCHEZ (Waitress), ED SWANSON (Angler with glasses), PATRICIA DECOU (Mary
Brown), MARK MASON (Man with the yellow hat), JACKIE HALLEX.

## "It's very hard to get lost in America these days and even harder to stay lost."

We know the story from the brothers Grimm: young people get lost in a wood and struggle with a witch. In the contemporary adaptation *The Blair Witch Project* there is however no tempting gingerbread and the witch doesn't get pushed into the oven – instead film students Heather (Heather Donahue), Michael (Michael Williams) and Joshua (Joshua Leonard) set off into the woods in Maryland with their camera to investigate stories of a witch, and they come to a sticky end. First the three youngsters ask people in the village of Blair about the stories, then they go off into the woods to look. It soon becomes ominously clear that they are being watched and they realise too late that they are lost.

*The Blair Witch Project* cost only a fraction of the cost of a normal Hollywood production. The plot is driven by the movie's own frugal production conditions. A horror movie disguised as a documentary, it begins with a text insert saying that in October 1994 three film students disappeared in the woods near Burkittsville, Maryland while making a documentary film and that the film material was found a year later. This material is what we are about to see. Unlike Danish Dogme films such as *The Celebration* (*Festen*, 1998), which base their stark simplicity on a pseudo-religious creed and a wish to take cinema back to its basics, in this case the movie's lack of technical sophistication is an integral part of its storyline.

Physical movement always has a psychological dimension in cinema: as the three students move further and further away from a normal investigative outing, they penetrate deeper and deeper into the woods and become more and more convinced that they are hopelessly lost. The nearer they get to the witch's house, the closer they are to the darkness within themselves. The would-be filmmakers become increasingly tense. They neither look nor act like future stars, but more like we would imagine ordinary film students: they are not particularly attractive, they're not necessarily very nice and they're ultimately a bit nerdy. This makes it all the more believable that we are seeing the material from their filming expedition: wobbly and unfocused images of a journey with no return, to which the pictures are the only witnesses. Their journey through the woods of Maryland is also an excursion into American history. This wild countryside on the East Coast was where the first settlers arrived, and it was here that James Fenimore Cooper's last Mohican roamed and hunted. It is a sad reflection on today's civilisation that the descendants of this pioneering generation are destroyed by their forefathers' legends. City-dwellers in the wilderness are mostly their own worst enemies, and they fall victim to their own fears rather than to the hostile environment. Trapped in a situation that seems increasingly hopeless, the three students mercilessly document each other's despair and psychic disintegration.

Its innovative marketing aside, the movie still basically functions as a relatively old-fashioned horror film. The three students tramp up hill and down dale, and live in terror of what they might find in front of their tent in the morning. But there is actually nothing to be seen – we can't make out anything for sure in the partly blackened pictures and the fear only exists where it is at its worst: in our own heads.

MH

## "*Blair* is the clearest example of a new phenomenon: the film's success was driven not by a conventional publicity campaign, but by a web site combined with word of mouth." *Süddeutsche Zeitung*

**MARKETING**

The Blair Witch Project cost 35,000 dollars and in the USA alone the movie made 140 million – profit margins which most investors can only dream of. The movie first attracted attention in January 1999 at the Sundance Festival, which is the El Dorado for US independent film. Artisan, a small distribution company, secured the distribution rights to *BWP* and began an unrivalled marketing campaign. Week after week the Internet site www.blairwitch.com published new titbits on the background to the mythology of the Blair Witch. When the movie was released in June 1999 only 27 copies were made, although this number was gradually increased. As copies were kept short, cinema screenings sold out in a few places and the word on the street spread. This is quite unlike the usual Hollywood practice where the market is flooded with as many copies as possible.

1 Face to face with terror – the observer is stuck there with his own fear.

2 Always aim for the other camera.

3 Michael (Michael Williams) and Joshua (Joshua Leonard) in the face of horror, which is always located somewhere near the camera.

4 Securing evidence of an expedition into the heart of darkness.

5 Seemingly realistic images of a fictional story.

# THE SIXTH SENSE

999 - USA - 106 MIN. - THRILLER, DRAMA, HORROR FILM

DIRECTOR  M. NIGHT SHYAMALAN (Manoj Nelliyattu Shyamalan) (*1970)
SCREENPLAY  M. NIGHT SHYAMALAN  DIRECTOR OF PHOTOGRAPHY TAK FUJIMOTO  MUSIC  JAMES NEWTON HOWARD  PRODUCTION  KATHLEEN KENNEDY, FRANK MARSHALL, BARRY MENDEL for HOLLYWOOD PICTURES, SPYGLASS ENTERTAINMENT.

STARRING  BRUCE WILLIS (Dr Malcolm Crowe), HALEY JOEL OSMENT (Cole Sear), TONI COLLETTE (Lynn Sear), OLIVIA WILLIAMS (Anna Crowe), TREVOR MORGAN (Tommy Tammisimo), DONNIE WAHLBERG (Vincent Grey), MISCHA BARTON (Kyra Collins), PETER ANTHONY TAMBAKIS (Darren), JEFFREY ZUBERNIS (Bobby), BRUCE NORRIS (Stanley Cunningham).

## "I don't want to be scared anymore."

Although death waits for us all, its nature is beyond our knowledge. No film of the 90s brings this closer to home than *The Sixth Sense*. Little Cole (Haley Joel Osment) has a secret: he has a sixth sense, and he can see the dead. They have chosen him to be their medium. They want to tell him of their torment and reveal the mysterious circumstances of their deaths. Dr Malcolm Crowe (Bruce Willis) is a child psychologist. He is also dead, shot by a former patient whose treatment failed. The unusual thriller that results from this situation strikes a subtle and moving balance between psychological drama, horror film, buddy movie, and melodrama. In it Bruce Willis, who alongside Stallone and Schwarzenegger is an action star par excellence, demonstrates an unexpected mastery of restrained feeling. The exceptional performance of Haley Joel Osment provides the perfect counterpart as the little boy whose daily encounters with the dead leave painful traces on his body.

Willis portrays the dead psychologist with a combination of melancholy and loneliness, making his vague sense of loss perceptible in every gesture and expression. He's quite unaware that he has joined the ranks of the dead. Only Cole can see him. They meet for the first time in a church near the home that Cole shares with his mother. Cole is tormented by his sixth sense and

Crowe offers assistance, not knowing that in fact it is Cole who will be of greater help to him in coming to grips with his past. The exchange between these two characters gives the film emotional plausibility, in spite of its being a ghost story which is not without horrifying moments of subtle terror. *The Sixth Sense* brings a new dimension to the mystery / ghost story horror genre. The nightmarish tale, with its surprise ending, is staged with remarkable creativity and assurance by Night Shyamalan. The plot plays with our expectations, exploiting the viewer's assumption that all that is seen is real, and that time, place and causality all correspond to his everyday experience. After Malcolm Crowe is shot in the stomach, the film fades into darkness. It fades in again to the figure of Crowe, who is sitting on a bench and observing a child in the distance. Further deception is provided by a subtitle, fixing the event in space and time. Nothing recalls the previous injury, and the world seems to be back in order. From this position of security, the viewer scarcely notices that Crowe no longer has any contact with his fellow humans, with the exception of Cole. Scenes showing Crowe together with other people are staged so cunningly that the audience takes it for granted that he is alive and is still treating Cole's case. In fact, the reverse is true and

## "The film is so well plotted and the ending so unforeseen that the surprise is complete. This is a film worth seeing several times over to grasp all its nuances." M. Night Shyamalan in: Le Figaro

the film is treating the case of Crowe, but to make the twist at the end of the movie work, the audience must believe that he is still in the world of the living.

In Tak Fujimoto, Shyamalan had one of Hollywood's most distinguished cameramen at his disposal, and it is his artistic mastery that is responsible to a large extent for the great visual power of the film. The calm camerawork together with the subdued colouring of the individual scenes blend to create an atmosphere of morbid foreboding. There is also plenty of visual quotation from other films, like the winding staircase from Hitchcock's *Vertigo*. Shyamalan also follows Hitchcock's lead in making a cameo appearance as hospital doctor.

Hitchcock's unusual habit of self-portrayal and his subversive brand of psycho-terror are not the only sources of inspiration for this movie. A number of visual shock effects, and the motif of the child's hallucinatory abilities are reminiscent of Stanley Kubrick's horror classic *The Shining* (1980), and the sudden inexplicable opening of kitchen cupboards remind us of Tobe Hooper's *Poltergeist* (1982). *The Sixth Sense* is an illustrious example of the

way filmmakers of the 90s are often masters of the art of quotation. By playing with repetition, ironic refraction, parody and reversal of meaning, directors open up new perspectives for themselves while at the same time offering audiences a fresh source of entertainment in finding points of comparison with their own knowledge of film. The name of the young protagonist "Cole" for example is a direct reference to the figure played by Bruce Willis in *Twelve Monkeys* (1995) by Terry Gilliam. The characters do much more than share a name – in both films their extraordinary stories are so implausible that they are held to be sane. Both figures find themselves in the same predicament, that they can both see dead people.

The childhood nightmares that make a nightmare of Cole's childhood are dispelled when he accepts his role as go-between and offers the dead his services. When realisation of his own death finally catches up with the shocked Crowe, he recalls Cole's words: "I see people – they don't know they're dead". This is the real moment of death for Crowe. The scene is consumed in brilliant white light, and our last visual impression is a short excerpt from his wedding video.                                                                                      BR

3

1   Young Cole (Haley Joel Osment) knows what Dr
    Malcolm Crowe (Bruce Willis) doesn't know yet.

2   The descent into hell is never-ending: the boy
    sees one frightening image after the other.

3   Childish fears and crippling fantasies of death:
    horror lurks behind the door at the top of the
    stairs.

**CAMERAMAN
TAK FUJIMOTO**

The visual power of Tak Fujimoto's images had a lasting influence on the cinema of the 90s. He trained at the International Film School in London and has left his mark on the style of a generation of cameramen. His impressive debut in 1973 with *Badlands* (director: Terrence Malick) was an early demonstration of his virtuosity and sense of style.
*Caged Heat* (1974) was the first of several collaborations with director Jonathan Demme. The originality of this director's American images is largely due to Fujimoto's rich colouring and judicious lighting. Above all, in *The Silence of the Lambs* (1991) Fujimoto developed his virtuoso games with space, with nearness and distance, and with the visible and the invisible to unique perfection.

# BEING JOHN MALKOVICH

1999 - USA - 112 MIN. - COMEDY

**DIRECTOR** SPIKE JONZE (*1969)
**SCREENPLAY** CHARLIE KAUFMAN **DIRECTOR OF PHOTOGRAPHY** LANCE ACORD **MUSIC** CARTER BURWELL, BÉLA BARTÓK **PRODUCTION** STEVE
GOLIN, VINCENT LANDAY, SANDY STERN, MICHAEL STIPE for GRAMERCY PICTURES, PROPAGANDA FILMS, SINGLE CELL
PICTURES.

**STARRING** JOHN MALKOVICH (John Horatio Malkovich), JOHN CUSACK (Craig Schwartz), CAMERON DIAZ (Lotte Schwartz),
NED BELLAMY (Derek Mantini), ORSON BEAN (Dr Lester), CATHERINE KEENER (Maxine), MARY KAY PLACE (Floris),
K. K. DODDS (Wendy), REGINALD C. HAYES (Don), BYRNE PIVEN (Captain Mertin).

## "I think, I feel, I suffer."

To be famous and desired. To be inside someone else, to see what he sees, to feel what he feels. To be a star, to enjoy his privileges and to bathe in his success, and yet remain incognito – that would be the perfect material for a fairytale, a play or a movie. Well clear the stage and raise the curtain, because the play's called *Being John Malkovich*.

Struggling puppeteer Craig Schwartz (John Cusack) could use more public and financial success for his virtuoso marionette theatre. The lonely "Dance of Despair" of his wooden hero, an expression of Craig's own mental state, is performed with astonishing perfection and intensity, but the public prefers something bigger. To get into television and become famous you need giant puppets, the sort that you would have to manipulate from the side of a bridge. This is the starting point for newcomer Spike Jonze's bizarre film comedy. The frustrated Craig is forced to work as a filing clerk for the Lester Corporation, where he meets and falls for the fetching Maxine. She, for her part, is more interested in Craig's wife Lotte (Cameron Diaz). The

vehicle for the self-centred preoccupations of all three becomes John Malkovich, who plays himself. This trick allows for a side-story about the identity of actors and the problems they have giving expression, face and body to countless different characters without losing themselves in the process.

The main story is dedicated to the kafkaesque idea that by crawling through a dwarf-sized door in the wall of the seven-and-a-halfth storey of an office building, it is possible to enter into the head of John Malkovich and take part in his life. Based on this unusual and arresting idea, *Being John Malkovich* becomes an ironic illustration of the theory that we only see ourselves through the eyes of others. A convoluted amorous quadrangle develops. John Cusack and Cameron Diaz play the young couple whose relationship falls apart after Craig's discovery. At first they take turns sliding through the dark corridor beyond the small door that leads into the skull of John Malkovich. He is seduced by Maxine. Maxine actually has her sights on Lotte,

1   The anguish of not being master in your own house: John Malkovich.

2   The light at the end of the tunnel is called John Malkovich.

3   Queue here for bliss.

# "Hollywood hasn't dared to entrust itself so casually to an absurd initial idea for many years." *Frankfurter Allgemeine Zeitung*

who for her part is not averse to Maxine's advances. Together, they stage their sexual adventure with the help of John Malkovich's body, cuckolding Craig at the same time. In contrast to her character in Tom DeCillo's media satire *Living in Oblivion* (1995, a film whose high spirits are shared by *Being John Malkovich*) Catherine Keener's portrayal of the clever Maxine is coldly erotic. Thanks to her business sense the hole in the wall leading to John Malkovich's brain becomes a source of income, and the secret passage becomes an insider attraction for anyone willing to pay money to have a prominent identity for a change, even if it's only for fifteen minutes. That's the length of the visits, and afterwards visitors find themselves miles away lying in the dirt beside the New Jersey turnpike. When Malkovich finally discovers the unscrupulous business, it's already too late. His ego is no longer master in its own abode. Craig has taken possession of his mind, and Maxine changes her loyalties to Craig alias Malkovich, from whom she is expecting a child. Craig has finally made it: he's transformed Malkovich into a living puppet and he basks in the brilliance of his success. As if the story were not already full of supernatural situations, it then transforms into a tale of migrating souls like *Cocoon* (1985) where the undead are forced to change their host bodies from time to time. After Maxine's outrageous kidnap attempt, Craig leaves the body of John Malkovich to make room for the spirit of Captain Merten, the builder of the office building with the seventh-and-a-half floor. Craig's attempt to achieve happiness by exploiting John Malkovich's fame turns out to be an illusion of the mind.

BR

4

"It is precisely the vanity, which Malkovich portrays with remarkable self-irony and without exaggeration so that it always seems authentic, that makes many scenes so funny." *Frankfurter Allgemeine Zeitung*

**FILMS ABOUT FILMMAKING** The medium of film has always been preoccupied with different aspects of its own make-up,: from scriptwriting (*Sunset Boulevard*, Billy Wilder, 1950) to camerawork (*The Camera Man*, Buster Keaton. 1928), from directing (*Otto e Mezzo*, Federico Fellini, 1963) to acting (*Chaplin*, Richard Attenborough, 1992) and on-location shooting (*Living in Oblivion*, Tom DiCillo, 1995). But the movie business does more than examine aspects of its own creative process. In remakes and film quotations, directors consistently return to imagery created by other filmmakers, and thus construct their own history. The cinema of the 90s is particularly characterised by such self-reflective films, from *Cape Fear* (1991) to *Pulp Fiction* (1994).

4   Puppeteer Craig Schwartz (John Cusack) as a fake Mephistopheles.

5   Cameron Diaz in the role of the wife Lotte Schwartz discovers that she is in love with Maxine.

6   The shock of realisation: I am not myself.

7   Unscrupulous *femme fatale* Maxine (Catherine Keener) turns everybody's head.

5

DIRECTOR PAUL THOMAS ANDERSON (*1970)

SCREENPLAY PAUL THOMAS ANDERSON DIRECTOR OF PHOTOGRAPHY ROBERT ELSWIT MUSIC JON BRION, AIMEE MANN PRODUCTION PAUL THOMAS ANDERSON, JOANNE SELLAR for GHOULARDI FILM COMPANY, NEW LINE CINEMA, THE MAGNOLIA PROJECT.

STARRING JOHN C. REILLY (Jim Kurring), TOM CRUISE (Frank T. J. Mackey), JULIANNE MOORE (Linda Partridge), PHILIP BAKER HALL (Jimmy Gator), JEREMY BLACKMAN (Stanley Spector), PHILIP SEYMOUR HOFFMAN (Phil Parma), WILLIAM H. MACY (Quiz Kid Donnie Smith), MELORA WALTERS (Claudia Wilson Gator), JASON ROBARDS (Earl Partridge).

IFF BERLIN 2000 GOLDEN BEAR.

# "It would seem that we're through with the past, but it's not through with us."

According to Quentin Tarantino, the plot of *Pulp Fiction* (1994) is three stories about a story. Shortly before that, the film virtuoso Robert Altman gave the episodic movie new elegance with *Shorts Cuts* (1993), where many short stories revolve around a centre, overlap, move away from each other again and form new combinations. Although director Paul Thomas Anderson originally tried to play down the link, *Magnolia* can definitely be seen in relation to these earlier movies. The denial was probably just the reaction of a promising young filmmaker who wanted audiences to take a second look at his *Boogie Nights* (1997).

At the centre of the tragicomedy *Magnolia* is Big Earl Partridge (Jason Robards), a TV tycoon of the worst kind. He lies dying, a wilting magnolia. Earl is the key figure, the man behind the scenes and the origin of all evils. His name alone is a programme for the movie … Earl is the only figure who always stays in the same place, unable to move from his deathbed. When the camera looks down on him from above and the mighty fanfare from Richard Strauss's *Also sprach Zarathustra* sounds, it's not just an ironic reference to

his once all-powerful influence, but also to the end of Stanley Kubrick's *2001 – A Space Odyssey* (1968). There we see the astronaut David Bowman as an old man alone on a big bed, shortly before the next evolutionary leap transforms him into the famous foetus from the final shot of 2001 and the cycle of human development moves onto a higher plane. Earl's end also signifies new beginnings, but before that can come about all the suffering that he has brought into the world must be dealt with. And that is no easy task.

With great humour and sympathy, *Magnolia* tells the stories of all the people on whose lives he has had such a lasting influence. First of all comes Earl's son Frank (Tom Cruise) who trains frustrated men to become supermacho in his "Seduce and Destroy" seminars. He got this motto from his father, who destroyed his wife with his complete lack of consideration. Now, shortly before his death, the shallow patriarch searches for his lost son, who he had abandoned as a teenager when his mother fell ill with cancer. When the two come together at the end, their broken relationship is shown in all its misery. Earl's young wife Linda (Julianne Moore) only married him for his

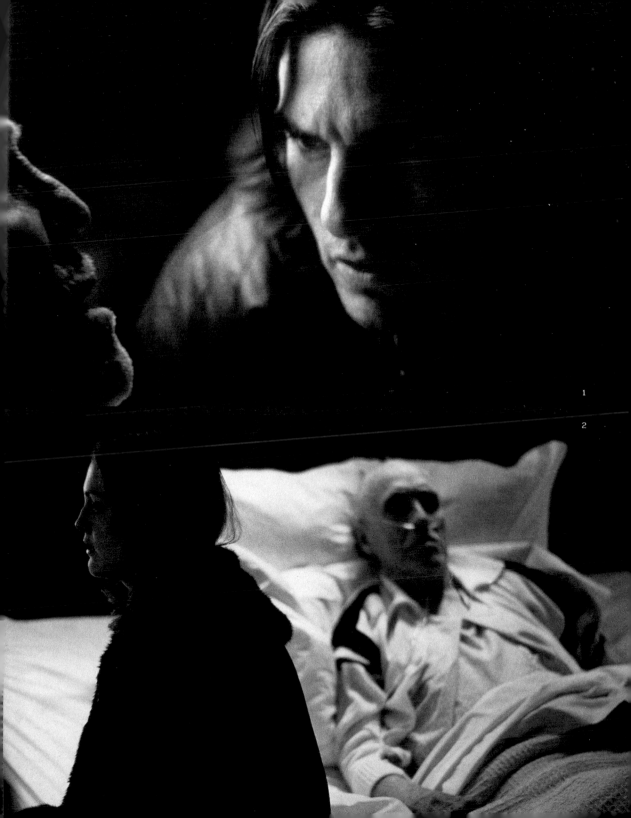

# "Almost exactly in the middle is *Magnolia* – which lasts for three hours and isn't a second too long – so close to its characters that we can almost feel their breath."

*Frankfurter Allgemeine Zeitung*

1  Prodigal son (Tom Cruise) and hated father (Jason Robards).

2  Relationship at an end: scenes from a marriage on its deathbed. Julianne Moore in the role of Linda Partridge.

3  The incarnation of law and order: good-natured police officer Jim Kurring (John C. Reilly).

4   Claudia (Melora Walters), abused by her own
    father and addicted to drugs, provides an opti-
    mistic ending to the film.

5   Phil (Philip Seymour Hoffman), the carer of ailing
    patriarch Earl, demonstrates patience and sensi-
    tivity.

6   Confessions under duress: homosexual Donnie
    (William H. Macy) becomes the victim of his inferi-
    ority complex.

money. She realises the shallowness of her own character and starts to go through a crisis of identity. Quiz master Jimmy Gator (Philip Baker Hall) presents the bizarre show "What Do Kids Know?" for Big Earl Partridge TV Productions, where three children compete against three adults answering general knowledge questions. Jimmy has absorbed his boss's way of thinking to such a degree that his extramarital affairs even include his daughter Claudia, who is now a cocaine addict and funds her habit with occasional prostitution. When the neighbours complain about her loud music, she gets a visit from a policeman who promptly falls in love with her, and even greater confusion ensues. Finally, there are the two child prodigies who have become famous through the quiz show. Former child star Donny now tries vainly to chat up a good looking barman and Stanley wets his pants at the show's decisive moment, as the production team's strict rules don't allow him to go to the lavatory before the broadcast.

The movie's interpersonal conflicts run along the fault lines between parents and children and men and women. All these relationships have been ruined by an inability to build up and maintain friendships, and by the impossibility of any real communication. *Magnolia* is an affectionate but cynical critique of the medium of television, and all the people in the movie seem to be trying to emulate its clichés. Behind everything is the television magnate Earl. The characters' lives are nothing more than television made flesh, absurd TV drama on the wrong side of the screen.

The movie begins with a macabre, satirical undertone and it becomes increasingly sarcastic and even cynical. An amused, concise voice-over at the beginning talks about the absurdity of life and denies the existence of coincidence, and the film goes on to prove that thesis. Although at first the episodes appear to be a transitory collection of unconnected events, a dense network of links gradually appears. The movie draws the audience into a

**PAUL THOMAS ANDERSON**   Paul Thomas Anderson first worked as a production assistant on television films, video productions and game shows in Los Angeles and New York, before leaving the New York University Film School after only two days to get back to the practical side of things again. He developed his short film *Cigarettes and Coffee* (1993) into his first feature film *Hard Eight*, which was presented at the 1996 Cannes Film Festival. *Boogie Nights* (1997) was nominated for three Oscars. His innovative directing style doesn't balk at confusing plots or complex characters, and he is not afraid to break taboos. Paul Thomas Anderson is considered one of the most promising young directors around today.

7　The strain of the TV quiz is written all over the face of young genius Stanley (Jeremy Blackman).

8　Donnie runs into more and more trouble.

9　Learning from children: a hard task even for compère Jimmy Gator (Philip Baker Hall)

whirl of failed relationships and unfulfilled yearnings for freedom, love and mutual respect. This descent influences the movie's images, and their rhythm becomes slower and their colours darker, and spectators start to feel that the downward spiral could go on forever. But *Magnolia* is anything but a pessimistic movie: shortly before the final catastrophe, all the figures suddenly begin to sing the same song wherever they happen to be. After the initial surprise, this absurd directorial idea turns out to be a wonderful trick, which counteracts the seemingly inevitable end with off-beat humour in a manner not dissimilar to the song at the end of *Monty Python's Life of Brian* (1979). When it rains frogs at the very end, spectators heave a sigh of relief along with the characters in the movie. This surreal event makes it clear that anything is possible in this movie. We may not be able to believe our eyes, but "it did happen" as the text under the pictures tells us. The event shakes the characters out of their lethargy and reminds them of the incredible opportunities that life can offer. And a small smile into the camera in the final shot holds the key to the way out of this crisis whose name is life.　　BR

"*Magnolia* takes a long run-up, then jumps and lands in the middle of our present. It is the first film of the new millennium." *Frankfurter Allgemeine Zeitung*

9

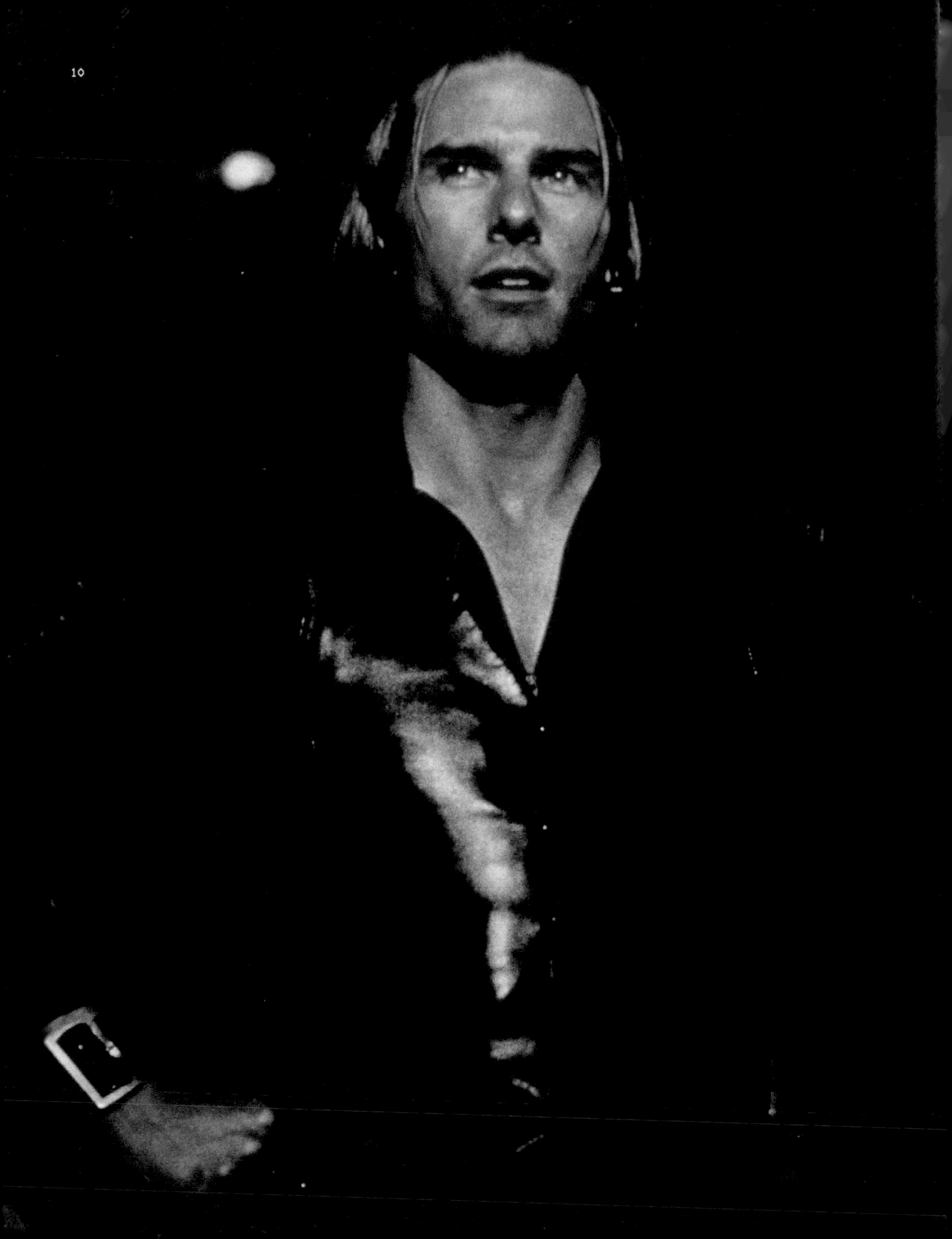

"The film pauses for a moment: suicides forget to press the trigger, addicts forget their fix, and those in pain their pain. Then the play is over, the world appears fresh once more, the dead are buried and the living are given a second chance." *Süddeutsche Zeitung*

10    Tom Cruise in the unusual role of a repulsive
advocate of machismo.

11    Victim of self-delusion: Julianne Moore is a
convincing Beauty and the Beast.

# INDEX OF FILMS

# GENERAL INDEX

This list contains the names of the people involved in the production of a film.
Production companies are in italics and film categories are preceded by a dash.
Numbers in bold refer to a glossary text.

# ABOUT THE AUTHORS

*Ulrich von Berg (UB)*, *1955, degree in American and Media Studies. Many years' experience as a movie journalist in all branches of the media. Editor and author of various books on film. Lives in Berlin.

*Malte Hagener (MH)*, *1971, degree in Literature and Media Studies. Editor and author of numerous academic articles. Lecturer in Film History at Amsterdam University. Lives in Hamburg and Berlin.

*Steffen Haubner (SH)*, *1965, studied Art History and Sociology. Has written many academic and press articles. Collaborator on the science and research section of the Hamburger Abendblatt. Lives in Hamburg.

*Jörn Hetebrügge (JH)*, *1971, studied German Literature. Author of many academic and press articles. Lives in Berlin.

*Annette Kilzer (AK)*, *1966, degree in Theatre Studies, German Studies and Philosophy. Has written many books and press articles. Lives in Berlin.

*Heinz-Jürgen Köhler (HJK)*, *1963, deputy editor-in-chief of the movie program for TV Today. Author of many academic and press articles. Lives in Hamburg.

*Steffen Lückehe (SL)*, *1962, Film Theorist. Member of the German Standards Committee for children's and young people's videos. Author of many articles in various papers and magazines. Lives in Mannheim.

*Nils Meyer (NM)*, * 1971, studied German Literature and Politics. Has written many articles in various papers and magazines. Lives in Berlin.

*Olaf Möller (OM)*, Author, translator, program curator. Writes for the national press. Lives in Köln.

*Anne Pohl (APO)*, *1961, active as a journalist since 1987. Author of numerous academic articles. Lives in Berlin.

*Burkhard Röwekamp (BR)*, *1965, researcher at the Institute for Contemporary German Literature and Media at the Philipps University in Marburg. Has taught numerous courses and published many articles on the aesthetics and theory of contemporary film. Lives in Marburg.

*Markus Stauff (MS)*, *1968, researcher at the Institute for Film and Television Studies at the Ruhr University in Bochum. Author of many academic articles. Lives in Bochum.

*Rainer Vowe (RV)*, *1954, historian, works for the EU Directorate General XII (Audio-Visuelles and the Institute for Film and Television Studies at the Ruhr University in Bochum. Numerous articles about the history of cinema and television. Lives in Bochum.

# CREDITS

Our thanks to the distributors, without whom many of these films would never have reached the big screen.

ARSENAL, ARTHAUS, BUENA VISTA, C/I VERTRIEBSGEMEINSCHAFT, COLUMBIA TRI STAR, CONCORDE, CONSTANTIN, HIGHLIGHT FILM, JUGENDFILM, KINOWELT, NIL FILM, PANDORA, POLYGRAM FILMS, PROKINO, SCOTIA, SENATOR, TOBIS, 20TH CENTURY FOX, UIP, WARNER BROS.

Academy Award® and Oscar® are the registered trademark and service mark of the Academy of Motion Picture Arts and Sciences.

We deeply regret it if, despite our concerted efforts, a distributor has been unintentionally overlooked and omitted. Obviously we will amend any such errors in the next edition if they are brought to the attention of the publishers.

# ACKNOWLEDGEMENTS

The creation of this book was made possible by the collaboration of a number of people. Heartfelt thanks go to *Thierry Nebois* of TASCHEN Verlag for the coordination work and his ability to keep track of everything. *Birgit Reber* and *Andy Disl* came up with a design concept that gives pride of place to the pictures, which are the true capital of a film book. My thanks to *Herbert Klemens* from the *Filmbild Fundus* for his help in accessing the original stills. But this book was only first made really possible by the stimulating texts from the authors. The keen-eyed editing work was done by *Corinna Dehne* and *Lioba Waleczek*. *Malte Hagener* attended to the technical editorial work with his customary meticulousness. The fact that this book got off the ground is thanks to the commitment and initiative of *Petra Lamers-Schütze*. And last but not least *Benedikt Taschen* has included the book in his programme and enthusiastically followed the publication's progress from start to finish. My personal thanks to him and everyone else mentioned here.

# ABOUT THIS BOOK

The 63 films selected for this book represent a decade of cinema. It goes without saying that this particular selection is based on a decision that could have turned out differently. Each film is presented by an essay, and additionally accompanied by a glossary entry devoted to one person or a cinematographic term. To ensure optimal access to all this information, an index for the films and a general index are provided at the back of the book.

# IMPRINT

ILLUSTRATIONS PAGES 2–14   THE SILENCE OF THE LAMBS / Jonathan Demme / COLUMBIA / TRI STAR / ORION PICTURES

To stay informed about upcoming TASCHEN titles, please request our magazine at www.taschen.com or write to TASCHEN America, 6671 Sunset Boulevard, Suite 1508, USA-Los Angeles, CA 90028, Fax: +1-323-463.4442. We will be happy to send you a free copy of our magazine which is filled with information about all of our books.

PHOTOGRAPHS               FILMBILD FUNDUS ROBERT FISCHER, Munich

PROJECT MANAGEMENT        PETRA LAMERS-SCHÜTZE, Cologne
EDITORIAL COORDINATION    THIERRY NEBOIS, Cologne
DESIGN                    SENSE/NET, ANDY DISL and BIRGIT REBER, Cologne
TEXTS                     ULRICH VON BERG (UB), MALTE HAGENER (MH), STEFFEN HAUBNER (SH),
                          JÖRN HETEBRÜGGE (JH), ANNETTE KILZER (AK), HEINZ-JÜRGEN KÖHLER (HJK),
                          STEFFEN LÜCKEHE (SL), NILS MEYER (NM), OLAF MÖLLER (OM), ANNE POHL (APO),
                          BURKHARD RÖWEKAMP (BR), MARKUS STAUFF (MS), RAINER VOWE (RV)
TECHNICAL EDITING         MALTE HAGENER, Berlin
ENGLISH TRANSLATION       DEBORAH CAROLINE HOLMES, Vienna (Texts), HARRIET HORSFIELD in association with
                          FIRST EDITION TRANSLATIONS LTD, Cambridge (Introduction), KATHARINE HUGHES,
                          Oxford (Captions)
EDITING                   JONATHAN MURPHY, Brussels
COLLABORATION             BRIGITTE LÖBACH, Cologne
PRODUCTION                UTE WACHENDORF, Cologne

PRINTED IN INDIA
ISBN 3–8228–4114–5